UPGRADING AND REPAIRING PCS: A+ CERTIFICATION STUDY GUIDE

Scott Mueller
Scott Berkel

201 West 103rd Street,
Indianapolis, Indiana 46290

Contents at a Glance

Upgrading and Repairing PCs: A+ Certification Study Guide

Copyright © 2000 by Que® Corporation

International Standard Book Number: 0-7897-2095-7

Library of Congress Catalog Card Number: 99-63039

Printed in the United States of America

First Printing: October 1999

01   00   99   4   3   2

Trademarks

Warning and Disclaimer

Publisher
Jim Minatel

Acquisitions Editor
Jill Byus

Senior Development Editor
Rick Kughen

Managing Editor
Lisa Wilson

Project Editor
Linda Seifert

Copy Editor
Kelly Talbot

Indexer
Bill Meyers

Proofreader
Billy Fields

Technical Editor
David Smith

Team Coordinator
Vicki Harding

Interior Design
Trina Wurst

Cover Design
Karen Ruggles

Layout Technician
Steve Geiselman

Contents

About the Authors

Scott Mueller is president of Mueller Technical Research, an international research and corporate training firm. Since 1982, MTR has specialized in the industry's longest running, most in-depth, accurate and effective corporate PC hardware and technical training seminars, maintaining a client list that includes Fortune 500 companies, the U.S. and foreign governments, major software and hardware corporations, as well as PC enthusiasts and entrepreneurs. His seminars have been presented to thousands of PC support professionals throughout the world.

Scott Mueller has developed and presented training courses in all areas of PC hardware and software. He is an expert in PC hardware, operating systems, and data-recovery techniques. For more information about a custom PC hardware or data recovery training seminar for your organization, contact Lynn at

Mueller Technical Research

21 Spring Lane

Barrington Hills, IL 60010-9009

(847) 854-6794

(847) 854-6795 Fax

Internet: scottmueller@compuserve.com

Web: http://www.m-tr.com

Scott has many popular books, articles, and course materials to his credit, including *Upgrading and Repairing PCs*, which has sold more than 2 million copies, making it by far the most popular PC hardware book on the market today. His two-hour video titled *Your PC—The Inside Story* is available through LearnKey, Inc. For ordering information, contact

LearnKey, Inc.

1845 West Sunset Boulevard

St. George, UT 84770

(800) 865-0165

(801) 674-9733

(801) 674-9734 Fax

If you have questions about PC hardware, suggestions for the next edition of the book, or any comments in general, send them to Scott via email at scottmueller@compuserve.com.

When he is not working on PC-related books or teaching seminars, Scott can usually be found in the garage working on vehicle performance projects. This year a Harley Road King is taking most of his time, and he promises to finish the Impala next.

Scott Berkel is a systems engineer and certified instructor for A+ and MCSE courses. On the CompTIA A+ side, he has been certified on both the DOS/Windows and Macintosh tracks as well as being a beta tester for the 1998 revisions of the exams. With more than 12 years of experience in the PC industry, Scott holds over 30 other certifications, including Microsoft's MCSE, MCT, MCP, CompTIA Network+, IBM PSE, two Novell CNA's, and a multitude of manufacturer-specific hardware certifications. He has authored and edited material on multiple projects for Que and other Macmillan Publishing companies, including the Top Score A+ Certification Software. Much of this material is used in the development and delivery of new training courses for fellow employees. Scott works as a Senior Consultant and Project Manager for Xerox Connect, Inc., a worldwide information technology services provider. He currently lives in Indianapolis, Indiana with his wife and two children.

Dedication

To Robyn and Christopher. Yes kids, Daddy is done typing and can come and play now. – Scott Berkel

Acknowledgments

I would like to thank the members of the team that worked on this project: Jill Byus for keeping me on target and not canceling the project before it really got started; Rick Kughen for his late nights of editing and patience with my writing style; David Smith for keeping me honest with his technical editing; and of course, Scott Mueller for his sage wisdom and the use of his bestselling material to create an exceptional A+ Study Guide.

I would also like to thank my friends and family for giving me both support and criticism during the long nights of writing. Lastly, I would like to thank Scott Holley, high-school English teacher extraordinaire. Mr. Holley taught this would-be artist that writing is not a chore but an enjoyable experience, and that words are simply a different medium in which to paint.

Tell Us What You Think!

As the reader of this book, *you* are our most important critic and commentator. We value your opinion and want to know what we're doing right, what we could do better, what areas you'd like to see us publish in, and any other words of wisdom you're willing to pass our way.

As a Publisher for *Que*, I welcome your comments. You can fax, email, or write me directly to let me know what you did or didn't like about this book—as well as what we can do to make our books stronger.

Please note that I cannot help you with technical problems related to the topic of this book, and that due to the high volume of mail I receive, I might not be able to reply to every message.

When you write, please be sure to include this book's title and author as well as your name and phone or fax number. I will carefully review your comments and share them with the author and editors who worked on the book.

Fax: 317.581.4666

Email: hardware@mcp.com

Mail: *Que*
          201 West 103rd Street
          Indianapolis, IN 46290 USA

Introduction

What Is This Book About?

This text is designed as a self-study preparation for the Computing Technology Industry Association's A+ Certification. This certification is the premiere certification for service technicians and engineers throughout the world. Designed as a standard by which to evaluate technicians with or without other formal training, the A+ has become very much in demand—especially since the release of updated exams in mid-1998. More information on the A+ certification, its objectives, and testing strategies can be found in Chapter 14, "Preparing for the Exam," as well as on CompTIA's Web site at http://www.comptia.org.

The content of this book is set up in three different parts:

> Part I: CompTIA Core Technologies Exam Preparation Material
>
> Part II: CompTIA Operating Systems Exam Preparation Material
>
> Part III: So You Think You're Ready to Take the Exam?

Parts I & II

As these book headings might indicate, Part I is strictly devoted to the hardware components of the system and its underlying design as applicable to CompTIA exam number 220-101. Part II is concerned with the DOS, Windows 3.x, and recently added (and heavily emphasized) Windows 95 material for CompTIA exam 220-102 and includes some necessary hardware references to relevant material in Part I.

Part III

After you finish reading this book, whether it is a refresher for your own hardware and software knowledge or a new learning experience, there are two additional chapters in Part III devoted to getting you to pass both the exams. These chapters include the previously mentioned "Preparing for the Exam," which includes the CompTIA objectives for both exams, background A+ certification information, and proven testing strategies for the exams, and a 50-question "Sample Test Questions," which will test your knowledge in the same way, format, and content as the CompTIA exams will. These chapters, combined with the Cram Session and Review Question sections at the end of each chapter, should provide you with the final preparation you need before walking into the testing center.

How Is this Book Related to *Upgrading and Repairing PCs, Eleventh Edition?*

Although it is written to prepare you for the A+ Certification on its own, this book will also be of use to you long after you pass the exam. Throughout this book, you will find not only special discussions about "Exam Tips" and comprehensive exam-preparation information, but also relevant tips gleaned from the author's experiences "In The Real World" and even more references that point to further, in-depth study in the most popular computer reference book of all time, now in it's 11th Edition, Scott Mueller's *Upgrading and Repairing PCs.*

Who Should Read This Book?

You. That is, if you have read through the previous section "What Is This Book About?" and you are still reading, chances are likely that you are exactly for whom this book was written.

If you are looking for an study guide that will help you pass the CompTIA A+ Certification, this book is for you.

If you are simply curious about the entry-level computer knowledge and certifications or if you are or want to be in the service, manufacturing, or training areas of the computer industry, this book is for you. Even if you already have your A+ certification and want a tool to bridge your A+ knowledge with the extensive material in Mueller's latest edition of *Upgrading and Repairing PCs*, this book is for you.

Conventions Used in This Book

Tips

Tip

Tips suggest alternative methods for accomplishing a task or provide additional information that will help you prepare for the A+ exams.

Notes

Note

Notes provide additional information about the current topic that are either ancillary to the topic at hand or are designed to provide additional insight into a topic.

Cautions

Caution

Cautions point out actions that could be counterproductive, at the least, and downright dangerous, at the most. When you see one of these, be sure to read it!

In the Real World

In the Real World

There is much that is in the exam objectives that is no longer encountered in today's computing environments. In addition, there is much that might be encountered that is not in the exam objectives. These discussions contain information gleaned from professional experiences "in the real world."

Chapter 1

Installation, Configuration, and Upgrading

Basic Components

To pass the A+ Certification Exam, you will need a basic understanding of system components, key concepts, and technological terminology. This chapter will provide an overview of these topics for your understanding.

A modern PC is both simple and complicated. It is simple in the sense that over the years, many of the components used to construct a system have become integrated with other components into fewer and fewer actual parts. It is complicated in the sense that each part in a modern system performs many more functions than did the same types of parts in older systems.

Here are the components needed to assemble a basic modern PC:

- System board (motherboard)
- Processor
- Firmware (ROM)
- Memory (RAM)
- Case and power supply
- Keyboard
- Mouse
- Video card
- Monitor (display)
- Floppy drive
- Hard disk
- CD-ROM, CD-R, or DVD-ROM drive
- Sound card

System Board

The system board, also called a motherboard, is the core of the system. It really is the PC; everything else is connected to it, and it controls everything in the system. Motherboards are available in several different shapes or form factors. The motherboard usually contains the following individual components (see Figure 1.1):

- Processor socket (or slot)
- Firmware and Chipset
- Level 2 cache (normally found in the CPU today)
- Memory SIMM or DIMM sockets
- Bus slots
- ROM BIOS
- Clock/CMOS battery
- Super I/O chip

The chipset contains all the primary circuitry that makes up the motherboard; in essence, the chipset *is* the motherboard. The chipset controls the CPU or processor bus, the L2 cache and main memory, the PCI (Peripheral Component Interconnect) bus, the ISA (Industry Standard Architecture) bus, system resources, and more. If the processor represents the engine of your system, the chipset represents the chassis in which the engine is installed. As such, the chipset dictates the primary features and specifications of your motherboard, including what types of processors, memory, expansion cards, disk drives, and so on the system supports.

The chipset plays a big role in determining what sorts of features a system can support. For example, what processors you can use, what types and how much memory you can install, what speeds you can run the machine, and what types of system buses your system can support are all tied in to the motherboard chipset. The ROM BIOS contains the initial POST (Power-On Self-Test) program, the bootstrap loader (which loads the operating system), drivers for items that are built in to the board (the actual BIOS code), and usually a system setup program (often called CMOS setup) for configuring the system. System boards and expansion busses are covered in detail in Chapter 4, "Motherboards/Processors/Memory."

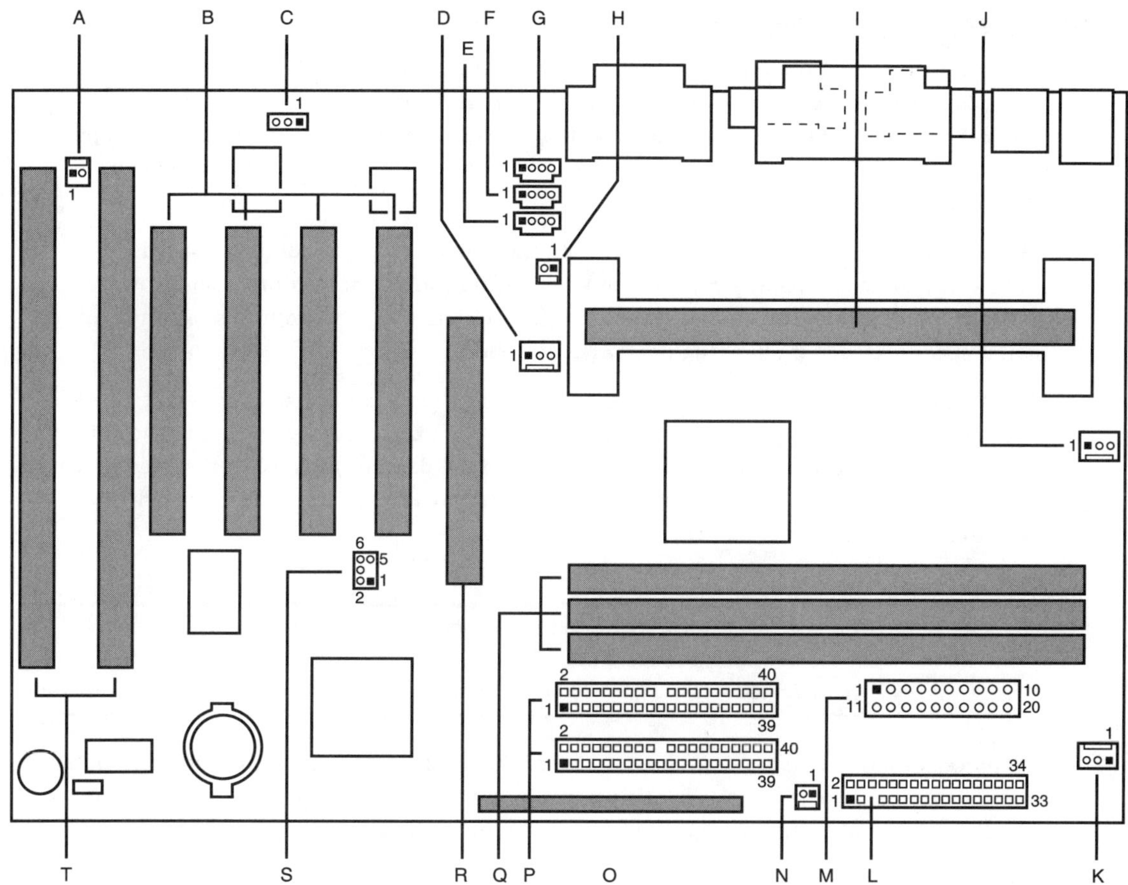

A	Wake on Ring (J1A1)	K	Fan 1 (J8M1)
B	PCI slots (J4D2, J4D1, J4C1, J4B1)	L	Diskette drive (J8K1)
C	Optional Wake on LAN technology (J1C1)	M	Power supply (J7L1)
D	Fan 3 (J3F2)	N	Optional SCSI LED (J8J1)
E	Optional Auxiliary Line In (J2F2)	O	Front panel (J8G2)
F	Optional telephony (J2F1)	P	Primary and secondary IDE (J7G1, J8G1)
G	Optional CD-ROM audio (J1F1)	Q	DIMMs (J6J1, J6J2, J7J1)
H	Optional chassis intrusion (J3F1)	R	A.G.P. (J4E1)
I	Slot 1 (J4J1)	S	PC/PCI (J6D1)
J	Fan 2 (J4M1)	T	ISA slots (J4B2, J4A1)

Figure 1.1 Typical system board connectors and components.

Processor/Coprocessor

The processor is often thought of as the "engine" of the computer. Also called the CPU (central processing unit), it is the single most important chip in the system because it is the primary circuit that carries out the program instructions of whatever software is being run. Modern processors contain literally millions of transistors, etched onto a tiny square of silicon called a die, which is about the size of your thumbnail.

Coprocessors are any additional chips to which specific instructions can be offloaded. Historically, and consequently for the exam, this term means a math coprocessor. However, many video cards and sound cards today also have other, different types of coprocessors on them to handle specialized video rendering or synthesized audio.

Most CPUs today are so fast that the rest of the system simply cannot keep up with them. To lessen the impact of this problem, many processors have extra memory built in to the chip in the form of a level 1 (L1) cache. By keeping this full with the data for the next anticipated process, the CPU can be kept from being idle for too long. This greatly increases the efficiency of the computer.

In the Real World

Most newer (Pentium Celeron/II/III class) systems include the L2 cache inside the processor rather than on the motherboard. In the newest and best designs, the L2 cache is actually a part of the processor die just like the L1 cache, whereas in others it is simply a separate chip (or chips) in the processor module or on the system board.

The processor has the distinction of being one of the most expensive parts of most computers, even though it is also one of the smallest parts. In most modern systems, the processor costs from 2–10 times more than the motherboard it is plugged in to.

Note

Microprocessors are also covered in detail in Chapter 4.

Firmware

Firmware is simply a program that is embedded in a silicon chip rather than stored on a floppy disk. This firmware contains the ROM BIOS, POST, and CMOS Setup utilities.

CMOS

CMOS, or Complementary Metal-Oxide Semiconductor, is the primary hardware configuration component in today's computers. Originally, configuring a system board required physical switch settings to change components. Now, the CMOS utility program can be invoked during startup from the ROM BIOS, and the configuration parameters are stored indefinitely in the CMOS chip. Because this chip requires constant power to retain the configuration, a battery must be installed in the computer to provide this power.

BIOS

ROM BIOS stands for read-only memory basic input/output system. This simply means that it translates on the most basic level the software requests into hardware commands. BIOS contains the Power-On Self-Test and system routines and initializes the system with them to load, or *boot,* an operating system from one of the disk drives into the main RAM memory so that the system can run normally and perform useful work.

Upgrading BIOS

Upgrading BIOS can be accomplished by one of two methods. The oldest method required the user to open the computer chassis, locate the ROM BIOS chip(s), and remove and replace them with the manufacturer's upgraded version. Most systems today use flash ROM BIOS. This enables the user to download a piece of software that, when run, overwrites the existing BIOS using a special address and code to access the flash ROM.

In the Real World

In the real world, flash ROMs are very user-friendly. However, beware of a system or power failure when flashing the BIOS. The resulting corrupt BIOS will render the system completely inoperable. Because there is no way to recover gracefully from the failed BIOS upgrade on most systems today, most manufacturers will require that you send them the motherboard so that they can physically replace the flash ROM chip.

POST

When the POST, or Power-On Self-Test, is run, the resulting hardware settings are compared to the settings stored in CMOS for accuracy. If anything is mismatched, the system halts, and the user is prompted to reconfigure the computer with the proper settings. If no changes have been made, POST also provides some basic troubleshooting to determine what devices have failed since the previous boot-up.

Memory

Memory comes in two different classes and many different forms. The classes are RAM and ROM and are described in the following text. Regardless of form or function, memory of any type is simply a place for data storage.

ROM

ROM, as explained previously, is read-only memory. One application of this class of memory is the BIOS chip previously described. However, all devices also utilize a ROM chip of their own to provide for the basic storage necessary to have a basic initialization program.

ROM retains its memory even with the power removed from the chip. It is slower and less flexible than its counterpart, RAM.

RAM

The system memory is often called RAM (for random-access memory). This is the primary memory, which holds all the programs and data the processor is using at a given time. RAM requires power to maintain storage, so when you turn off the computer, everything in RAM is cleared; when you turn it back on, the memory must be reloaded with programs for the processor to run.

Newer operating systems allow several programs to run at one time, with each program or data file that is loaded using some of the main memory. Generally, the more memory your system has, the more programs you can run simultaneously. This "software side" of RAM is covered in more depth in Chapter 10, "Memory Management."

RAM is normally purchased and installed in a modern system in SIMM (single inline memory module) or DIMM (dual inline memory module) form, although some other forms might be encountered on the exam. Memory can also have different access methods or architecture on these modules. These include SRAM, SDRAM, EDO RAM, VRAM, and many others.

In the Real World

There is a new memory module being used in higher-end systems today called a RIMM. RIMM memory uses RamBus technology on a DIMM-sized memory module. The benefits to this new RDRAM include a chip-to-chip memory bus and internal speeds at over 800MHz.

For more information on RIMM and RamBus technology, see Scott Mueller's *Upgrading and Repairing PCs, Eleventh Edition*.

Formerly very expensive, memory prices have dropped recently, significantly reducing the cost of memory as compared to other parts of the system. Even so, the cost of the recommended amount of memory for a given system is usually equal to or greater than that of the motherboard.

Memory is covered in greater detail in Chapter 4.

Controllers

Controllers are comprised of circuitry that, surprise, controls I/O devices. Some of these controllers are associated with specific cabling and ports and will be discussed in a later section as well. A controller not only controls the hardware device, but it also provides a pathway for the data to flow between the device and the CPU.

Keyboard

The keyboard controller is, by default, on the system board. Generally an oblong, rectangular chip, the keyboard controller is usually soldered onto the system board. Replacement requires purchasing a new system board.

Parallel Port

The parallel port is an interface into the system for external peripherals and I/O devices. This port provides for simultaneous communication of one byte over eight individual data lines for distances under 15 feet. Most commonly associated with printers, this port will be discussed in a later section in more detail.

Serial Port

As opposed to parallel ports, serial ports provide a connection over two data wires, one transmit and one receive. The data is sent in series, one bit after another—hence, the name "serial." Although this is a slower process, the cabling can handle more power through it to provide for much longer distances. Distances up to 50 feet are not unheard of.

Universal Serial Bus

A new high-speed serial-bus architecture for desktop and portable systems is becoming more prevalent: the Universal Serial Bus (USB). This technology provides for the dynamic configuration and communication with a wide variety of peripherals over a proprietary 12Mbps shared connection (see Figures 1.2 and 1.3). By taking full advantage of plug-and-play technology, these devices are automatically configured on-the-fly by the operating system, eliminating the device conflicts that will be discussed in the next chapter.

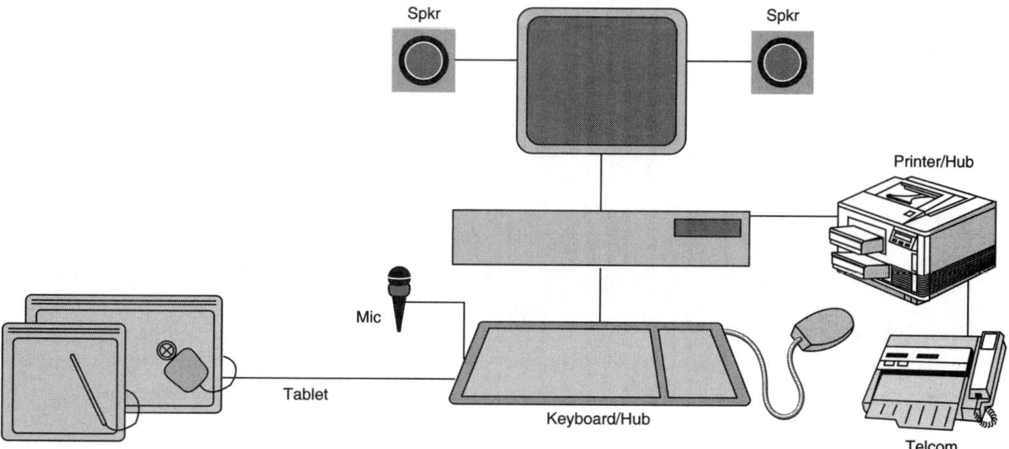

Figure 1.2 A USB connector.

Figure 1.3 A PC can use multiple USB hubs to support a variety of different peripherals on the same shared line.

In the Real World

Although not on the exam, IEEE 1394, also known as Firewire or i.Link, is on a track to surpass and replace USB and virtually all other peripheral connections available today.

IEEE 1394 (or just 1394 for short) is a relatively new bus technology standard designed on Apple and Texas Instruments' FireWire; it is the result of the large data-moving demands of today's audio and video multimedia devices. It is extremely fast, with data transfer rates of up to an incredible 400Mbps, and even faster speeds are being developed.

Both USB and IEE 1394 are discussed in much more detail in Scott Mueller's *Upgrading and Repairing PCs, Eleventh Edition*, Chapter 16, "Serial, Parallel, and Other I/O Interfaces."

Video

The video card controls the information you see on the monitor. A video adapter provides the interface between your computer and your monitor and transmits the signals that appear as images on the display. All video cards have four basic parts: a video chip or chipset, Video RAM, a DAC (digital-to-analog converter), and a BIOS.

- The video chip actually controls the information on the screen by writing data to the video RAM.
- The DAC reads the video RAM and converts the digital data there into analog signals to drive the monitor.
- The BIOS holds the primary video driver that allows the display to function during boot time and at a DOS prompt in basic text mode. More enhanced drivers are then usually loaded from disk to enable advanced video modes for Windows or applications software.

Throughout the history of the PC, there have been a succession of standards for video display characteristics that represent a steady increase in screen resolution and color depth. The following list of standards can serve as an abbreviated history of PC video-display technology:

MDA (monochrome display adapter)
HGC (Hercules Graphics Card)
CGA (Color Graphics Adapter)
EGA (Enhanced Graphics Adapter)
VGA (Video Graphics Array)
SVGA (Super VGA)
XGA (eXtended Graphics Array)

In the Real World

Many advancements have been made in the video industry, even since the release of the 1998 version A+ exams. Some of these advancements include S3 video acceleration chipsets, 3D video cards, Accelerated Graphics Port (AGP), and other special chipsets and adapters. For more information on these, refer to Scott Mueller's *Upgrading and Repairing PCs, Eleventh Edition*, Chapter 15, "Video Hardware."

If you are a gamer, pick up a copy of *Building the Ultimate Game PC*, published by Que, to learn more about 3D video cards.

Most of these standards were pioneered by IBM but were also adopted by the manufacturers of compatible PCs as well. Today, IBM is no longer the industry leader that it once was, and many of these standards are obsolete. Those that aren't obsolete are seldom referred to by these names anymore. The sole exception to this is VGA, which is a term that is still used to refer to a baseline graphics display capability supported by virtually every video adapter on the market today.

Storage

Storage interfaces include all drive controllers. Although this does include a floppy-disk drive interface, this section is devoted to the hard disk controllers and interfaces. The primary job of the hard disk controller or interface is to transmit and receive data to and from the drive. The different interface types limit how fast data can be moved from the drive to the system and offer different levels of performance.

These interfaces have different cabling and configuration options, and the setup and format of drives will vary as well. Special problems might arise when you are trying to install more than one drive of a particular interface type or (especially) when you are mixing drives of different interface types in one system.

Several types of hard disk interfaces have been used in PC systems over the years, as shown in the following table.

Interface	When Used
ST-506/412	1978–1989
ESDI	1986–1991
SCSI	1986–Present
IDE	1988–Present

As you can see, only IDE and SCSI remain popular today. It is these controllers that you will be tested over on the A+ examination. Both of these technologies will be covered in more detail in a later section of this chapter.

IDE

The IDE interface, which is the most commonly used storage device interface in modern systems, has evolved from a hard-disk–only interface to one that supports hard disks and many different types of removable media such as CD-ROM, CD-RW, DVD, Zip tape drives, and others.

IDE stands for Integrated Drive Electronics and refers to the fact that the interface electronics or controller is built in to the drives.

There are many different types of IDE/ATA interfaces. These include the following:

- IDE
- EIDE
- Ultra ATA/33
- Ultra ATA/66

SCSI

SCSI (pronounced "scuzzy") stands for Small Computer System Interface and is a general-purpose interface used for connecting many types of devices to a PC. SCSI is the most popular interface for attaching high-speed disk drives to higher performance PCs such as workstations or network servers. SCSI is also very flexible; it is not only a disk interface, but also a systems-level interface allowing many different types of devices to be connected to it. SCSI is a device bus that supports as many as 8 or 16 total devices.

Because SCSI is a bus and has a host adapter rather than a controller attached to the PC (the controller is on the drives), the bus must be terminated on both ends to avoid signal reflection and degradation from ghosting. This concept will be explained in the later section in this chapter on SCSI configuration.

There are many different types of SCSI interfaces and variations to the types. These include the following:

- SCSI
- SCSI-2
- SCSI-2 Fast
- SCSI-2 Wide
- SCSI-2 Fast/Wide
- SCSI-3/Ultra
- SCSI-3/Ultra Wide
- SCSI-3/Ultra2
- SCSI-3/Ultra2 Wide

In the Real World

Only the most basic of SCSI concepts (those of the SCSI-2 base variety) will be covered on the exam. In addition, the SCSI-3 specifications have yet to be finalized. These SCSI-3 variations are what the marketplace has developed without a ratified standard. These standards should be ratified sometime in 1999 by the ANSI Accredited Standard Committee.

IDE and SCSI Comparison

Table 1.1 shows a comparison of the speeds, data paths, and number of devices supported by the various IDE and SCSI interfaces.

Table 1.1   IDE and SCSI Comparison

Interface	Data Path	Speed in Mbps	Max. Devices	Connection
IDE	16-bit	8.3	2	40-pin daisy chain
EIDE	16-bit	16.6	4	2 40-pin daisy chains
ULTRA ATA	16-bit	33	4	2 40-pin daisy chains

Interface	Data Path	Speed in Mbps	Max. Devices	Connection
ULTRA ATA/66	16-bit	66	4	2 40-pin daisy chains
SCSI/SCSI-2	8-bit	5	7	50-pin daisy chain
SCSI-2 Fast	8-bit	10	7	50-pin daisy chain
SCSI-2 Wide	16-bit	10	7	68-pin daisy chain
SCSI-2 Fast/Wide	16-bit	20	7	68-pin daisy chain
SCSI-3 Ultra	8-bit	20	15	50-pin daisy chain
SCSI-3 Ultra Wide	16-bit	40	15	68-pin daisy chain
SCSI-3 Ultra2	8-bit	40	15	50-pin daisy chain
SCSI-3 Ultra2 Wide	16-bit	80	15	68-pin daisy chain

More in-depth information on the IDE and SCSI interfaces can be found in Chapters 7, "The IDE Interface," and 8, "The SCSI Interface," of the eleventh edition of *Upgrading and Repairing PCs*.

I/O Devices

This section will discuss the various input and output devices commonly found on PCs. Although some are strictly for input and others strictly for output, some have aspects of both. The more common devices include the following:

- Keyboard
- Mouse
- Monitor
- Printers
- Modems
- Multimedia
- Storage devices

Additional information on I/O Devices and interfaces can be found in Chapters 16, "Serial, Parallel, and Other I/O Interfaces," and 17, "Input Devices," of the eleventh edition of *Upgrading and Repairing PCs*.

Keyboard

The keyboard is the primary device on a PC that is used by a human being to communicate with and control a system. It is also one of the only two devices that are tested by POST and has a controller built in to the system board by default.

Keyboards are available in a large number of languages, layouts, sizes, and shapes and have numerous special features or characteristics. Common additional keys today include the "Windows" key, which launches the Windows 95/98 Start Menu (see Figure 1.4).

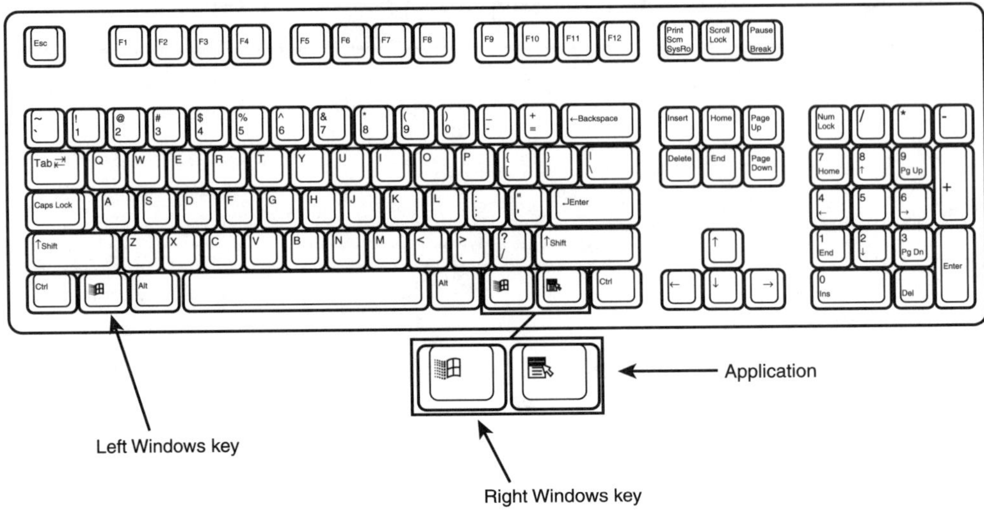

Figure 1.4 104-key Windows keyboard layout.

Note

Keyboards are covered in greater detail in Chapter 17 of the eleventh edition of *Upgrading and Repairing PCs* and will be covered in various troubleshooting sections in this text.

Mouse

With the advent of computer operating systems that used a Graphical User Interface (GUI), it became necessary to have a device that enabled a user to point at or select items that were shown on the screen. Although there are many different types of pointing devices on the market today, the first and most popular device for this purpose is the mouse. By moving the mouse across a desktop or tabletop, a corresponding pointer can be moved across the computer screen, allowing items to be more easily selected or manipulated than they can be with a keyboard alone. This is a relative-positioning device, as opposed to the absolute positioning seen in digitizing tablets.

Standard mice, as used on PCs, have two buttons: one for selecting items under the pointer and the other for activating menus. Mice are also available with a third button, a wheel, or a stick, which can be used for scrolling the display or other special functions.

Mice can be connected using a serial port, a standard PS/2 port, or a proprietary bus connection in addition to the new USB and Firewire types.

Monitor

This output device is required for a system to function. In most systems, the monitor is housed in its own protective case, separate from the system case and chassis. In portable systems and some low-cost PCs, however, the monitor is built in to the system case. Monitors are generally classified by three major criteria: diagonal size in inches, resolution in pixels, and refresh rate in hertz (Hz).

Desktop monitors, using CRT's, usually range from 14 inches to 21 inches diagonal measure (although the actual viewable area is smaller than the advertised measure by about 1/20th of the actual measured distance from corner to corner). LCD monitors in portable systems today range from 11 inches to 15 inches and can be passive matrix or active matrix. There are larger LCD panel screens available, but rather than a portable system, these provide a smaller footprint desktop monitor (and at a significantly higher cost, too).

In the Real World

Although passive and active matrix LCD panels are not specifically covered on the A+ tests, you will encounter them in the real world.

Passive matrix screens are becoming obsolete because of the poorer quality images they provide. In a passive matrix screen, the crystals are "excited" by a grid of wires. A charge is sent down a horizontal and a vertical wire to meet and light up the crystal at the intersection. Because liquid crystals retain their charge longer than the phosphorescent pixels in a CRT, any motion on the screen will leave a trail of ghost images behind that gradually fade out.

Active matrix screens, on the other hand, have the same type of grid, but rather than activating the liquid crystals, they activate a thin-film transistor, or TFT. This transistor maintains a charge to the crystals while it is activated but removes the charge completely when the signal stops. This immediate "off" switch on the crystals provides ghost-free motion on an LCD display.

More in-depth information on CRTs and LCDs can be found in Chapter 15 of the eleventh edition of *Upgrading and Repairing PCs.*

Resolution ranges from 640×480 pixels (horizontal by vertical) to 1,600×1,200 pixels. Each pixel in the monitor is made up of a trio of dots, one each for the colors red, blue, and green.

Because of the technology underlying the CRT, a monitor must be *refreshed* quite often. To explain this, a little understanding of the working of a CRT will be necessary.

Cathode-Ray Tubes (CRTs) are vacuum-filled glass bubbles with a flat end to display an image. The inside of the flattened portion of the screen is coated with a phosphorous substance in a precise pattern of red, green, and blue dots that form thousands of triangles called pixels. A pulsing electron beam is emitted from the back side of the tube and deflected in a specific pattern on the screen. The colored dots that the beam touches momentarily (for about 1/50th of a second) light up. This creates the first image. The beam follows a pattern that is a repeating, sweeping motion from one side to the other while sequentially stepping from the top of the screen to the bottom (see Figure 1.5). This occurs so rapidly that the beam traverses the screen from top to bottom many times per second. Each pass is called a *cycle*. To provide for the appearance of a solid picture with no flickering, the cycle must be repeated, or refreshed, at least 60 times per second. The number of cycles completed per second is known as the *refresh rate*. The more cycles completed per second creates a progressively better image.

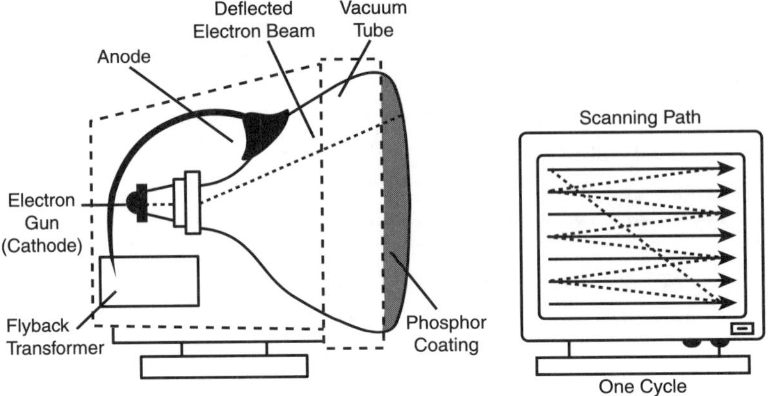

Figure 1.5 CRT cross section and scanning path.

An average monitor is capable of refreshing 60 times per second (60Hz), whereas higher quality monitors might refresh at 100Hz. The refresh rate measures how often the display of the screen is redrawn from the contents of the video adapter memory. Both the resolution and refresh rate of the monitor are tied to the capability of the system video adapter. Most monitors are capable of supporting several different resolutions and refresh rates (with the common exception of LCD screens in portables).

Monitors are covered in detail in Chapter 15 of the eleventh edition of Scott Mueller's *Upgrading and Repairing PCs*.

Printers

The capability to produce a printed version (often called a hard copy) of a document is a primary function of a PC, so printers have become a required accessory. This is not to say, however, that every PC requires its own printer. One of the main reasons for the rise in local area networking in the business world has been the capability to share printers among multiple users.

Due in part to this network market, there is a wide variety of printers on the market supporting a multitude of both features and speeds. This section touches on the underlying concepts of printer technology and the basic types of printers available today. For more information, see Chapter 5, "Printers," of this text or Chapter 22, "Printers and Scanners," of *Upgrading and Repairing PCs, Eleventh Edition*.

There are three basic types of printer technologies used with PCs that will be covered on the exam. There are several other printing technologies available today, but these bit-image formation methods will be your focus for the exam:

Laser

Laser printers function by creating an electrophotostatic image of an printed page on a photosensitive drum with a laser beam. When an ultrafine black plastic powder called toner is applied to the drum, it adheres only to the sensitized areas corresponding to the letters or images on the page. The drum spins and is pressed against a sheet of paper, transferring the toner to the page and creating the image. This is the same basic technology used by copiers. Laser printers print faster and at higher quality than the other two methods and are consequently more expensive.

Inkjet

Inkjet printers, as their name implies, have tiny nozzles that spray ink onto a page. Different manufacturers use different technologies to accomplish this, and a few of these methods will be discussed in Chapter 5. As the ink is sprayed onto the page, a degree of absorption occurs and the dots merge together. Although the inkjet has much less resolution than the laser printer, this side-effect tends to cause the letters to seem more fully formed for the resolution than their dot matrix counterparts.

Dot Matrix

Dot matrix printers use an array of round-headed pins to press an inked ribbon against a page. The pins are arranged in a rectangular grid (called a matrix); different combinations of pins form the various characters and images. Because of the forceful contact with the page, the dot matrix printer is singularly suited to producing multipart carbon forms, a feat which no other common printer technology can produce today.

Modems

For PCs that are not connected to a network by some other means, a modem has become virtually a standard piece of equipment. For many home users, connecting to the Internet is their primary reason for owning a computer. Whether for business, entertainment, or just keeping in touch with friends and family, a modem connection takes an isolated system and makes it a part of a worldwide network.

The word *modem* (from modulator/demodulator) basically describes a device that converts the digital data used by computers into analog signals suitable for transmission over a telephone line, and it converts the analog signals back to digital data at the destination. The typical PC modem is an asynchronous device, meaning that it transmits data in an intermittent stream of small packets. The receiving system takes the data in the packets and reassembles it in a form the computer can use.

More information on modems can be found in Chapter 7, "Basic Networking," and again in Chapter 13, "Networks."

Multimedia

What is multimedia? The term embraces a number of PC technologies, but it primarily deals with video, sound, and storage. Basically, PC multimedia means the capability to merge images, data, and sound on a computer into a unified perceptual experience. In a practical sense, multimedia usually means adding an audio adapter and a CD-ROM drive to your system. Because CD-ROMs are covered under storage devices and video devices have already been discussed, this topic will cover audio hardware and can be enhanced with some study of *Upgrading and Repairing PCs*, Chapter 20, "Audio."

Audio hardware is comprised of these components (see Figure 1.6):

- Sound card
- Speakers
- Microphone

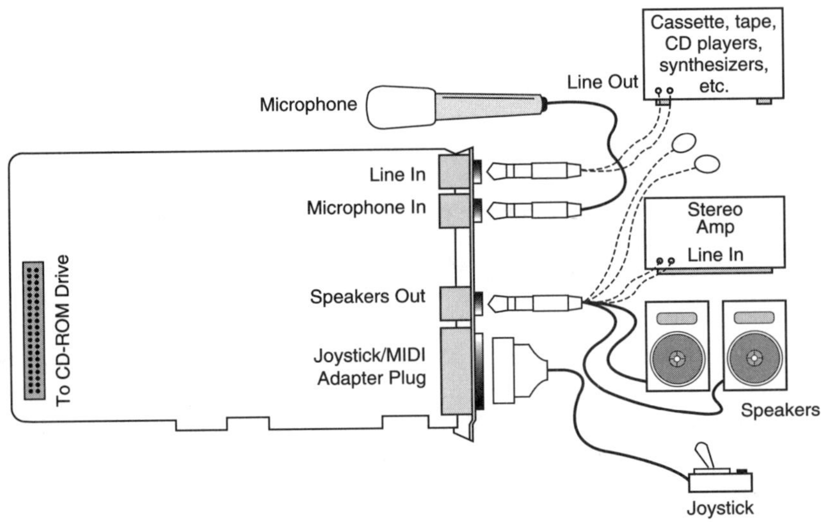

Figure 1.6 Common sound card connections and multimedia components.

Sound cards

Today's PC audio hardware usually takes the form of an audio adapter on an expansion card that you install into a bus slot in the computer. As with video adapters, some systems today include the audio hardware directly on the motherboard. The adapter provides jacks for speakers, a microphone, and sometimes other devices such as joysticks and MIDI hardware. On the software side, the audio adapter requires the support of a driver that you install either directly from an application or in your computer's operating system.

Tip

The line in, line out, microphone, and speaker connectors on an audio adapter all use the same 1/8-inch minijack socket. The four jacks are usually labeled, but when setting up a computer on or under a desk, these labels on the back of the PC can be difficult to read. One of the most common reasons why a PC fails to produce any sound is that the speakers are plugged into the wrong socket.

Over the past few years, some manufacturers of audio adapters have fought for dominance over the market, and there are several popular brands. Historically, the leader in the field has been Creative Labs, whose Sound Blaster audio adapters continue to dominate the marketplace and have established the de facto SoundBlaster Pro standard for the industry.

Speakers

Sound cards offer little or none of the amplification needed to drive external speakers. Although some sound cards have small 4-watt amplifiers, they are not powerful enough to drive quality speakers. Also, conventional speakers sitting near your display might create magnetic interference, which can distort colors and objects onscreen or jumble the data recorded on nearby floppy disks or other magnetic media.

To solve these problems, computer speakers need to be small, efficient, and self-powered. Also, they should be provided with magnetic shielding, either in the form of added layers of insulation in the speaker cabinet or electronic cancellation of the magnetic distortion.

Microphone

Virtually all audio adapters have an audio input jack and/or a microphone jack. With a microphone, you can record your voice. Using the Sound Recorder application included with all versions of Microsoft Windows, you can play, edit, or record a sound files in the WAV format. From the Windows Sounds Control Panel, you can assign specific WAV files to certain Windows events.

Storage Devices

Computers are all about data storage, whether long-term (magnetic or optical media) or short-term (memory). They store raw data and they store processed data. Memory will be covered extensively in Chapter 4. This section will cover the various magnetic and optical storage devices used for long-term storage in computers today.

Floppy Disk

The floppy drive is a simple, inexpensive, low-capacity, removable media magnetic storage device. For many years, floppy disks were the primary medium for software distribution and system backup. However, with the advent of CD-ROM and DVD-ROM discs as the primary method of installing or loading new software in a system and with inexpensive high-capacity tape drives for backup, the floppy drive is not used very often in most modern systems, except perhaps by a system builder, installer, or technician. Because the floppy drive is the first device from which a

PC attempts to boot, it is still the primary method that is used for loading initial operating systems' startup software and core hardware diagnostics. Recent advancements in technology have created new types of floppy drives with up to 120MB or more of storage, making the drive much more usable for temporary backups or for moving files from system to system. See Figures 1.7 and 1.8.

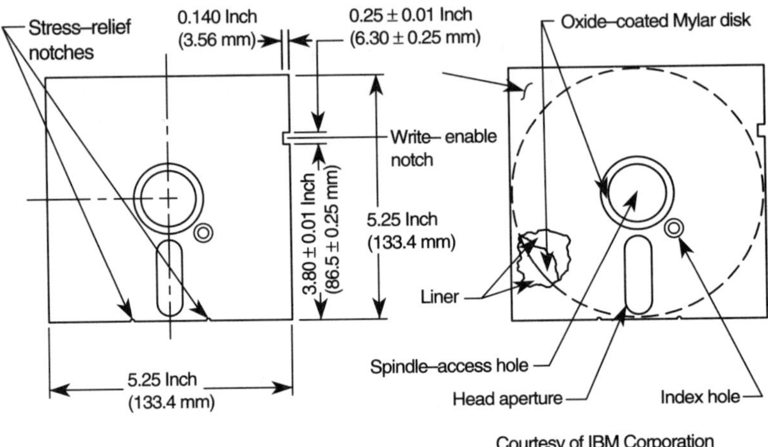

Figure 1.7 5 1/4-inch floppy diskette.

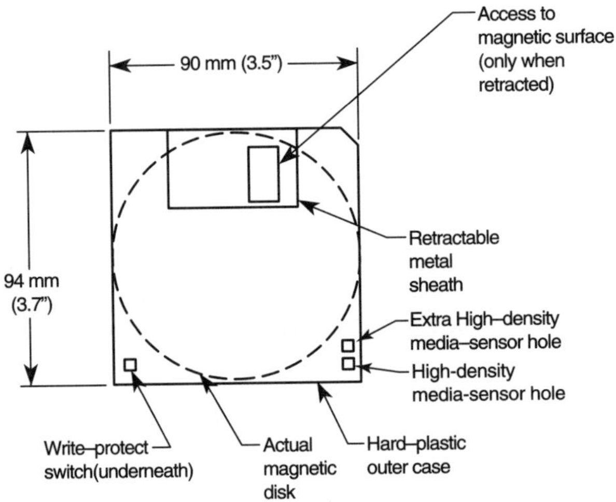

Figure 1.8 3 1/2-inch floppy diskette.

Floppy disks store the data on a magnetic medium by changing the polarity of the area directly under the *read/write heads*. This data is arranged in concentric circles called *tracks,* which are divided into pie-shaped pieces called *sectors* much like a hard disk. Unlike a hard disk drive, to read and write to the disk properly, the read/write heads must be in direct contact with the magnetic medium. Because of the contact between the heads and disk, a buildup of the magnetic material from the disk eventually forms on the heads. The buildup should periodically be cleaned off the heads as part of a normal service program.

To retrieve the data from a diskette, the computer must know which side of the disk the data is on as well as the specific track and sector location. This map is stored in the *FAT*, or file allocation table, at the first track and sector of the disk.

Floppy disks come in several different physical sizes and capacities. Some of the more common drive comparisons are listed in Table 1.2.

Table 1.2   Common Drive Comparisons

Physical Size	Type	Tracks xSectors	Capacity
5.25"	Double Sided-Double Density	40×9	360KB
5.25"	Double Sided-High Density	80×15	1.2MB
3.5"	Double Sided-Double Density	80×9	720KB
3.5"	Double Sided-High Density	80×18	1.44MB
3.5"	Double Sided-Extra Density	80×36	2.88MB

There is another type of floppy disk drive that has been left out of the preceding chart. This is called the LS-120. The LS-120 is a magneto-optical device that, although backward-compatible with other floppy technologies, can use specialized 3.5" optical diskettes to achieve 120MB in the same form factor. This device is thought to replace both floppy and ZIP drive technology in one device.

Floppy disk technologies are discussed in greater depth in Chapter 11 of *Upgrading and Repairing PCs*.

Hard Disk

The hard disk is the primary archival storage memory for the system. It contains copies of all programs and data that are not currently active in main memory. A hard drive is so named because it consists of spinning platters of aluminum or ceramic that are coated with a magnetic media and sealed in a special, filtered unit. Hard drives can be created with many different storage capacities, depending on the density, size, and number of platters. Most desktop systems today use drives with 3 1/2-inch platters, whereas most laptop or notebook computers use 2 1/2-inch platter drives.

The basic physical construction of a hard disk drive consists of spinning disks with heads that move over the disks and store data in tracks and sectors. The heads read and write data in concentric rings called tracks, which are divided up into segments called sectors, which normally store 512 bytes each (see Figure 1.9).

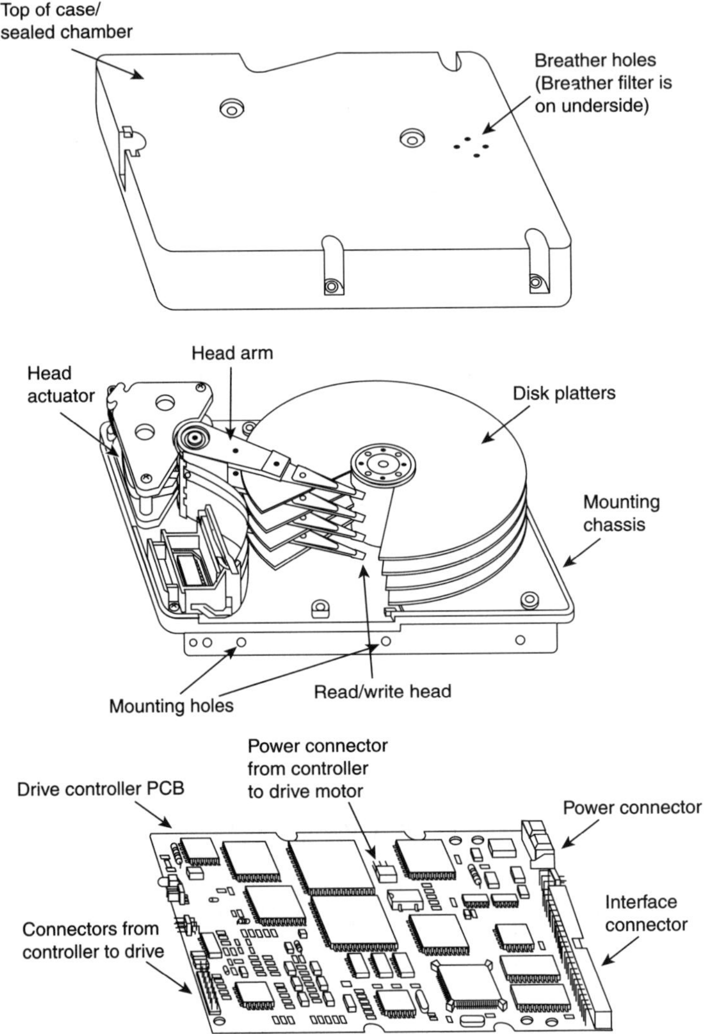

Figure 1.9 Hard disk components.

Hard disk drives usually have multiple disks, called platters, that are stacked on top of each other and spin in unison, each with two sides on which the drive stores data. Most drives have at least two or three platters, resulting in four or six sides, and some drives have up to 11 or more platters. The identically positioned tracks on each side of every platter together make up a cylinder (see Figure 1.10). A hard disk drive normally has one head per platter side, with all the heads mounted on a common carrier device or rack. The heads move radialy in and out across the disk in unison; they cannot move independently because they are mounted on the same rack.

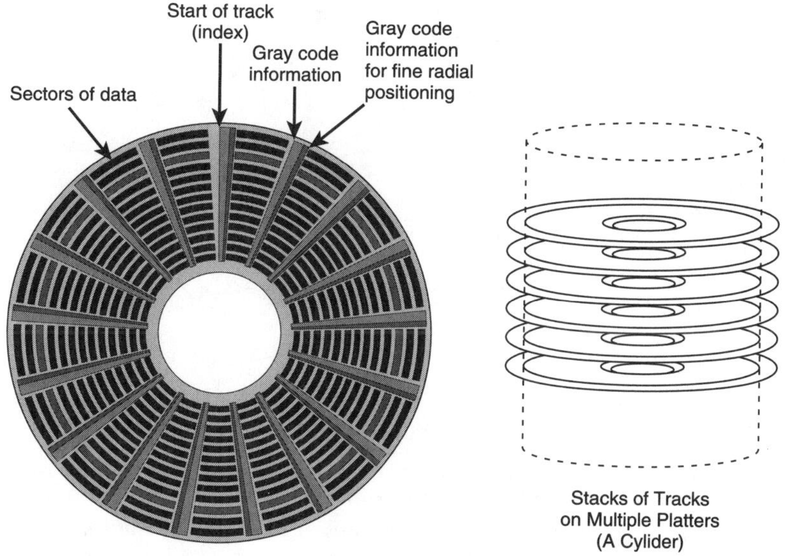

Figure 1.10 Tracks, sectors, and cylinders.

The heads in most hard disk drives do not (and should not!) touch the platters during normal operation. When the heads are powered off, however, in most drives they land on the platters as they stop spinning. While the drive is running, a very thin cushion of air keeps each head suspended a short distance above or below the platter. If the air cushion is disturbed by a particle of dust or a shock, the head may come into contact with the platter while it is spinning at full speed. When contact with the spinning platters is forceful enough to do damage, the event is called a *head crash*. The result of a head crash can be anything from a few lost bytes of data to a completely ruined drive.

Hard disk drives have several chapters devoted to them in *Upgrading and Repairing PCs, Eleventh Edition*, including Chapter 9, "Magnetic Storage Principles," and Chapter 10, "Hard Disk Drives."

Optical Storage (CD/DVD)

CD- (Compact Disc) and DVD- (Digital Versatile Disc) ROM (Read Only Memory) drives are relatively high-capacity, removable media optical drives. These devices use laser light reflected from a disc in a pulsing pattern to indicate data as shown in Figure 1.11. They are primarily a read-only medium, which means the drives can only read information, and the data on the discs cannot be altered or rewritten. There are writeable or rewriteable versions of the discs and drives available, but they are much more expensive than their read-only counterparts, and they therefore are not included as standard in most PCs. CD-ROM and DVD-ROM are the most popular media for distributing software or large amounts of data because they are very inexpensive when produced in quantity and they can hold a great deal of information.

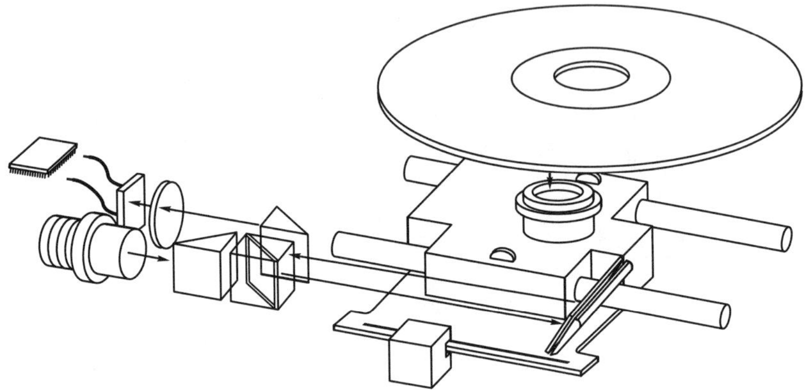

Figure 1.11 Laser transmission, reflection, and reception during data retrieval.

The CD-ROM is a read-only optical storage medium capable of holding up to 682MB of data (approximately 333,000 pages of text), 74 minutes of high-fidelity audio, or some combination of the two on a single side of a 5-inch disc. The CD-ROM is very similar to the familiar audio compact disc and can, in fact, play in a normal audio player. The result, however, would be noise—unless audio tracks accompany the data on the CD-ROM (see the CD PLUS coverage, later in this chapter). Accessing data from a CD-ROM is quite a bit faster than floppy disk but is considerably slower than a modern hard drive. The term CD-ROM refers to both the discs themselves and the drive that reads them.

DVD offers an initial storage capacity of 4.7GB of digital information on a single-sided, single-layer disc the same diameter and thickness of a current CD-ROM. With MPEG-2 (Motion Picture Experts Group, standard 2) compression, that's enough to contain 135 minutes of video—enough for a full-length, full-screen, full-motion feature film, including three channels of CD-quality audio and four channels of subtitles. With only one audio track, a single disk could easily hold 160 minutes of video or more. This initial capacity is no coincidence; the creation of DVD was driven by the film industry, which has long sought a storage medium cheaper and more durable than videotape.

Additional optical storage information can be found in Chapter 13, "Optical Storage," of the eleventh edition of *Upgrading and Repairing PCs*. That chapter covers CD-ROM, CD-R, CD-RW, DVD, WORM, and many other optical technologies and intricacies.

Tape

Tape backup drives are the most simple and efficient device for backing up your system. With a tape backup drive installed in your computer, you insert a tape into the drive, start your backup software, and select the drive and files you want to back up. The backup software copies your selected files onto the tape while you attend to other business. Later, when you need to retrieve some or all of the files on the backup tape, you insert the tape in the drive, start your backup program, and select the files you want to restore. The tape backup drive takes care of the rest of the job.

Tape drives are designed more for offline storage than a direct read/write medium for the end user. This is because the streaming tape is written and read in a linear fashion. This means that if you want to retrieve something from the end of the tape, the entire tape must unroll and reroll past the read/write head. Sequential access is relatively fast, but random access time suffers greatly due to this.

QIC (quarter-inch cartridge), DAT (Digital Audio Tape), and DLT (Digital Linear Tape) are the three most common tape standards. ZIP and JAZZ devices are removable interactive tape media and are included here, although they sacrifice capacity for speed. All these standards vary in capacity depending on the drive, tape, and compression used, but the ranges are listed in Table 1.3.

Table 1.3　QIC, DAT, and DLT Capacities

Tape Standard	Capacity Range
QIC	40MB–13GB
DAT	2GB–12GB
DLT	20GB–80GB
ZIP	100MB–120MB
JAZZ	1GB–2GB

Power Supply

The basic function of the power supply is to convert the type of electrical power available at the wall socket to the type the computer circuitry can use. The power supply in a conventional desktop system is designed to convert the American 120v, 60Hz, AC (alternating current) power into +3.3v, +5v, and +12v DC (direct current) power. Usually, the digital electronic components and circuits in the system (motherboard, adapter cards, and disk-drive logic boards) use the +3.3v or +5v power, and the motors (disk drive motors and any fans) use the +12v power. The power supply must deliver a good, steady supply of DC power so the system can operate properly.

Most power supplies today (with the notable exception of ATX) use the P8 and P9 motherboard connectors. These systems have the connectors installed end-to-end so that the two black-colored wires (ground connections) on both power cables are next to each other. Note that the designations P8 and P9 are not fully standardized, although most use those designations because that is what IBM used on the originals. Some power supplies have them labeled as P1/P2 or possibly something else. Because these connectors usually have a clasp that prevents them from being inserted backward on the pins on the motherboards, the major concern is getting them in the correct order and not missing a pin on either side. Following the black-on-black rule keeps you safe. You must take care, however, to make sure that no unconnected motherboard pins are between or on either side of the two connectors when you install them. A properly installed connector connects to and covers every motherboard power pin. If any power pins are showing on either side of the connectors, the entire connector assembly is installed incorrectly, which can result in catastrophic failure for the motherboard and everything plugged into it at the time of power-up. Figure 1.12 shows an example of a standard slim-tower version of the AT power supply.

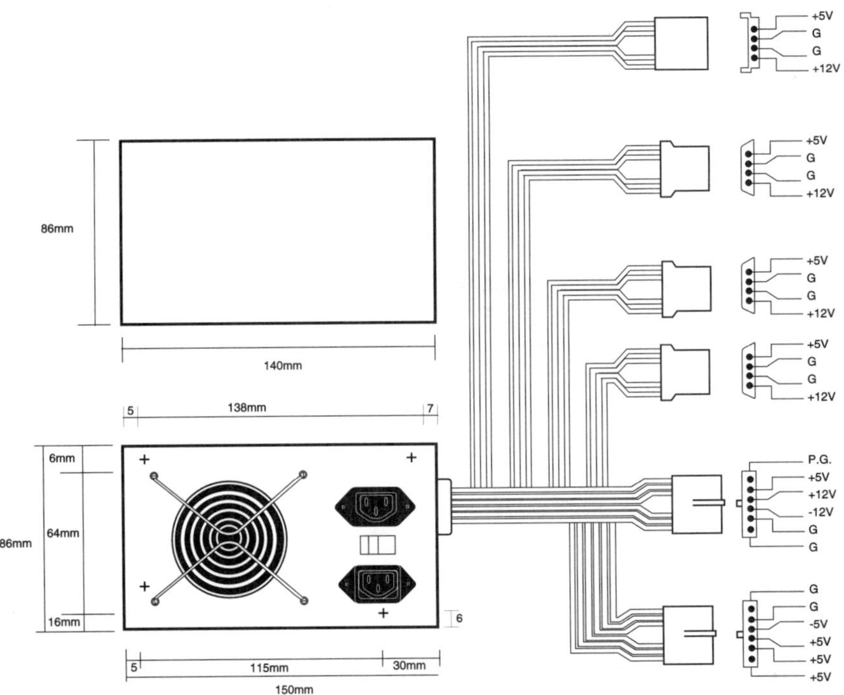

Figure 1.12 AT-style power supply.

ATX power supplies have redesigned the p8/p9 connections into a single power connection and include the 3.3v signal, as shown in Figure 1.13.

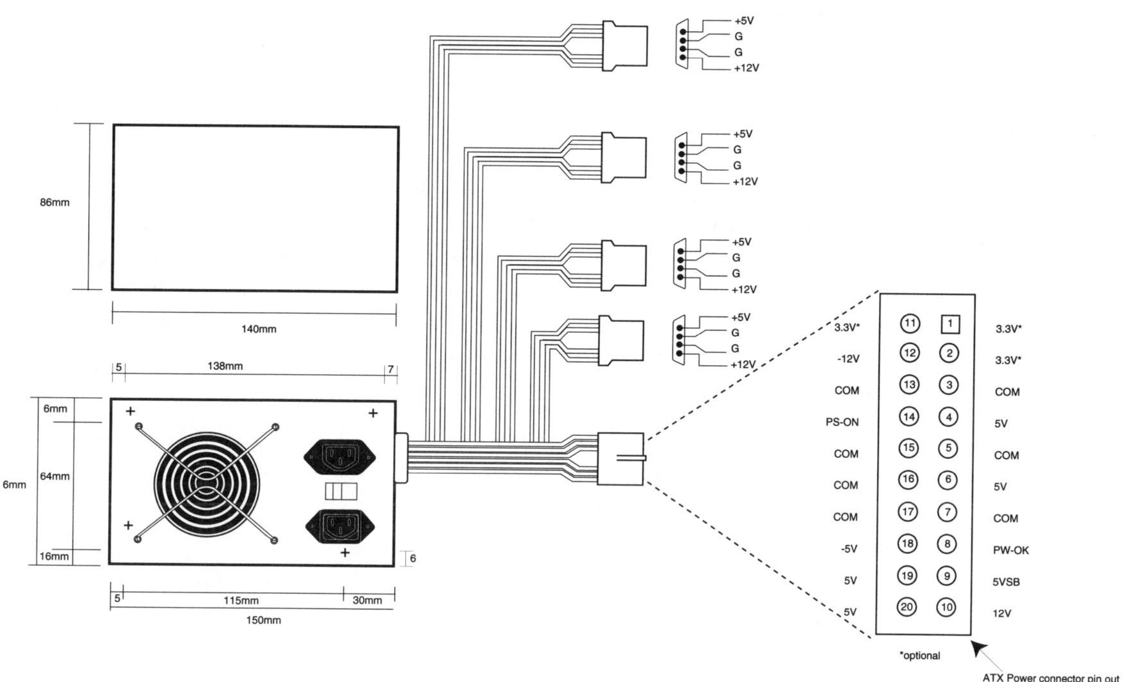

Figure 1.13   ATX-style power supply.

Various colors also indicate the voltage that the wire is carrying. Most manufacturers adhere to these standard colors as listed in Table 1.4.

Table 1.4   Standard Voltages by Wire Color

Color	Voltage
Orange	+3.3v
Red	+5v
Yellow	+12v
White	-5v
Blue	-12v
Black	Ground

Field Replacement Procedures

Following all the proper ESD precautions and safety measures is a must for any replacement process. In addition, there are a few things that you should do before beginning:

1. Ensure that the system is backed up.

2. Observe how the system is designed and configured. This includes physical configuration as well as CMOS/BIOS configuration and operating system versions and configurations.

3. Document everything that you see. Draw cabling diagrams, print reports from diagnostic software such as Microsoft Diagnostics, record CMOS settings, and draw jumper and physical settings on any components you intend to replace.

System Board

When you are installing your system's motherboard, unpack the motherboard and check to make sure that you have everything that should be included. Before a new motherboard can be installed, it must be set up properly to accept the processor. Some motherboards have jumpers that control both the CPU speed and the voltage supplied to it. If these are set incorrectly, the system might not operate at all, might operate erratically, or might possibly even damage the CPU. If you have any questions about the proper settings, contact the vendor who sold you the board before making any jumper changes.

The motherboard attaches to the case with one or more screws and often several plastic standoffs. If you are using a new case, you might have to attach one or more metal spacers or plastic standoffs in the proper holes before you can install the motherboard. Use the following procedure to install the new motherboard in the case:

1. Find the holes in the new motherboard for the metal spacers and plastic standoffs. You should use metal spacers wherever there is a ring of solder around the hole. Use plastic standoffs where there is no ring of solder (see Figure 1.14). Screw any metal spacers into the new case in the proper positions to align with the screw holes in the motherboard.

2. Insert any plastic standoffs directly into the new motherboard from underneath until they snap into place.

3. Install the new motherboard into the case by setting it down so that any standoffs engage the case. Often, you will have to set the board into the case and slide it sideways to engage the standoffs into the slots in the case. When the board is in the proper position, the screw holes in the board should be aligned with all the metal spacers or screw holes in the case.

4. Take the screws and any plastic washers that were supplied with the new motherboard and screw the board into the case.

There are several connections that must be made between a motherboard and the case. These include LEDs for the hard disk and power, an internal speaker connection, a reset button, a power button, and a deturbo button on some systems. Most modern motherboards also have several built-in I/O ports that have to be connected. This includes dual IDE host adapters, a floppy controller, dual serial ports, and a parallel port. Some boards also include additional items such as built-in video, sound, or SCSI adapters.

If the board is an ATX type, the connectors for all the external I/O ports are already built in to the rear of the board. If you are using a Baby-AT–type board, you might have to install cables and brackets to run the serial, parallel, and other external I/O ports to the rear of the case. If your motherboard has onboard I/O, use the following procedures to connect the cables:

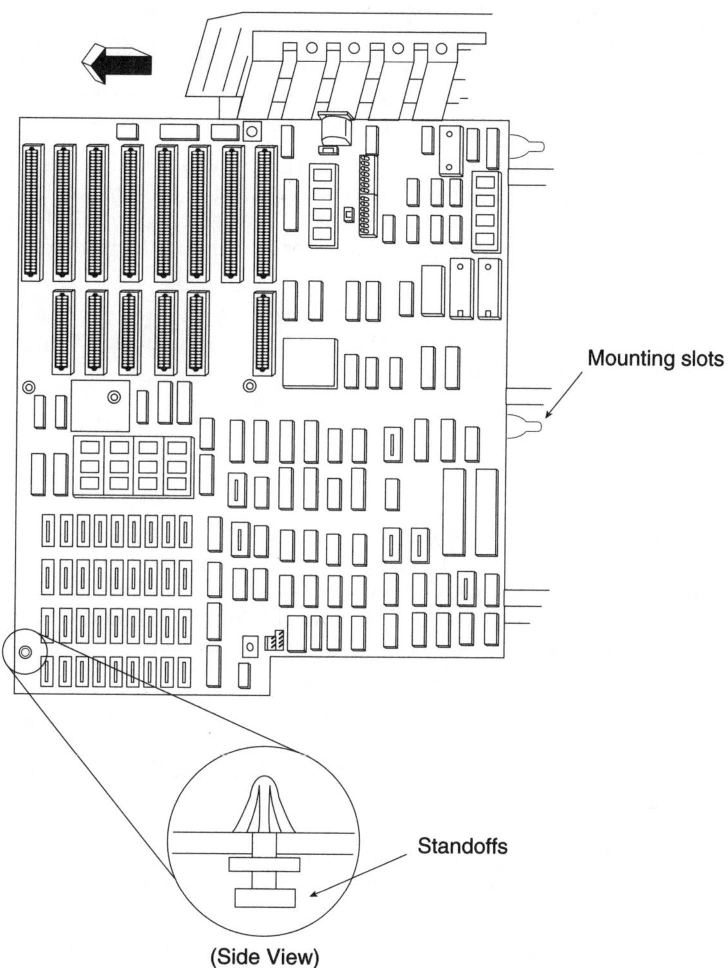

Figure 1.14 System board standoffs and mounting slots.

1. Connect the floppy cable between the floppy drives and the 34-pin floppy controller connector on the motherboard.

2. Connect the IDE cables between the hard disk, IDE CD-ROM, and the 40-pin primary and secondary IDE connectors on the motherboard. Normally, you will use the primary IDE channel connector for hard disks only and the secondary IDE channel connector to attach an IDE CD-ROM or other device, such as a tape drive.

3. On non-ATX boards, a 25-pin female cable port bracket is normally used for the parallel port. There are usually two serial ports: a 9-pin, and either another 9-pin or a 25-pin male connector port. Align pin 1 on the serial and parallel port cables with pin 1 on the motherboard connector and plug them in.

4. If the ports don't have card slot-type brackets or if you need all your expansion slots, there might be port knockouts on the back of the case that you can use instead. Find ones that fit the ports and push them out, removing the metal piece covering the hole. Unscrew the hex nuts on each side of the port connector and position the connector in the hole. Install the hex nuts back in through the case to hold the port connector in place.

5. Most newer motherboards also include a built-in mouse port. If the connector for this port is not built in to the back of the motherboard (usually next to the keyboard connector), you will probably have a card bracket type of connector to install. In that case, plug the cable into the motherboard mouse connector and then attach the external mouse connector bracket to the case.

6. Attach the front panel switch, LED, and internal speaker wires from the case front panel to the motherboard. If they are not marked on the board, check where each one is on the diagram in the motherboard manual.

Processor

To attach processors, follow these steps:

1. Refer to the motherboard manufacturer's manual to set the jumpers, if any, to match the CPU you are going to install. Look for the diagram of the motherboard to find the jumper location, and look for the tables for the right settings for your CPU. If the CPU was supplied already installed on the motherboard, the jumpers should already be correctly set for you, but it is still a good idea to check them.

2. For socketed processors, find pin 1 on the processor; it is usually denoted by a corner of the chip that is marked by a dot or a bevel. Next, find the corresponding pin 1 of the ZIF socket for the CPU on the motherboard; it is also usually marked on the board, or there might be a bevel in one corner of the socket. Insert the CPU into the ZIF socket by lifting the release lever, aligning the pins on the processor with the holes in the socket, and lowering it down into place. If the processor does not go all the way into the socket, check for possible interference or pin alignment problems. When the processor is fully seated in the socket, push the locking lever on the socket down to secure the processor.

3. For slotted processors, the same process applies except that the processor unit package is placed into a keyed edge connector rather than a lever-driven Zero Insertion Force socket.

4. If the CPU does not already have a heat sink attached to it, attach it now. Most heat sinks will either clip directly to the CPU or to the socket with one or more retainer clips. Be careful when attaching the clip to the socket; you don't want it to scrape against the motherboard, which might damage circuit traces or components. In most cases, it is a good idea to put a dab of heat sink thermal transfer compound (normally a white-colored grease) on the CPU before installing the heat sink. This prevents any air gaps and allows the heat sink to work more efficiently.

Memory

Modern motherboards use either SIMMs or DIMMs. Depending on the module type, it will have a specific method of sliding into and clipping to the sockets. Normally, you install modules in the lowest numbered sockets or banks first. Note that some boards will require modules to be installed in pairs or even four at a time. Consult the motherboard documentation for more information on which sockets to use first and in what order and how to install the specific modules the board uses.

Memory modules are normally keyed to the sockets by a notch on the side or on the bottom, so they can go in only one way.

Caution

Be careful not to damage the connector. If you damage the motherboard memory connector, you could be facing an expensive repair. Never force the module; it should come out easily. If it doesn't, you are doing something wrong.

Figures 1.15, 1.16, and 1.17 show the insertion techniques and locking mechanisms for SIMM and DIMM memory modules.

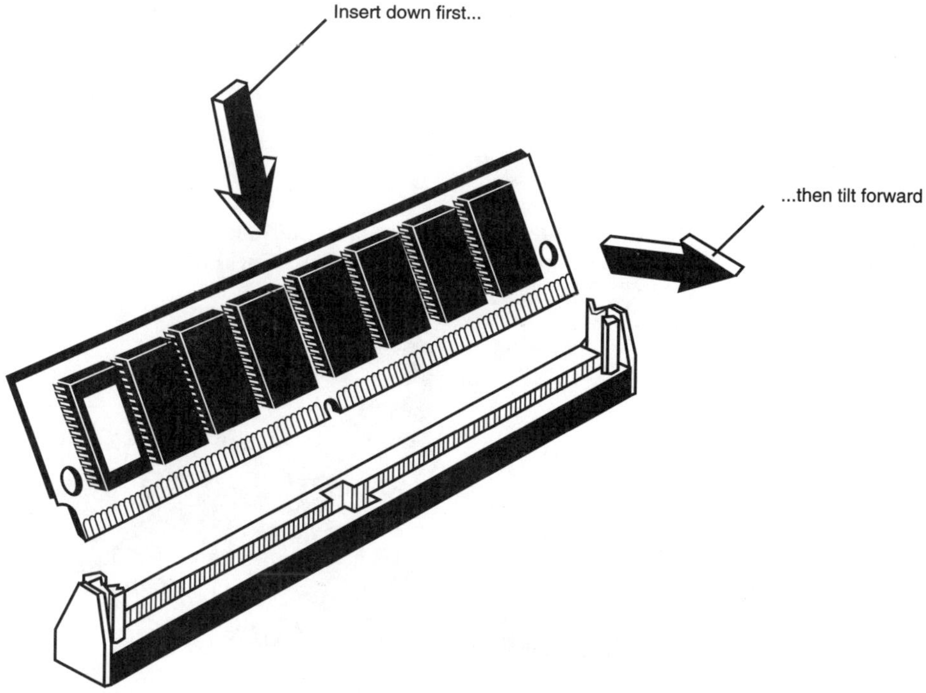

Figure 1.15 The notch on this SIMM is shown on the left end. Insert the SIMM at an angle and then tilt it forward until the locking clips snap into place.

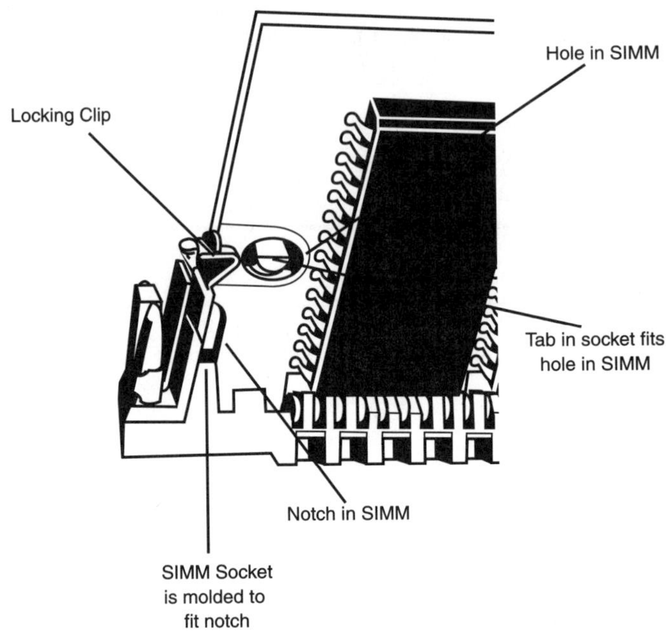

Figure 1.16 This close-up shows the backside of the SIMM inserted in the SIMM socket with the notch aligned, the locking clip locked, and the hole in the SIMM aligned with the tab that sticks out from the socket.

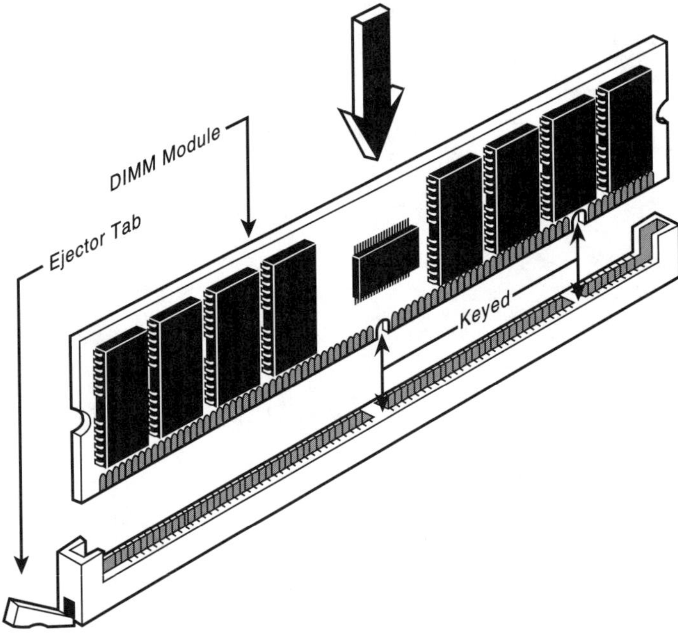

Figure 1.17 DIMM keys match the protrusions in the DIMM sockets.

Expansion Card

Most systems use expansion cards for video, network interface, sound, and SCSI adapters. These cards are plugged into the bus slots present on the motherboard (see Figure 1.18). To install these cards, follow these steps:

1. Insert each card by holding it carefully by the edges, making sure not to touch the chips and circuitry. Put the bottom-edge finger connector into a slot that fits. Firmly press down on the top of the card, exerting even pressure, until it snaps into place.

2. Secure each card bracket with a screw.

3. Attach any internal cables you might have removed earlier from the cards.

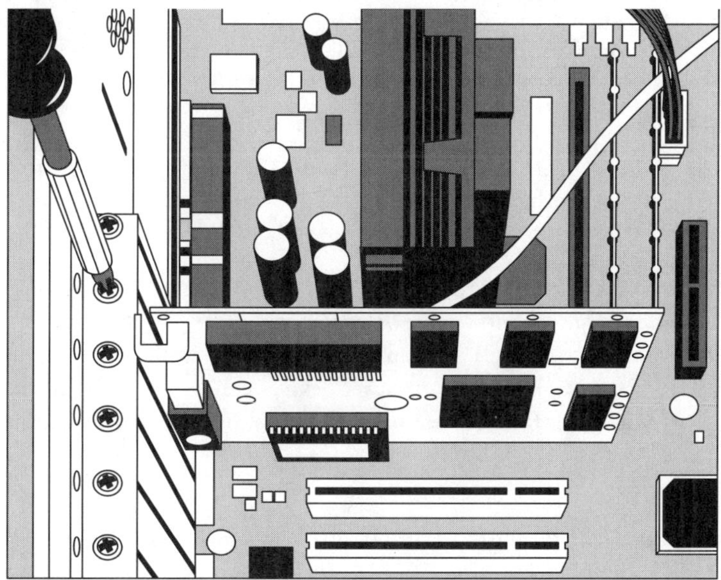

Figure 1.18 Insert the adapter into the slot and screw it into place.

Storage Devices

The key to replacing a storage device is the recovery and transfer of the data on the original device. If this device is backed up, you can simply replace it using the steps listed under the IDE and SCSI sections later in this chapter. If the device has not been backed up and cannot be recovered, all the data it previously held is gone. Some recovery facilities are available, but the cost for this process is so exorbitant that only the most critical of data is ever recovered.

I/O Devices

External peripherals should be powered down and disconnected before removing them. Likewise, the reinstallation of a peripheral requires that the device be powered down (the computer powered off as well in some cases) and that the device be reconnected. Other configuration should not be necessary if the unit is replaced with an identical piece.

Power Supply

Newer ATX-style motherboards have a single-power connector that can go on only one way. Baby-AT and other-style board designs usually have two separate six-wire power connectors from the power supply to the board, which might not be keyed and therefore might be interchangeable. Even though it might be possible to insert them several ways, only one way is correct! These power leads are usually labeled P8 and P9 in most systems. The order in which you connect them to the board is crucial; if you install them backward, you might cause damage to the motherboard when you power it up. Many systems use a CPU cooling fan, which should also be connected. To attach the power connectors from the power supply to the motherboard, do the following:

1. If the system uses a single ATX-style power connector, plug it in; it can go on only one way. If two separate six-wire connectors are used, the two black ground wires on the ends of the connectors must meet in the middle. Align the power connectors such that the black ground wires are adjacent to each other, and plug the connectors in. Consult the documentation with your board to make sure the power supply connection is correct.

2. Plug in the power lead for the CPU fan if one is used. The fan will either connect to the power supply via a disk drive power connector, or it might connect directly to a fan power connector on the motherboard.

Device Configuration

Device configuration requires knowledge of system resources and how they are used. You will need to know not only what resources you have available, but what resources the device you are working with can use, as well as what all other devices can or are using in the case of a conflict. Having the proper documentation is a must for manual resource configuration.

Resources

System resources are the communications channels, addresses, and other signals used by hardware devices to communicate on the bus. At their lowest level, these resources typically include the following:

- Memory addresses
- IRQ (interrupt request) channels
- DMA (direct memory access) channels
- I/O port addresses

These resources are required and used by many different components of your system. Adapter cards need these resources to communicate with your system and to accomplish their purposes. Not all adapter cards have the same resource requirements. A serial communications port, for example, needs an IRQ channel and I/O port address, whereas a soundboard needs these resources and normally at least one DMA channel as well. Most network cards use a 16KB block of memory addresses, an IRQ channel, and an I/O port address.

As your system increases in complexity, the chance for resource conflicts increases dramatically. Modern systems with sound cards and network cards can really push the envelope and become a configuration nightmare for the uninitiated.

IRQ

Interrupt request channels (IRQs), or hardware interrupts, are used by various hardware devices to signal the processor that a request must be fulfilled. This procedure is the same as a student raising his hand to indicate that he needs attention.

Through the use of interrupts, your system can respond to external events in a timely fashion. Each time a serial port presents a byte to your system, an interrupt is generated to ensure that the system reads that byte before another comes in (see Table 1.5).

Table 1.5 shows the typical uses for interrupts in the 16-bit ISA, EISA, and MCA buses, and it lists them in priority order from highest to lowest.

Table 1.5   16/32-Bit ISA/PCI Default Interrupt Assignments

IRQ	Standard Function	Bus Slot	Card Type	Recommended Use
0	System timer	No	-	-
1	Keyboard controller	No	-	-
2	2nd IRQ controller cascade	No	-	-
3	Serial port 2 (COM2:)	Yes	8/16-bit	COM2:/internal modem
4	Serial port 1 (COM1:)	Yes	8/16-bit	COM1:
5	Sound/parallel port 2 (LPT2:)	Yes	8/16-bit	Sound card
6	Floppy disk controller	Yes	8/16-bit	Floppy controller
7	Parallel port 1 (LPT1:)	Yes	8/16-bit	LPT1:
8	Real-time clock	No	-	-
9	Available (appears as IRQ 2)	Yes	8/16-bit	Network interface card
10	Available	Yes	16-bit	USB
11	Available	Yes	16-bit	SCSI host adapter
12	Motherboard mouse port/available	Yes	16-bit	Motherboard mouse port
13	Math coprocessor	No	-	-
14	Primary IDE	Yes	16-bit	Primary IDE (hard disks)
15	Secondary IDE/available	Yes	16-bit	Secondary DE (CD-ROM/tape)

Notice that interrupts 0, 1, 2, 8, and 13 are not on the bus connectors and are not accessible to adapter cards. Interrupts 8, 10, 11, 12, 13, 14, and 15 are from the second interrupt controller and are accessible only by boards that use the 16-bit extension connector because this is where these wires are located. IRQ 9 is rewired to the 8-bit slot connector in place of IRQ 2, which means that IRQ 9 replaces IRQ 2 and therefore is available to 8-bit cards, which treat it as though it were IRQ 2.

DMA

DMA (Direct Memory Access) channels are used by high-speed communications devices that must send and receive information at high speed. Essentially, this provides a separate channel to the RAM, bypassing the CPU, where the device takes control of memory directly.

DMA channels sometimes can be shared if the devices are not the type that would need them simultaneously. For example, you can have a network adapter and a tape backup adapter sharing DMA channel 1, but you cannot back up while the network is running.

DMA actually can decrease the efficiency of today's PCs because of the speed with which the processors can handle RAM requests. DMA should be used sparingly and should be disabled if you notice device performance decreases. Table 1.6 shows the typical uses for the DMA channels.

Table 1.6   16/32-Bit ISA/PCI Default DMA-Channel Assignments

DMA	Standard Function	Bus Slot	Card Type	Transfer	Recommended Use
0	Available	Yes	16-bit	8-bit	Integrated sound
1	Available	Yes	8/16-bit	8-bit	8-bit sound
2	Floppy disk controller	Yes	8/16-bit	8-bit	Floppy controller
3	Available	Yes	8/16-bit	8-bit	LPT1: in ECP mode
4	1st DMA controller cascade	No	—	16-bit	
5	Available	Yes	16-bit	16-bit	16-bit sound
6	Available	Yes	16-bit	16-bit	ISA SCSI adapter
7	Available	Yes	16-bit	16-bit	Available

Note that PCI adapters don't use these ISA DMA channels. These are only for ISA cards.

The only standard DMA channel used in all systems is DMA 2, which is universally used by the floppy controller. DMA 4 is not usable and does not appear in the bus slots. DMA channels 1 and 5 are most commonly used by ISA sound cards such as the Sound Blaster 16. These cards use both an 8- and a 16-bit DMA channel for high-speed transfers.

Note

Although DMA channel 0 appears in a 16-bit slot connector extension and therefore can only be used by a 16-bit card, it only does 8-bit transfers! Because of this, you will generally not see DMA 0 as a choice on 16-bit cards. Most 16-bit cards (like SCSI host adapters) that use DMA channels have their choices limited to DMA 5 through 7.

I/O

Your computer's I/O ports enable communications between devices and software in your system. They are equivalent to two-way radio channels. If you want to talk to your serial port, you need to know what I/O port (radio channel) it is listening on. Similarly, if you want to receive data from the serial port, you need to listen on the same channel it is transmitting on.

Table 1.7 shows the commonly used motherboard and chipset-based I/O port usage. Bus-based devices normally use the addresses from 100h on up. Table 1.7 lists the commonly used bus-based device addresses and also some common adapter cards and their settings.

Table 1.7   Motherboard, Chipset-based, and Bus-based Device Port Addresses

Address (hex)	Size	Description
0000 - 000F	16 bytes	Chipset - 8237 DMA 1
0020 - 0021	2 bytes	Chipset - 8259 interrupt controller 1
002E - 002F	2 bytes	Super I/O controller configuration registers
0040 - 0043	4 bytes	Chipset - counter/timer 1
00A0 - 00A1	2 bytes	Chipset - 8259 interrupt controller 2
0170 – 0177	8 bytes	Secondary IDE interface
01F0 - 01F7	8 bytes	Primary IDE / AT (16-bit) hard disk controller
0200 – 0207	8 bytes	Gameport or joystick adapter
0220 – 0233	20 bytes	Creative Labs Sound Blaster 16 Audio (default)
023C - 023F	4 bytes	MS bus mouse (default)
0270 – 0273	4 bytes	Plug and play I/O read ports
0278 - 027F	8 bytes	Parallel port 2 (LPT2)
02E8 - 02EF	8 bytes	Serial port 4 (COM4)
02EC - 02EF	4 bytes	Video, 8514 or ATI standard ports
02F8 - 02FF	8 bytes	Serial port 2 (COM2)
0330 – 0331	2 bytes	MPU-401 MIDI port (default)
0330 – 0333	4 bytes	Adaptec SCSI adapter (default)
0378 - 037F	8 bytes	Parallel port 1 (LPT1)
03B0 - 03BB	12 bytes	Video, mono/EGA/VGA standard ports
03E8 - 03EF	8 bytes	Serial port 3 (COM3)
03F0 - 03F5	6 bytes	Primary floppy controller
03F8 - 03FF	8 bytes	Serial port 1 (COM1)
04D0 - 04D1	2 bytes	Edge/level triggered PCI interrupt controller
0CF8 - 0CFB	4 bytes	PCI configuration address registers
0CF9	1 byte	Turbo and reset control register
0CFC - 0CFF	4 bytes	PCI configuration data registers
FF00 - FF07	8 bytes	IDE bus master registers
FF80 - FF9F	32 bytes	Universal Serial Bus (USB)
FFA0 – FFA7	8 bytes	Primary bus master IDE registers

To find out exactly what port addresses are being used on your motherboard, consult the board documentation or look these settings up in the Windows device manager.

Physical Configuration Versus Plug and Play

Physical configuration can be accomplished on many devices using backs of switch settings, jumper blocks, or even a proprietary software program that writes directly to the card.

Jumpers are used to shortcut to protruding pins to complete a circuit, whereas switches are used to make a similar internal connection to complete a circuit. The proprietary program runs a configuration routine much like CMOS, but it makes changes to the chip on the adapter in question. These changes are written to the chip and saved as the new configuration.

Plug and play works completely differently. This configuration option, although it has some problems occasionally, seems to be the chosen design today. To use plug and play, you will need three things:

- Plug and play–compliant adapter card.
- Plug and play–compliant BIOS.
- Plug and play–compliant operating system. (Currently, only Windows 95, 98, and 2000 have this functionality.)

Manual resource allocation is a heavily tested component of the A+ examination.

Peripheral Ports, Associated Cabling, and Their Connectors

This section covers the primary peripheral input/output ports, cables, and connectors on a modern PC system. This includes serial ports, parallel ports, Universal Serial Bus (USB), IEEE-1394, as well as video, SCSI, Game, and other standard ports.

Ports

A port is an interface between the system and an external device, a "window" outside of the computer case itself, so to speak. A port is the specification of how data is transferred and in what format to the peripheral devices that are attached to it through the cables and connectors. A port can have several different types of standard connectors (see Table 1.8).

Table 1.8 Ports and Connectors

Port	Connector
Video	DB15 Female (3 ROWS) VGA
	DB9 Female Monochrome, CGA, EGA
Parallel	DB25 Female at Computer
	Centronics 36 Female at Printer
Serial	DB25 Male at computer
	DB9 Male at computer
Game/Joystick	DB15 Female (2 ROWS) at computer
Network	RJ 45 (8 wire)
	BNC Coaxial Thinnet
Modem	RJ 11 (4 wire)
SCSI	DB25 Female at computer
	Centronics 50 Female at device
	HD50 SCSI Regular
	HD68 SCSI Wide
Keyboard	DIN5 AT Style
	DIN6 PS/2 Style
Mouse	DIN6 PS/2 Style

Connectors

A connector is the physical specification of the jack that the cable plugs into. It is through this connector that the port can attach to the cable and the peripheral device.

Common connectors include the DB, HD, DIN, and RJ series. Several of these are depicted in Figures 1.19 and 1.20.

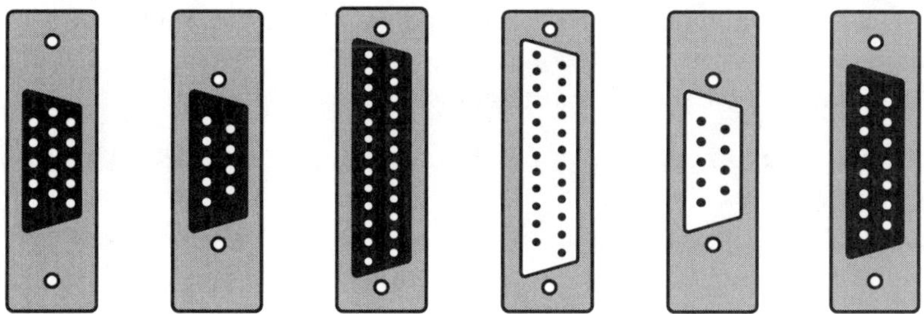

Figure 1.19 Various connectors, including VGA, parallel, serial, and game ports.

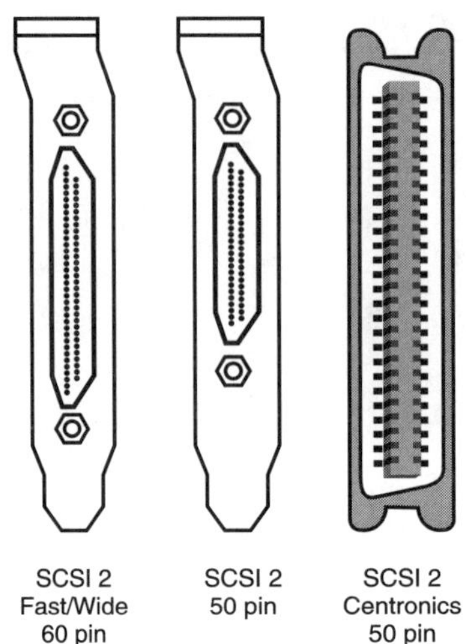

Figure 1.20 SCSI connectors.

Cables

A cable is merely an extension of the connector on the back of the computer. Sometimes, the cable will rearrange the signals on the connector by twisting the wires inside the cable into a different configuration at the other end. Sometimes, the cable is simply a "straight-through" cable, which is to say that there is no twist.

Serial cables are generally limited to 50 feet, but parallel cables are limited to 10–15 feet for accurate data transfer. Other cables have their own specifications for pin mappings, as well as maximum lengths.

Hard Disk Installation and Configuration

A hard disk is a key component in today's computers. Without it, no Windows-based operating system can be installed. The installation of software will be covered in Part II of this text, but the actual installation of the hard disk subsystem will be discussed here.

A hard disk subsystem is comprised of three components interconnected together. They are the following:

- System interface
- Controller
- Drive

Because they are the predominant technology today, both IDE and SCSI drives will be discussed in the following text and are discussed in greater depth in Chapter 14, "Physical Drive Installation and Configuration," of the eleventh edition of *Upgrading and Repairing PCs*.

IDE

The primary interface used to connect a hard disk drive to a modern PC is called IDE. This stands for Integrated Drive Electronics and refers to the fact that the interface electronics or controller is built in to the drives themselves. Placing the controller, including the digital to analog encoder/decoder (endec) on the drive gives IDE drives an inherent reliability advantage over interfaces with separate controllers. Today IDE is used to connect not only hard disks, but also CD-ROM drives, DVD drives, high-capacity floppy drives, and tape drives. Even so, IDE is still thought of primarily as a hard disk interface, and it evolved directly from the separate controller and hard drive interfaces that were used prior to IDE. More IDE interface information can be found in Chapter 7 of the eleventh edition of *Upgrading and Repairing PCs* as well.

Addressing and Termination

Because IDE interfaces support only two drives per interface, addressing the drives is fairly simple. In a single-channel, dual-drive setup, IDE drives are addressed as either Channel 0, Drive 0 or Channel 0, Drive 1. What tends to confuse the issue is that both drives have controllers on them. To function properly, one controller must have priority over the other one. This is known as a master and a slave, as shown in Figure 1.21. All IDE drives have a manual setting to define whether they are the master or the slave.

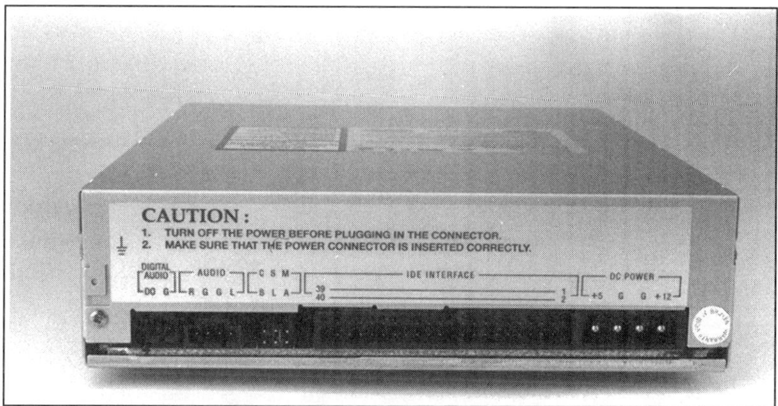

Figure 1.21 Master/slave addressing jumpers and other connections for IDE devices.

In the Real World

There is a third setting known as cable select. Although rarely used, this setting allows a twist in the cable to determine the master and the slave by configuring both drives as cable select (CS).

Physical Installation

The procedure for the physical installation of a hard disk drive is much the same as that for installing a floppy disk drive. You must have the correct screws, brackets, and faceplates for the specific drive and system before you can install the drive.

CMOS Configuration

For IDE drives, virtually all new BIOS versions in today's PCs have automatic typing. The BIOS sends a special Identify Drive command to all the devices connected to the IDE interface during the system startup sequence; the drives are intelligent enough to respond with the correct parameters. The BIOS then automatically enters the parameter information returned by the drive. This procedure eliminates errors or confusion in parameter selection.

If you are dealing with a motherboard that does not support automatic typing, you must enter the appropriate drive information in the system BIOS manually. The BIOS has a selection of pre-configured drive types, but these are woefully outdated in most cases, providing support only for drives holding a few hundred megabytes or less. In nearly every case, you will have to select the user-defined drive type and provide values for the following settings:

- Cylinders
- Heads
- Sectors per track
- Write precompensation

The values that you use for these settings should be provided in the documentation for the hard disk drive, or they might be printed on the drive itself. It's a good idea to check for these settings and write them down because they may not be visible after you've installed the drive. You should also maintain a copy of these settings in case your system BIOS should lose its data due to a battery failure. One of the best places to store this information is inside the computer. Taping a note with vital settings such as these to the inside of the case can be a lifesaver.

Note

The setup parameters for over 1,000 popular drive models are included on the CD-ROM with the eleventh edition of *Upgrading and Repairing PCs*, in the section "Technical Reference." Additionally, there is a generic table of parameters included that will work (although they might not work optimally) with any IDE drive up to 528MB.

SCSI

SCSI (pronounced "scuzzy") stands for Small Computer System Interface and is a general-purpose interface used for connecting many types of devices to a PC. SCSI is the most popular interface for attaching high-speed disk drives to higher performance PCs such as workstations or network servers. SCSI is also very flexible; it is not only a disk interface, but also a systems-level interface allowing many different types of devices to be connected. SCSI is a device bus that supports as many as 8 or 16 total devices (minus 1 for the host adapter).

Addressing and Termination

SCSI drives are not too difficult to configure, but they are more complicated than IDE drives. The SCSI standard controls the way the drives must be set up. You need to set two or three items when you configure a SCSI drive:

- SCSI ID setting (0–7 or 0–15)
- Terminating resistors

The SCSI ID setting is very simple. Up to eight SCSI devices can be used on a single narrow SCSI bus or up to 15 devices on a wide SCSI bus, and each device must have a unique SCSI ID address. The host adapter takes one address, so the rest are free for up to seven SCSI peripherals. Most SCSI host adapters are factory-set to ID 7 or 15, which is the highest priority ID. All other devices must have unique IDs that do not conflict with one another. Some host adapters boot only from a hard disk set to a specific ID. Older Adaptec host adapters required the boot hard disk to be ID 0; newer ones can boot from any ID.

Setting the ID usually involves changing jumpers on the drive. If the drive is installed in an external chassis, the chassis might have an ID selector switch that is accessible at the rear. This selector makes ID selection a simple matter of pressing a button or rotating a wheel until the desired ID number appears. If no external selector is present, you must open the external device chassis and set the ID via the jumpers on the drive according to the Table 1.9.

Table 1.9   SCSI ID Jumper Settings with the Most Significant Bit to the Left

SCSI	ID	Jumper	Settings
0	0	0	0
1	0	0	1
2	0	1	0
3	0	1	1
4	1	0	0
5	1	0	1
6	1	1	0
7	1	1	1

1 = Jumper On, 0 = Jumper Off

SCSI termination is very simple. Termination is required at both ends of the bus; there are no exceptions. If the host adapter is at one end of the bus, it must have termination enabled. If the host adapter is in the middle of the bus and if both internal and external bus links are present, the host adapter must have its termination disabled, and the devices at each end of the bus must have terminators installed. Unfortunately, the majority of problems that are found in SCSI installations are the result of improper termination.

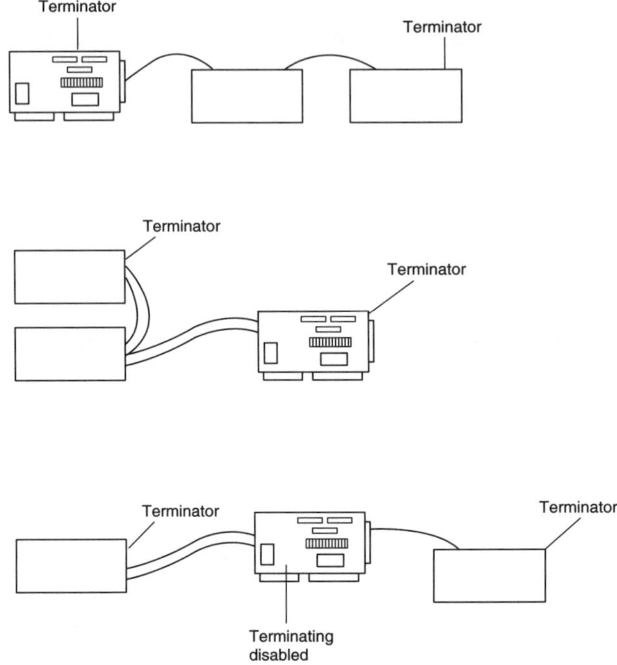

Figure 1.22 Examples of various SCSI termination scenarios.

Physical Installation

SCSI drives usually require a host adapter card that you must install in a bus slot like any other card. A few motherboards have integrated SCSI adapters, but these are rare. Configuring a SCSI host adapter card involves setting the different system resources that the adapter requires. As with most expansion cards, a SCSI host adapter will require some combination of the system resources.

The procedure for the physical installation of a SCSI hard disk drive is the same as that for installing an IDE disk drive. You must have the correct screws, brackets, and faceplates for the specific drive and system before you can install the drive.

CMOS Configuration

SCSI devices have no CMOS type. In fact, because the host adapter will initiate the boot device itself, CMOS should be set to "No Drives Defined."

I/O Device Configuration

The most common I/O devices include the following:

- Keyboard
- Mouse
- Monitor
- Printers
- Modems
- Multimedia

This section will discuss the installation and configuration of these devices.

Keyboard

As required devices, keyboards have relatively simple installation and configuration procedures. After you have verified that you have the proper keyboard, either the AT style or the PS/2 style, simply plug it in and turn on the computer.

Mouse

Mice are also fairly simple. There are more types available and more ports to plug them into; including serial, proprietary bus, or PS/2 styles. Mice require a driver in older operating systems, but in Windows 95, 98, and NT, it is a fairly simple plug-and-play operation.

Monitor

Monitors also have very little configuration necessary to function. Some monitors have additional features that require special configuration, but for the most part, this, too, is a plug-and-play setup.

Printers

Printers require little, if any, configuration when using parallel connections. Serial printers, on the other hand, require intensive configuration of the communication parameters such as speed, start and stop bits, and parity; some serial printers even require proprietary serial cables. Printers are covered in much more detail in Chapter 5.

Modems

Modems require hardware and software configuration to function properly over a serial port. Modems are covered in more detail in Chapter 7.

Multimedia

Audio equipment, such as microphones and speakers, require no additional hardware configuration, although the software configuration in a non–plug-and-play computer can be quite frustrating.

Review

The following study points and test questions will help you prepare for the A+ exams.

Cram Session

- The system board is the heart of the computer. It contains the processor, firmware, memory, bus slots, and might have other interfaces built in to it.

- The processor is the brain or engine of the computer, although some instructions can be offloaded to a coprocessor.

- CMOS is the repository for the system configuration. BIOS checks the system settings with what is found by the POST to verify system integrity.

- Memory is storage in the form of RAM, short-term storage, and ROM, long-term storage. RAM loses its data when the power is turned off, whereas ROM retains it indefinitely.

- Serial communication is data moving one bit at a time. Parallel communication is data moving 8 bits, or 1 byte, at a time.

- USB is designed to provide a shared bus connection for all external peripherals, eliminating the resource-allocation nightmare currently in use.

- The CRT is a turn-of-the-century technology in desktop monitors.

- LCD panels create an image by exciting a crystal with an electric current, causing it to light up.

- Laser printers use the electrophotographic process to create a printed image, much like a copier.

- Inkjet printers fire streams of ink at the page in patterns to form characters.

- Dot matrix printers strike the ribbon and page with print wires, creating coarse, bit-image characters.

- Modems are devices that convert digital data into analog signals suitable for transmission over a telephone line and that convert the analog signals back to digital data at the destination.

- Hard disks are fixed, rewriteable magnetic storage. Floppy disks provide smaller, removable, rewriteable storage. All magnetic media stores data in tracks, sectors, and cylinders as defined by the format process.

- Optical technology uses light beams to reflect off of pits in the media to represent binary data. DVD and CD devices both use this technology, albeit in different ways.

- Power supplies provide five distinct voltage levels and a common ground. These voltages are +12, -12, +5, -5, and +3.3 volts.

- Field replacement procedures vary from device to device, but all replacement procedures should include backing up relevant data and observing and recording configuration settings throughout the system—especially on the device being replaced.

- System resources are the various communication channels, addresses, and other signals used by hardware devices to communicate on the bus. They are IRQ channels, DMA channels, and I/O port addresses. Each device in the system must use a system resource setting that is not shared with other devices.

- Plug-and-play configuration requires three distinct plug-and-play–compliant components: operating system, BIOS, and Adapter. Without all three, plug and play will not function.

- IDE and SCSI are the primary hard disk technologies used today. Both technologies require adapter interface installation, drive termination/addressing, and CMOS configuration before the drive can be formatted and recognized in the computer.

Review Questions

1. Which components would most likely be found on a system board?

2. What are the voltages found in a power supply?

3. What is the difference between RAM and ROM?

4. What does CRT stand for? How does it work?

5. What is a modem used for?

6. What hard drive types are the most commonly used today?

7. How do floppy and hard disk drives store data?

8. Which tape standard has the largest capacity and is used in most businesses today?

9. How should a processor be installed into a ZIF socket?

10. What IRQs are normally used for parallel ports?

11. DMA provides a communication channel between what devices?

Review Answers

1. A system board is the heart of the computer. The CPU, RAM, expansion bus, CMOS, and keyboard controller always exist on the system board. Except for the video controller, all components necessary to start the machine are present.

2. There are 5 voltages found in power supplies today: +5, -5, +12, -12, and sometimes 3.3v for ATX systems.

3. RAM provides a temporary storage area for data, and it is purged when the power is turned off. ROM provides long-term storage in the form of data "burned" into the chip itself. RAM has many uses, whereas ROM has one use.

4. CRT=Cathode Ray Tube. An electron gun fires repeatedly at the phosphor-coated glass to create an image by lighting up the specific pixels it hits.

5. Modems are used to convert digital signals into analog signals for transmission through the phone lines to a remote computer. There must also be a modem on the receiving end.

6. IDE and SCSI are the most used hard disks today. These are the only types that will be tested over.

7. These drives store data in magnetic fields on a magnetic medium divided into tracks and sectors. The read/write heads use a magnetic pulse to alter the polarity of the media directly beneath them.

8. Digital Linear Tape, or DLT, can quickly store up to 80GB on a single tape. For this reason, most businesses today use this type.

9. A ZIF, or Zero Insertion Force, socket has a lever that releases the tension on the connecting pins of the CPU. When the lever is disengaged, the CPU can be freely removed or inserted with very little force. To lock the CPU back into place, simply lower the lever.

10. IRQs are listed in a table in this chapter. IRQs 7 and 5 are used for the first and second parallel ports in that order. IRQ 5 is normally available because most systems do not have a second parallel port installed.

11. Direct Memory Access, or DMA, is a direct communication channel between an adapter or device and the system RAM. This channel allows the adapter to bypass the overworked CPU and control the memory directly.

Chapter 2

Diagnosing and Troubleshooting

Troubleshooting Basics

No matter how well-built your PC is and how well-written its software is, something is eventually going to go wrong, and there might not always be a support system available to resolve the problem for you.

Troubleshooting is an imprecise science. To be sure, there are steps that you must take to resolve the problem, but many of these steps are just generalities that you should think about during your troubleshooting, rather than step-by-step instructions in a manual.

Troubleshooting involves several things:

- A basic understanding of system components and the interaction between components
- The ability to interact with the customer and the system to gather useful information
- System configuration and manufacturer's documentation
- A logical troubleshooting pattern

The majority of this book is concerned with giving you the hardware and software knowledge that you will need, and later sections in this chapter will give you some common errors and their solutions to add to that knowledge. What the following section will give you is the logical troubleshooting framework that you need to complete the basics.

Define

First, you need to identify what the problem is. This section relies heavily on your ability to interpret what the user is saying the problem is and what your diagnostics are telling you. These two information sources might be in complete and total disagreement.

To get the correct information from the user, you will need to ask open-ended questions to start. What is the computer doing or not doing? When did this begin happening? Did any error messages appear?

For more information on this subject, Chapter 8, "Customer Satisfaction," discusses user interaction and information gathering, and the Software diagnostics section at the end of this chapter helps you to obtain information from the system itself.

Isolate

Rather than jumping to conclusions (unless you have dealt with the exact same problem before for this user), you need to isolate the cause of the problem. To isolate the problem, all the information acquired in the definition phase is used. All documentation for the system should be available, especially system configuration settings and manufacturer documentation. One defining question is a key in your information gathering: Has anything been changed recently? This is the best place to begin isolation.

As with any other problem you have ever solved, you begin eliminating all possibilities until you are left with the only possible cause of the problem. At that point, you have completed the isolation phase.

In the Real World

Don't forget to isolate the user as a possible cause of the problem! In fact, depending on the user community in your place of business, over half of the reported errors can be attributed to user error. More information on this error and how to handle it professionally can be found in Chapter 8.

Hardware Versus Software

Computers are composed of two broad areas: hardware and software. The point at which these meet, namely the software that controls the hardware and hardware that passes information to the software, is difficult to define at times. This is especially true when troubleshooting a problem.

This being the case, one of the first steps that you must take when diagnosing and troubleshooting a given error is to determine which part is at fault. Is the driver for the network card flaky? Are there improper jumper settings on the card? The easiest way to determine this is to reboot the machine. This resets the operating system and all the related software, including the drivers.

If, after rebooting the machine, it begins to work, you have a software problem on your hands. If it doesn't, you might have a hardware problem. This is a very simplistic example, however. The only real way to determine the problem is to follow your diagnostic process as discussed above. A good technician will be able to use his experience, diagnostic steps, and a few good guesses to categorize and solve the problem.

Tip

This is not only an exam tip, but is certainly true in the real world as well. Most problems in computer systems are related to the fine line between software and hardware configuration in the area of resource conflicts. Resources and resource conflicts were discussed in Chapter 1 "Installation, Configuration, and Upgrading." You can also learn more about resolving resource conflicts in Chapter 4, "Motherboards and Buses," of Upgrading and Repairing PCs, Eleventh Edition.

Resolve

The resolution phase of problem solving is simply an extension of the isolation phase. As you'll recall, isolation eliminates one variable at a time until the true problem is found. When the true problem is found, eliminating it requires fixing it. After it is fixed, proper resolution techniques include duplicating the problem again and fixing it again for verification.

Document

After the problem is fixed, the last step in the resolution phase is documenting the solution. Although documentation throughout the entire troubleshooting process should be done, this documentation step is the most important. In it you should record all the documentation from the first two phases and the solution as well. This enables a faster response and resolution for similar problems in the future.

Common Errors

Experience is something that must be gained by each individual technician through the course of her career. Nothing can be substituted for real experience. That said, there is nothing wrong with building your experience on the knowledge garnered from other technicians' experience. The following sections contain some common errors (aside from resource conflicts) and common resolutions for system components. This is not an exhaustive list by any means, but it will help you prepare both for the exam and for real-life systems troubleshooting.

System Board (Motherboard)

As the heart of the computer, the system board has many interconnections that might be difficult to diagnose. The best method for testing the system board is running manufacturer or third-party benchmark and diagnostic tools.

System boards that have more integrated components, such as parallel, serial, IDE, SCSI, video, and other controllers, are more prone to failure. The boards are also generally more expensive than other standardized clone system boards.

Note

Motherboards are covered in exhaustive detail in Chapter 4, "Motherboards and Buses," of Upgrading and Repairing PCs, Eleventh Edition.

CMOS

The single most common problem with CMOS is loss of configuration information. The most common cause of this is a dead battery, but other power supply fluctuations can cause this as well. You will recall from Chapter 1 that CMOS maintains the system settings in memory while the system is off. To do this, CMOS requires power from a small, wafer-style battery (although older systems used cylindrical and even AA type batteries) that is mounted on the system board. When this battery is drained, CMOS will be reset every time the computer is turned off. The most common symptom of this is a 161, 162, or 163 error from the POST test as described in the section "POST Visual Error Codes" later in this chapter. To resolve the problem, the battery must be replaced and the configuration re-entered and saved again.

BIOS

BIOS errors are very rare. When one does happen, it is more of a problem with the code that was written to the chip than of the chip corrupting the code. The recommendation to replace the BIOS is generally given by the manufacturer or posted on its Web page.

To replace the BIOS, you must either replace the socketed chip with a new one form the manufacturer or, more commonly, run a flash BIOS upgrade on systems that support FlashROM. FlashROM, as discussed in Chapter 1, is an electrically erasable, electrically programmable memory chip. The program that the manufacturer provides can erase the current ROM and write the new version to the chip.

Note

The BIOS is covered in detail in Chapter 5, "BIOS," of *Upgrading and Repairing PCs, Eleventh Edition*.

POST Error Codes

Whenever you start up your computer, it automatically performs a series of tests that checks the primary components in your system, such as the CPU, ROM, motherboard support circuitry, memory, and major peripherals such as the expansion chassis. These tests are brief and are designed to catch hard (not intermittent) errors. The POST procedures are not very thorough compared with available disk-based diagnostics. The POST process provides error or warning messages whenever it encounters a faulty component.

Although the diagnostics performed by the system POST are not very thorough, they are the first line of defense, especially when it comes to detecting severe motherboard problems. If the POST encounters a problem severe enough to keep the system from operating properly, it halts the system boot process and generates an error message that often identifies the cause of the problem. These POST-detected problems are sometimes called fatal errors because they prevent the system from booting. The POST tests normally provide three types of output messages: audio codes, onscreen text messages, and hexadecimal numeric codes that are sent to an I/O port address.

POST Audio Error Codes

POST audio error codes take the form of a series of beeps that identify the faulty component. When your computer is functioning normally, you should usually hear one short beep when the system starts up at the completion of the POST, although some systems (such as Compaq's) do not do this. If a problem is detected, a different number of beeps sound—sometimes in a combination of short and long tones. These BIOS-dependent codes can vary among different BIOS manufacturers. Table 2.1 lists the beep codes for IBM systems and the problem indicated by each series of beeps. Award BIOS (from Award Software, Inc.) uses many of the same codes as the IBM BIOS.

Table 2.1   IBM POST Audio Error Codes and Indicated Problem

Audio Code	Sound	Problem (Fault Domain)
One short beep	.	Normal POST-system okay
Two short beeps	..	POST error-error code
No beep		Power supply, system board, or defective speaker
Continuous beep	- - - -	Power supply, system board
Repeating short beeps	....	Power supply, system board
One long, one short beep	-.	System board
One long, two short beeps	-..	Display adapter (MDA, CGA)
One long, three short beeps	-...	Enhanced Graphics Adapter (EGA)
Three long beeps	- - -	3270 keyboard card

. = *short beep*

- = *long beep*

POST Visual Error Codes

On most PCs, POST also displays the results of its system memory test on the monitor. The last number displayed is the amount of memory that tested successfully. For example, a system might display the following message:

```
32768 KB OK
```

If an error is detected during the POST procedures, an error message might be displayed onscreen following the memory test. These messages usually are in the form of a numeric code several digits long—for example, 1790-Disk 0 Error. You should check the documentation for your motherboard or system BIOS for information about these errors. The major BIOS manufacturers also maintain Web sites where this information should be available. The table below has the commonly accepted code categories. For example, two different manufacturers might call a floppy drive error 612 and 691, but they will both generally be in the 600–699 range. This range is listed in the table as 6xx.

Table 2.2   Post Visual Error Codes

Visual Error Code or Range	Probable Error
1xx	System board or BIOS
16x	CMOS, options, or time not set
2xx	Memory
3xx	Keyboard
6xx	Floppy drive
7xx	Math coprocessor
9xx	Parallel port
11xx	Serial port
17xx	Hard drive
73xx	Drive controller

Processor/Coprocessor

The CPU can commonly be misdiagnosed when conflicts concerning memory, DMA, and IRQs repeatedly arise. There are times when the CPU itself can fail, however. The most common cause for CPU failure is overheating. The CPU generates heat rapidly and requires heat radiation devices (heat sinks) and cooling fans to dissipate the heat. If the cooling fans fail or the ventilation on the computer's case is blocked (which happens quite often), the CPU will quickly overheat past working tolerances. The only resolution for this is to create better ventilation, and replacement if the processor has been permanently damaged.

Also, as your system heats and cools, it expands and contracts, and the physical expansion and contraction can cause components that are plugged in to sockets to gradually work their way out of those sockets. This process is called *chip creep*. To correct its effects, you must find all socketed components in the system and make sure that they are properly reseated.

Note

Processors are covered in detail in Chapter 3, "Microprocessor Types and Specifications," of *Upgrading and Repairing PCs, Eleventh Edition*.

Memory

Although there are expensive chip testers available, the only troubleshooting generally available to you for memory is a software diagnostic and the tried-and-true replacement technique.

The replacement technique simply means that given one suspect part and an identical good part, you should swap the two and see where the problem goes. If the problem follows the part, the part is bad, but if the problem stays with the system, the original part is not.

In the Real World

The replacement technique does not verify that either the replaced part or the system it was removed from is good. Without placing the suspect part in an identical system and testing it there, this method is generally only good for verifying that the system and replaced part had a problem when put together. This means that the replaced part might not necessarily be the only problem. Make sure that testing occurs on the removed part in a good system as well as the good part in the suspected system.

Most memory problems go away after a reboot. These are operating-system or soft-memory errors. Only if an error repeats after rebooting is it an actual hard memory error that requires replacement.

Keyboard and Mouse

Keyboards and mice today cannot be repaired. At an average cost of $10 for the keyboard or mouse and an average cost of $75/hour for service, why bother? Most problems can be prevented with the preventative maintenance procedures in the next chapter.

Video

As detailed under the preceding section on memory, the replacement technique is the best method for troubleshooting video problems. Table 2.3 gives some common symptoms and their causes.

Table 2.3   Video Troubleshooting

Symptom	Possible Cause
Dark screen	The monitor's power cable is unplugged or off, or the brightness is turned down too low.
White screen	The monitor's data cable is unplugged, or the brightness is turned up too high.
Distorted video	Horizontal and vertical controls are not aligned, or there is a magnetic source or electrical motor nearby.
Random garbage or snow	There is a bad video card or cable.

As indicated in Table 2.3, the most common error is the magnetic distortion attributed to desktop speakers, fans, or fluorescent lighting.

Printers

Printer troubleshooting is covered extensively in Chapter 5, "Printers."

Modems

Troubleshooting modems is usually a matter of testing cabling. Modems can fail because of a bad data cable to the computer, which often results in corrupt data being delivered. They can also fail because of a bad connection over the dial-up connection. Although this can corrupt the data as well, most modems have error correction built in to them. The most common symptom of a bad phone connection is decreased transmission speeds or dropped communication altogether.

Although the cable from the PC to the modem can be replaced, the dial-up connection might not be able to be fixed. Some local telephone providers only guarantee enough bandwidth and clarity for a human conversation, which might not be good enough for a modem connection.

Multimedia

Other than the problems associated with plugging multimedia peripherals into the wrong jack on the sound card, there are very few common multimedia hardware errors. Typically, sound problems are related to software configuration or driver failures.

Note

Audio hardware is covered in detail in Chapter 20, "Audio Hardware," of *Upgrading and Repairing PCs, Eleventh Edition*.

Floppy Disk

As opposed to during preventative maintenance, floppy-cleaning kits should be your first reactive solution. These kits are abrasive and should not be used unless errors are apparent. Aside from this, today's prices have made floppy drives another throwaway component. Rather than making expensive repairs, it is more cost-effective to simply replace the drive.

Hard Disk

Hard disk drives have several common problems that can be remedied. Hard drives in all the operating systems covered by the A+ examination use FAT partitioning, which you will learn more about in the second part of this book. Most of these procedures apply only to FAT systems and ensure that your hard disk works efficiently. Some of these procedures actually minimize wear and tear on your drive, which will prolong its life. Additionally, a high level of data protection can be implemented by performing some simple commands periodically.

Media Recovery

If you are experiencing many data read errors or bad sectors, media recovery might be your next step. Media recovery is what the DOS CHKDSK/Scandisk, Windows 9x Scandisk, or third-party utilities, such as Norton's Disk Doctor, perform. They begin by checking the drive for corruption in the partition tables and file structures. Scandisk (CHKDSK does not perform this function) then verifies the media beneath the data through a series of tests. If a bad sector is found, the data in it is copied to a new sector and the failed sector is flagged as bad (see Figure 2.1).

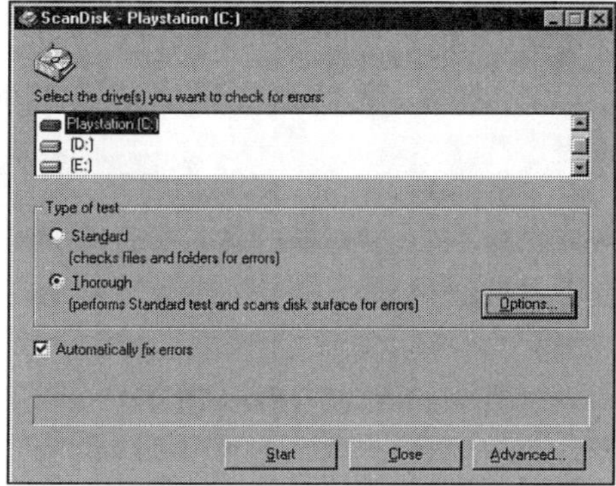

Figure 2.1 ScanDisk launch options.

It is a good idea to run a disk repair program such as Windows 9x's ScanDisk or Norton Disk Doctor before attempting disk defragmentation, even if you are not experiencing any problems. There are many scheduling and custom scanning options available as indicated in Figure 2.1. This ensures that your drives are in good working order before you begin the defragmentation process.

Defragmenting Files

Over time, as you delete and save files to a hard disk, the files become fragmented. This means that they are split into many noncontiguous areas on the disk. One of the best ways to protect both your hard disk and the data on it is to periodically defragment the files on the disk using a utility such as Microsoft's DEFRAG (see Figure 2.2) or Norton's SpeedDisk. The reasoning for this is that by ensuring that all the files are stored in contiguous sectors on the disk, head movement and drive wear and tear will be minimized. This has the added benefit of improving the speed at which the drive retrieves files by reducing the head thrashing that occurs every time it accesses a fragmented file.

Tape Drive

Similar to floppy disk drives, tape drives must be cleaned regularly. Errors related to data corruption and tape format can easily be attributed to an improperly cleaned tape device. More information on this and other cleaning issues can be found in Chapter 3, "Safety and Preventative Maintenance," of this book and Chapter 25, "PC Diagnostics, Testing, and Maintenance," of Scott Mueller's *Upgrading and Repairing PCs, Eleventh Edition*.

Power Supply

Common power supply failures include overheating and overloading; both of these are readily seen. When a power supply fails, the system loses power and shuts down. Some high-end servers have redundant power supplies and early warning features to prevent overloading and overheating.

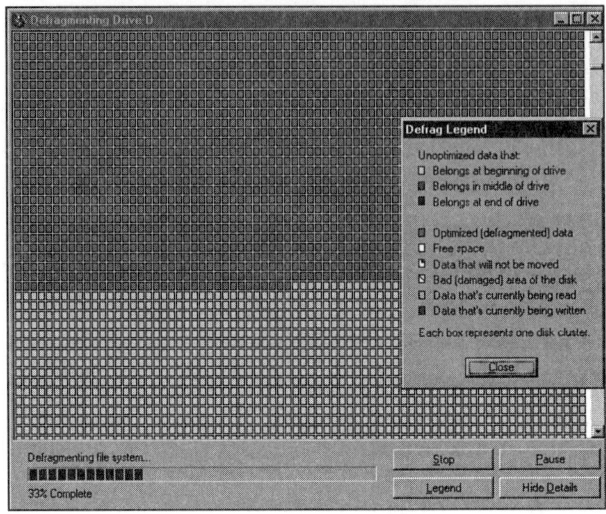

Figure 2.2 Defragmentation program with sector legend.

Note

See Chapter 21, "Power Supply and Chassis/Case," of *Upgrading and Repairing PCs, Eleventh Edition*, for more information on troubleshooting power supplies.

Another common failure can be heard as a grinding or whining fan. Most power supplies today are closed systems and unqualified technicians should not open these units. Rather than replacing these individual fans, replacement of the entire power supply is the preferred method today.

Diagnostic and Repair Tools

To troubleshoot and repair PC systems properly, you need a few basic tools. If you intend to troubleshoot and repair PCs professionally, there are many more specialized tools you will want to purchase. These advanced tools enable you to more accurately diagnose problems and make jobs easier and faster. The basic tools that should be in every troubleshooter's toolbox are the following:

- Simple hand tools for basic disassembly and reassembly procedures, including a flat blade and Phillips screwdriver (both medium and small sizes), tweezers, an IC extraction tool, and a parts grabber or hemostat
- Diagnostics software and hardware for testing components in a system
- A multimeter that provides accurate measurements of voltage and resistance
- Chemicals, such as contact cleaners, component freeze sprays, and compressed air for cleaning the system
- Foam swabs, or lint-free cotton swabs if foam isn't available
- Small nylon wire ties for "dressing" or organizing wires

Physical Tools

In this section, you'll learn about the tools required to assemble a kit that is capable of performing basic, board-level service on PC systems. One of the best ways to start such a set of tools is to purchase a small kit sold especially for servicing PCs.

The following list shows the basic tools that you can find in one of the small PC tool kits that sell for about $20:

- **3/16-inch and 1/4–inch nut drivers**   These are used to remove the hexagonal-headed screws that secure the system-unit covers, adapter boards, disk drives, and power supplies in most systems. The nut drivers work much better than conventional screwdrivers because they are hard to strip.

- **Small- and medium-sized Phillips and standard blade screwdrivers**   Because some manufacturers have substituted slotted or Phillips-head screws for the more standard hexagonal-head screws, standard screwdrivers can be used for those systems.

- **Chip inserter and extractor**   These are rarely needed these days because memory chips are mounted on SIMMs or DIMMs and processors use ZIF (zero insertion force) sockets or other user-friendly connectors.

- **Tweezers and claw tool**   The tweezers and parts grabber can be used to hold any small screws or jumper blocks that are difficult to hold in your hand. The parts grabber (see Figure 2.3) can retrieve screws that have fallen into the system; usually, you can remove the part without completely disassembling the system.

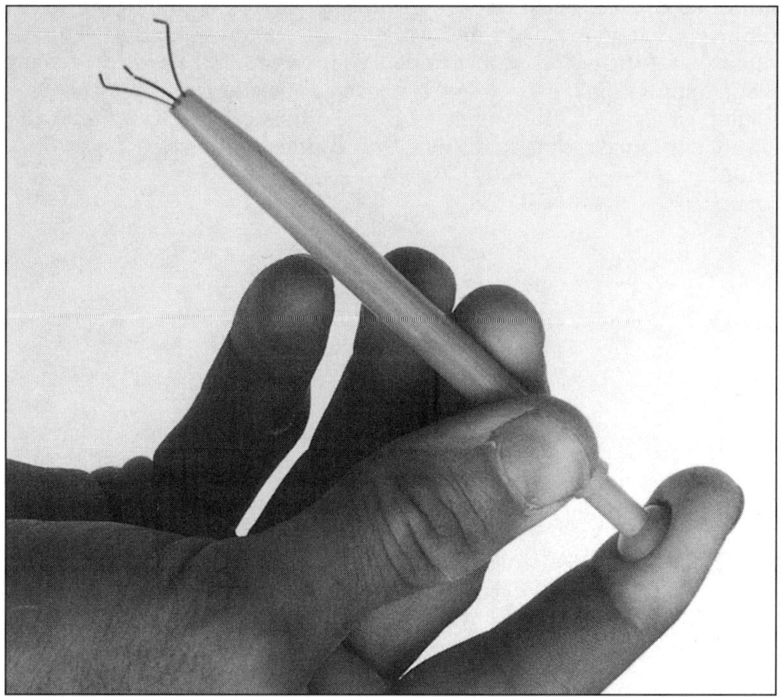

Figure 2.3 The claw tool has three small metal prongs that can be extended to grab a part.

- **T10 and T15 Torx drivers**   This is a special, star-shaped driver that matches the special screws found in most Compaq systems and in many other systems as well. You can also purchase tamper-proof Torx drivers that can remove Torx screws with the tamper-resistant pin in the center of the screw.

Caution

When working in a cramped environment such as the inside of a computer case, screwdrivers with magnetic tips can be a real convenience, especially for retrieving that screw you dropped into the case. However, although I have used these types of screwdrivers many times with no problems, you must be aware of the damage that a magnetic field can cause to memory chips and magnetic storage devices such as hard drives and floppy disks. Laying the screwdriver down on or near a floppy or working too close to a hard drive can damage the data on the disk.

You can also supplement this standard tool set with pliers, wire strippers, and a small flashlight, although these are not really necessary to work on today's computer equipment.

Electrical Tools

Two more considerations for your tool kit include the following:

- **ESD (electrostatic discharge) protection kit**   This kit consists of a wrist strap with a ground wire and a specially conductive mat with its own ground wire. Using a kit such as this when working on a system will help ensure that you never accidentally damage any of the components with a static discharge.

- **Analog or digital multimeter**   Although not necessary for most computer repairs, a multimeter is very useful at times. For example, if you wanted to verify the voltage and current output of the power supply to determine whether it needed replacing or the input voltage coming from the wall outlet needed to be checked, a multimeter could do this. In addition, when the multimeter is set to the ohms reading, it can test cabling continuity. (Infinite resistance means that there is no connection.) Figure 2.4 shows a standard digital multimeter.

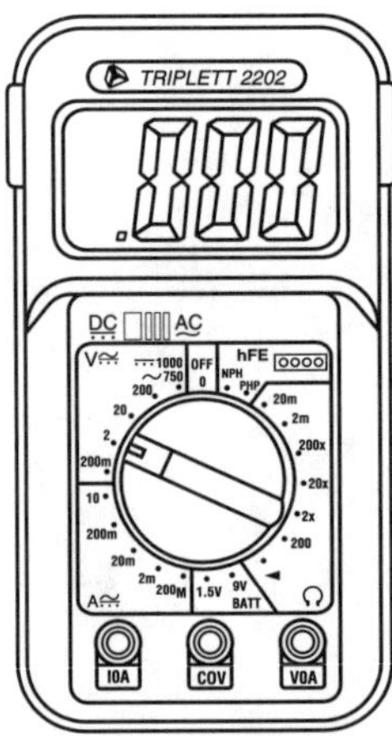

Figure 2.4 A typical digital multimeter set to measure voltage.

Basics of Electricity

Electricity is simply the shuffling of electrons in a given medium and using their natural tendency to equalize to perform work. This text will not delve deeply into this topic, but I (and CompTIA) would recommend that anyone working with electrical equipment understand the basics.

Voltage is electrical potential. (Imagine that this is the temperature of the electrons.) This simply means that one contact has "hotter" electrons on it than the other contact. When the two are brought together to complete a circuit, the hot electrons flow to equalize the temperature between the two. Voltage is measured in volts and is often represented as V (voltage) or E (energy). Because the entire value for voltage is represented in each and every electron, voltage can be measured by connecting the meter in parallel with the intact circuit—in other words, connected on either side of the component in the circuit that you want to measure.

Current is the rate or total amount of electrons that flow from the "hot" side to the "cold" side to heat up the "cold" side to a common equal temperature during a given unit of time. Current is measured in amperes and is represented as I or α. Because current is representative of all electrons flowing through a circuit in a given time, the meter must be inserted into the circuit, that is, connected in series to complete the circuit.

Resistance is an attribute of the actual wires or other components in the circuit. This causes the electrons to lose some potential because they have to work to move through the wire. Resistance is measured in ohms and is represented by R or Ω. Resistance can really only be measured in an incomplete and unpowered circuit or on a component that has been removed from the circuit.

The most basic formula of electricity is Ohm's law. This is the theory that Voltage = Current $\times$ Resistance or V=IR. Using basic algebra and given two of the values in a simple electrical circuit, you can solve to find the third value.

Tip

It is important to have a grasp of the basics of electricity for the exam. There will be a few questions over Ohm's law, as well as some questions concerning connecting a voltmeter or ammeter to a circuit.

Software Tools

There are three types of software-diagnostics categories. These are manufacturer diagnostics, third-party diagnostics, and operating-system diagnostics.

Manufacturer Diagnostics

Many of the larger manufacturers—especially high-end, name-brand manufacturers such as IBM, Compaq, Hewlett-Packard, Dell, and others—make special diagnostics software that is expressly designed for their systems. This manufacturer-specific software normally consists of a suite of tests that thoroughly examines the system. In some cases, you can download these diagnostics from the manufacturer's online services, or you might have to purchase them. Many vendors, such as Gateway, include a limited version of one of the after-market packages that has been customized for use with their systems. In some cases, the diagnostic software is installed on a special partition on the hard drive and can be accessed during startup. This is a convenient way for system manufacturers to make sure that you always have diagnostics available.

Third Party

A large number of third-party diagnostics programs are available for PC systems. Specific programs are available to test memory, floppy drives, hard disks, video adapters, and most other areas of the system. These include Norton, Q/A Plus, and CheckIt, among many others.

Many of these programs can run in a batch mode, which enables you to run a series of tests without operator intervention. You then can set up automated test suites, which can be especially useful when burning in a system or executing the same tests on many systems.

Much more information on third-party diagnostics and comparisons between them can be found in Chapter 25 of the eleventh edition of *Upgrading and Repairing PCs*.

Operating System Diagnostics

In many cases, it might not be necessary to purchase third-party diagnostic software because your operating system has all the diagnostic tools you need. Windows 95, 98, and NT include a large selection of programs that enable you to view, monitor, and troubleshoot the hardware in your system.

These tools include Microsoft Diagnostics (MSD and WinMSD), the Windows 9x Device Manager, Windows 9x System Monitor and Windows NT Performance Monitor, and Windows 9x System Information and Windows NT Diagnostics.

Note

Many of these Windows 9x tools will be discussed in Chapter 12, "Diagnostics and Troubleshooting," and in Chapter 25 of *Upgrading and Repairing PCs, Eleventh Edition*. Discussions on Windows NT tools and utilities are not covered on the A+ examination but can be found in Que's *Network+ Exam Guide*.

Review

Cram Session

Following are some key ideas you should keep in mind when readying yourself for the A+ exams:

- The three phases of troubleshooting are definition, isolation, and resolution.

- The definition phase involves data gathering from a variety of sources including the user, system configuration logs, and manufacturer documentation.

- Isolation involves the cyclical approach to troubleshooting to eliminate variables (or possibilities) one by one.

- Resolution involves not only fixing the problem, but duplicating it and documenting the confirmed resolution.

- The differences between a software error and a hardware error are often found by performing a reboot. Software errors usually disappear after a reboot. Hardware and configuration errors do not.

- The exam will give you POST error codes. Knowing what categories they fall into will be essential for the exam. Review Tables 2.1 and 2.2.

- The replacement technique for troubleshooting means taking a suspected part out of a problematic system and placing it into a known good system *as well as* placing a known good part in the suspected system. This dual replacement approach is the only true way to isolate a problem through replacement testing.

- Electromagnetic interference is a monitor's worst problem and its most common. This causes distortion of image and color variations.

- Modems fail due to data and telephone cabling more often than internal failures.

- Hard disks require software optimization to resolve problems with efficiency. These include media recovery and disk defragmentation.

- Many physical, electrical and software tools are required to be prepared to properly diagnose a problem.

- Electricity is all about excited electrons moving in a conductor doing work for you. Voltage is electrical potential. Current is the rate at which electrons flow by. Resistance is the natural...well, um, *resistance* of a wire to allow electrons to flow through it.

- There are three categories of software diagnostics. They are manufacturer, third party, and operating system.

Review Questions

1. What are the three phases of the troubleshooting model?

2. What types of questions are used for information gathering?

3. At what point is the isolation phase turned into the resolution phase?

4. What is the single most common type of error?

5. What is the easiest way to eliminate a soft memory error?

6. What is the last step in the resolution phase, and possibly the most important?

7. What visual error code range is related to memory errors?

8. What is the replacement technique of computer troubleshooting?

9. What is the most common video problem?

10. Given a circuit that has a 3.3 volt battery and an amperage of 600mA, what is the resistance?

Review Answers

1. The troubleshooting model is made up of three stages called definition, isolation, and resolution. A fourth stage, documentation, occurs throughout the course of the first three.

2. Open-ended questions are used to get the user to explain the situation in his own words. Close-ended questions are used to confirm what you believe the user to be saying.

3. When you have lost something, you always find it in the last place you look because when it is found, you stop looking for it. The same is true for the isolation phase. After you have eliminated all other possibilities, the last possibility, no matter how improbable, is the truth. This is what you pass into the resolution phase.

4. The most common error is the one that happens between the chair and the keyboard. It is common for user error to be cited for well over half of the support calls at almost any help desk.

5. Rebooting will eliminate soft errors in RAM, but a hard error, which is actually a malfunctioning chip, will not disappear with a reboot.

6. Documenting the entire process, paying special attention to the resolution of the problem, is the most important part of the resolution process.

7. 2xx. See Table 2.2 for other ranges.

8. The replacement technique for troubleshooting means taking a suspected part out of a problematic system and placing it into a known good system *as well as* placing a known good part in the suspected system.

9. Distortion due to electromagnetic interference. Desk fans, speakers, and especially cubicle shelf fluorescent lights are common culprits.

10. V=IR. Algebra says that to solve for R, divide V by I. 3.3 volts divided by .6 amps equals 5.5 ohms.

Chapter 3

Safety and Preventative Maintenance

Preventative Maintenance Procedures and Products

Preventative maintenance is the key to obtaining years of trouble-free service from your computer system. A properly administered preventative maintenance program pays for itself by reducing problem behavior, data loss, and component failure and by ensuring a long life for your system. How often you should perform active preventative maintenance procedures depends on the system's environment and the quality of the system's components. If your system is in a dirty environment, such as a machine shop floor or a gas station service area, you might need to clean your system every three months or less. For normal office environments, cleaning a system every one to two years is usually fine. However, if you open your system after one year and find dust bunnies inside, you should probably shorten the cleaning interval.

Preventative maintenance is all about cleaning. Dust buildup on the internal components can lead to several problems. One is that the dust acts as a thermal insulator, which prevents proper system cooling. Excessive heat shortens the life of system components and adds to the thermal stress problem caused by greater temperature changes between the system's power-on and power-off states. Additionally, the dust can contain conductive elements that can cause partial short circuits in a system. Other elements in dust and dirt can accelerate corrosion of electrical contacts, resulting in improper connections. In all, the regular removal of any layer of dust and debris from within a computer system benefits that system in the long run.

There are some software-based preventative measures that I will discuss as well, but primarily, PM is designed to proactively provide a proper computing environment. In the following sections, I will discuss the common needs and resolutions to a proper PM practice.

Cleaning Supplies

To properly clean the system and all the boards inside requires certain supplies and tools. In addition to the tools required to disassemble the unit, you should have these items:

- **Standard cleaner**   You should be sure that your cleaning solution is designed to clean computers or electronic assemblies. In most cases, this means that the solution should be chemically pure and free from contaminants or other unwanted substances. You should not, for example, use drugstore rubbing alcohol for cleaning electronic parts or contacts because it is not pure and could contain water or perfumes. The material must be moisture-free and residue-free. The solutions should be in liquid form, not in spray form. Sprays can be wasteful, and you almost never spray the solution directly on components. Instead, wet a foam or chamois swab used for wiping the component. These electronic-component cleaning solutions are available at any good electronics parts store.

- **Contact cleaner**   These chemicals are similar to the standard cleaners but include a lubricating component. The lubricant eases the force required when plugging and unplugging cables and connectors, reducing strain on the devices. The lubricant coating also acts as a conductive protectant that insulates the contacts from corrosion. These chemicals can greatly prolong the life of a system by preventing intermittent contacts in the future.

- **Canned air**   When using these compressed air products, make sure that you hold the can upright so that only gas is ejected from the nozzle. If you tip the can, the raw propellant will come out as a cold liquid, which not only is wasteful but can damage or discolor plastics. You should only use compressed gas on equipment that is powered off to minimize any chance of damage through short circuits.

- **A small brush and lint-free swabs**   Use cleaning swabs to wipe off electrical contacts and connectors, disk drive heads, and other sensitive areas. The swabs should be made of foam or synthetic chamois material that does not leave lint or dust residue. Unfortunately, proper foam or chamois cleaning swabs are more expensive than typical cotton swabs. Do not use cotton swabs because they leave cotton fibers on everything they touch. Cotton fibers are conductive in some situations and can remain on drive heads, which can scratch disks. Foam or chamois swabs can be purchased at most electronics supply stores.

- **Computer vacuum cleaner**   There are special vacuum cleaners specifically designed for use on and around electronic components. They are designed to minimize electrostatic discharge (ESD) while in use. If you are using a regular vacuum cleaner and not one specifically designed with ESD protection, you should take precautions such as wearing a grounding wrist strap. Also, if the cleaner has a metal nozzle, be careful not to touch it to the circuit boards or components you are cleaning.

In the Real World

Many people have recommended using a soft pencil-type eraser for cleaning circuit-board contacts. Testing has proven this to be bad advice for several reasons. One reason is that any such abrasive wiping on electrical contacts generates friction and ESD. Also, the eraser will wear off the gold coating on many contacts, exposing the tin contact underneath, which will rapidly corrode when exposed to air.

These simple cleaning tools and chemical solutions enable you to perform most common preventative maintenance tasks.

Keyboard and Mouse

Keyboards and mice are notorious for picking up dirt and garbage. To prevent problems for keyboards, it is a good idea to periodically clean the keyboard with a vacuum cleaner. An alternative method is to turn the keyboard upside down and shoot it with a can of compressed air. This will blow out the dirt and debris that has accumulated inside the keyboard and possibly prevent future problems with sticking keys or dirty key switches.

If a particular key is stuck or is making intermittent contact, you can soak or spray that switch with contact cleaner. The best way to do this is to first remove the keycap and then spray the cleaner into the switch. This usually does not require complete disassembly of the keyboard.

Most mice are easy to clean. In most cases, there is a twist-off locking retainer that keeps the mouse ball retained in the body of the mouse. By removing the retainer, the ball will drop out. After removing the ball, you should clean it with one of the cleaners. I would recommend a pure cleaner instead of a contact cleaner with lubricant because you do not want any lubricant on the mouse ball. Then you should wipe off the rollers in the body of the mouse with the cleaner and some swabs.

Periodic cleaning of a mouse in this manner will eliminate or prevent skipping or erratic movement. I also recommend a mouse pad for most ball-type mice because the pad will prevent the mouse ball from picking up debris from your desk.

Monitor

Monitors require little preventative maintenance other than occasionally cleaning the screen with a household nonstreaking glass cleaner. Beware spraying the cleaner directly onto the screen as the fluid could run down underneath the display casing and into the inside circuitry.

Another simple preventative maintenance task is to keep all ventilation clear of obstructing objects. This applies to all computer cases, not just the monitor.

Printers

Printers vary to some degree in procedures for maintenance and cleaning among the different major types. The three types that I will discuss here, and again in Chapter 5, "Printers," are dot matrix, ink jet, and laser.

Dot Matrix

Dot matrix printers require a vacuum or compressed-air cleaning to get rid of the large amounts of paper dust that these printers accumulate. The printer rollers also require a rubber restorative to rejuvenate the friction needed to advance the paper. The print head should be cleaned with an electrical contact cleaner and lint-free pad to provide for a small amount of lubrication among the print wires.

Inkjet

These printers require the same external maintenance as the dot matrix printers with the exception of the print head. The actual printing mechanism in an inkjet printer is maintained by a self-cleaning cycle built in to the printer's design. This cycle should be run after a few days' use. Different manufacturers recommend different cleaning times and cycles, but most printers have automated this task completely. The cycle can still be forced in the event of a problem.

Laser

For laser printers, the best preventative maintenance regimen results from purchasing a printer that uses toner cartridges with the drum and developer assemblies built in. These are the components that regularly come in contact with the toner, so replacing them on a regular basis ensures that these vital parts are clean and undamaged. You should take extra care to clean the inside of the printer whenever you replenish the toner, following the manufacturer's recommendations. Some printers include a special brush or other tool for this purpose.

Tip

Remember to be careful with the toner because it is very difficult to remove from skin and clothing. If you do get toner on your clothing, wash your clothes in cold water because hot water might melt the toner into your clothes permanently.

Circuit Boards

First clean the dust and debris off the board and then clean any connectors on the board. To clean the boards, it is usually best to use a vacuum cleaner designed for electronic assemblies and circuit boards or a duster can of compressed gas. The dusters are especially effective at blasting any dust and dirt off the boards.

Cleaning the connectors and contacts in a system promotes reliable connections between devices. On a motherboard, you will want to clean the slot connectors, power supply connectors, keyboard and mouse connectors, and speaker connector. For most plug-in cards, you will want to clean the edge connectors that plug in to slots on the motherboard and any other connectors, such as external ones mounted on the card bracket.

Floppy Drives

Floppy disk drives are particularly vulnerable to the effects of dirt and dust. A floppy drive is essentially a large hole in the system case through which air continuously flows. Therefore, these drives accumulate a large amount of dust and chemical buildup within a short time.

Floppy disk drive–cleaning units are commonly used to clean the interior of the drive. These kits contain a floppy diskette that has a cloth disk instead of a magnetic medium inside. The cleaner included is applied to the cloth diskette and inserted into the drive. As the drive attempts to read the diskette (which, of course, it can't) the cloth spins across the R/W heads, cleaning and polishing them.

Hard Drives

Because hard drives are sealed devices, very little physical cleaning can be done aside from dusting it off occasionally. Software-based hard disk preventative maintenance procedures protect your data and ensure that your hard disk works efficiently. Some of these procedures actually minimize wear and tear on your drive, which will prolong its life. These procedures include optimization and defragmentation of the hard disk drive. Both of these topics were discussed in Chapter 2, "Diagnosing and Troubleshooting."

Optical Discs

CD-ROMs, DVD-ROMs, and CD-R and CD-RW devices can be maintained in much the same way as the floppy disk maintenance procedures detail. There are special kits available with which to clean the drive heads.

As with the floppy kits, these should be used reactively instead of proactively due to the abrasive nature of the cleaning process.

Tape Drives

Tape drives have more well-defined cleaning cycles. This is due to the nature of the tape drive. It is very easy to get accurate predictions on the amount of use that they receive. Because of this, a scheduled preventative maintenance program for tape drives can be used, even though the cleaning process is nearly as abrasive as the floppy cleaning process. Generally, after a week's worth of backups, a cleaning tape should be inserted and run according to the manufacturer's specifications, although this interval might differ greatly depending upon the amount of use the device receives. It is not uncommon to see a cleaning tape run nightly after the drive has been used for 8–10 hours.

Power Supply

Power supplies are another relatively maintenance-free component. Aside from the occasional compressed air dusting, most technicians should not perform any repairs or maintenance on the internal components of a power supply.

Environmental and Safety Hazards

Environmental hazards to electronic and computer equipment include these eight categories:

- **Heat**   Overheating can be caused by electrical or power concerns, but it is primarily due to a lack of cleaning dirt and dust from the system in proper preventative maintenance procedures. Overheating can also be caused by poor ventilation of the computer casing.

In the Real World

If you see a monitor with a discolored case, take this as a warning sign. Commonly, users place papers or other objects on top of the monitor, which is exactly where the vents are located.

- **Humidity**   Extremely high or low humidity can cause concern for the computer technician. High humidity can cause condensation on the equipment, whereas low humidity can lead to static electricity.

- **Water**   Obviously, water and live electrical computer components don't mix. In some cases when a fire has been detected, computers have been destroyed not by the heat or flames, but by the sprinkler systems.

- **Food and Drink**   These can be extremely serious or extremely mild problems. Beware in particular of regular soda spilled into the computer circuits. Soda not only has a caustic nature, but regular (non-diet) soda has so much sugar in it that a sticky and caustic substance is released into the computer.

- **Magnetic Interference**   Magnetic fields can induce an electrical current into an adjacent circuit, causing unknown amounts of damage. In addition, magnetic media can be permanently erased or corrupted when placed into a magnetic field.

- **Static Electricity**   This is discussed in its own topic in the following section. Primarily, static causes damage that might not surface for a long period of time. There are various methods to eliminate or neutralize the static.

- **Smoke**   Cigarette smoke contains chemicals that can conduct electricity and can cause corrosion of computer parts. The smoke residue can infiltrate the entire system, causing corrosion and contamination of electrical contacts and sensitive components such as floppy drive read/write heads and optical drive lens assemblies.

- **Power**   Surge protectors, UPS, SPS, and line-conditioning devices are all created to deal with possible power source problems. These topics are discussed later in this chapter.

Electricity

There are many potential hazards with electricity. All of them can be avoided by simply understanding electricity and dispelling the myths and fears. This book will not go deeply into the specifics of electricity, but its concepts and components are essential to preparing for a career as a computer technician. More on the basics of electricity and its use in troubleshooting can be found in Chapter 2.

High Voltage and Current

As a warning, you should avoid both high voltage and high current. Although of the two, high current is far more deadly. High voltage can hurt and even kill, but so can an inordinately small amount of current.

Caution

For your safety, you should not use any form of ESD protection when working with high voltage or high current. ESD wrist straps and mats ground you to either the equipment being serviced, or possibly the ground plug in an electrical socket. By providing this convenient common ground, you are giving the high voltage an easy path to the ground—through you! In fact, you should wear shoes with rubber or insulated soles and no jewelry of any type. You should always, always, always unplug and discharge the equipment you are working on.

For more information on ESD, see the section "Electrostatic Discharge" later in this chapter.

Discharging a CRT

Discharging a CRT is certainly test material, although few service technicians today need to dive this deeply into a replaceable part.

Caution

You should never attempt to repair a CRT monitor unless you are a qualified service technician. Touching the wrong component can be fatal. The display circuits can hold extremely high voltages for hours, days, or even weeks after the power is shut off. You will need to drain the CRT and capacitors before servicing.

After following the other common safety and service techniques, such as removing jewelry and adhering to the high voltage techniques discussed previously, you can begin the process of discharging the CRT.

After removing power and disassembling the case, you will need a small high voltage probe. This probe will measure the power coming off a high voltage circuit and run it through a high ohm resistor to strain off the power. To connect it to the high voltage circuit, ground one end and slide the other underneath the suction cup that is attached to the top of the CRT, as shown in Figure 3.1. You might hear a slight pop when the probe makes contact, and the meter on the probe will jump to the top of the scale and gradually come back down. When the meter reads zero again, the circuit and tube are fully drained.

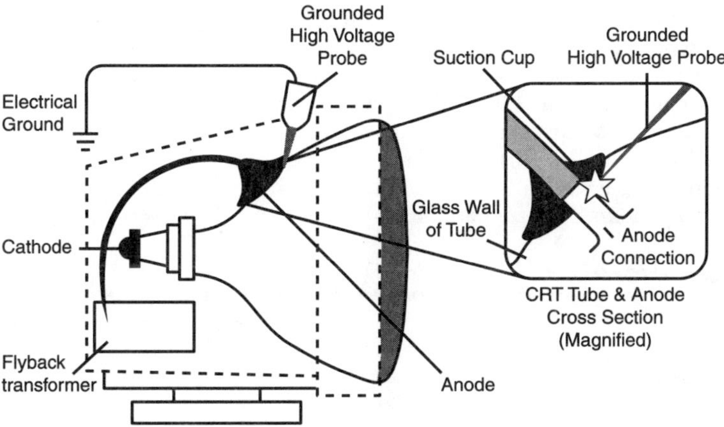

Figure 3.1 Discharging a CRT using a high-voltage probe.

The CRT will attempt to drain the other capacitors in the system to build its charge back up, so a second application of the probe might be necessary.

Electrostatic Discharge

Electrostatic discharge, or ESD, is dangerous to the computer components that you come into contact with. This occurs when any two surfaces contact each other. This includes anything from your necktie to your tools to your hand itself contacting the circuit boards in the computer. When your tie rubs against your shirt, electrons are transferred from one surface to the other. Because electricity always seeks a common level, or common ground, when either surface contacts another surface, the electrons jump across to level the charges between the two materials.

When you are working on the internal components of a computer, you need to take the necessary precautions to prevent accidental static discharges to the components. At any time, your body can hold a large static voltage charge that can easily damage components of your system. This damaging charge can be from as low as 25 volts to as much as 30,000 volts. Because you cannot physically feel electricity less than 5,000 volts, you can easily damage a circuit without your knowledge. The damage can be so small that it might not show up for a few days, weeks, or even years.

There are two ways to eliminate ESD. They are charge neutralization and charge equalization:

- Charge neutralization eliminates ESD by eliminating the ability for the electrons to rub off onto other surfaces, consequently disabling the surfaces to build up a static charge. This is accomplished by blowing ionized air particles over the equipment being worked on. This can be readily explained: Imagine a thin layer of oil keeping two gears from wearing down by rubbing off on each other. This is what the ionized air does to the equipment. Because of the expense, size, and controlled environment that this process requires, it is not commonly used in the field.

- Charge equalization is the most commonly used ESD prevention technique. Charge equalization works in a completely different way than ionized neutralization. Rather than eliminating the static buildup on components, a common ground is sought. For example, if one component acquires a 100v buildup, no discharge will occur to other devices that have a 100v buildup. The discharge will only happen when a device with less of a charge is contacted. To accomplish this, a conductor is used to connect you to your components so that no "pop" happens when you do come into contact with the circuit boards. This is generally in the form of an ESD strap and kit.

In the Real World

Beware—some people suggest touching the power supply in a system that has the power cable still attached to eliminate ESD. Although this method does work temporarily, the ESD charge will build constantly in the intervals between touching the power supply. In addition, some circuits on the motherboard might be fully powered even while the power switch is off. This can cause even more potential damage. This erroneous method is commonly used as a distracter on the exam. In this case, the exam and the real world agree: ESD wrist straps and mats are the only electrically safe environment in which to handle computer components.

These kits consist of a wrist strap and mat. The wrist strap is shown in Figure 3.2, with ground wires for attachment to the system chassis. When you are going to work on a system, you place the mat next to or partially below the system unit. Next, you clip the ground wire to both the mat and the system's chassis, tying the grounds together. You then put on the wrist strap and attach that wire to a ground.

Figure 3.2 A typical ESD kit with wrist strap and mat.

Because the mat and system chassis are already wired together, you can attach the wrist-strap wire to the system chassis or to the mat. If you are using a wrist strap without a mat, clip the wrist-strap wire to the system chassis. When clipping these wires to the chassis, be sure to use an area that is free of paint so that a good contact can be achieved. As you install or remove disk drives, adapter cards, and especially delicate items such as the entire motherboard, SIMMs, or processors, you should place these components on the static mat. This setup ensures that any electrical charges are carried equally by you and any of the components in the system, preventing the sudden flow of static electricity that can damage the circuits.

Power Interruptions

Power interruptions can come in many forms. Brownouts, surges, blackouts, and spikes are the four most common power fluctuations. These are described as follows:

- **Spikes** Spikes are momentary jumps in power to normally unreachable levels, often several hundred to thousands of volts. These often occur with lighting storms or poor power sources but can also be caused by shorts and surges through the power lines.

- **Surges** These can be caused by a power station running "hot" or simply by the draw on the lines decreasing from other areas of your building or neighborhood. This is a rolling rise in power levels for an extended period of time.

- **Brownouts** The opposite of surges, this is a decrease in the overall power available over a period of time. This can last as short as the time it takes the air conditioner compressor to turn on and off or as long as the entire evening. Most power companies have scheduled brownouts in the early morning hours because fewer people have the power on during that time.

- **Blackouts** Blackouts can be caused by something as terrible as storms tearing down power lines or as mundane as you forgetting to pay the electric bill. It amounts to a complete loss of power, regardless of the length of time it lasts.

Power interruptions and fluctuations can be resolved by several devices. These include surge suppressors and backup power supplies in the form of standby power supplies and uninterruptible power supplies. These are explained as follows:

- **Surge suppressors** These do exactly as their name indicates. They can stop any excess of power coming through the line within reason. Although more commonly used to stop spikes, surges greater than the tolerance of the device can be halted as well. These devices often have a circuit breaker or fuse that will turn off the power if an abnormally high level is reached. Unfortunately, these cannot protect against brownouts or blackouts.

- **Standby power supplies** SPS devices have a battery backup to provide power if the line voltage drops to less than tolerances. The battery and its charging circuit are connected in parallel with the power source going through to the computer. When the line voltage drops, there is a slight lag in switching over to the battery, which has to provide DC power to a power inverter that converts it to AC voltage to be sent to the computer. This circuit is shown in Figure 3.3. Often, the switching times are measured in milliseconds, which is enough to maintain power to the computer. Unfortunately, if the switching device or line sensors fail, there is no warning and no backup power provided.

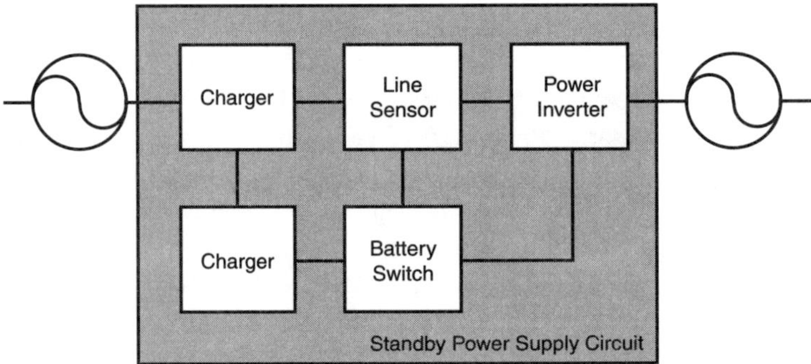

Figure 3.3 The charging and power circuits for a SPS device.

- **Uninterruptible power supplies**   UPS devices are similar to SPS devices, except that their batteries and charging circuits are connected in series with the power to the computer. This means that the AC line coming into the UPS goes directly to the battery charging circuit. The battery constantly provides DC power to the inverter, which converts it back into AC power for the computer to use. This circuit is shown in Figure 3.4. The biggest benefit to UPS devices is that they have no switching time and provide constant, steady, reliable power to the computer at all times.

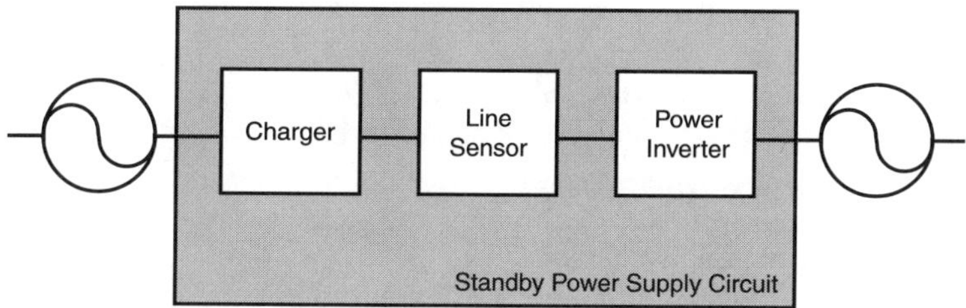

Figure 3.4 The charging and power circuits for a UPS device.

Lasers

Laser printers have several safety devices that will keep you from viewing the laser directly while power is applied. Lasers can seriously damage your retina, in some cases to varying degrees of blindness. Do not disable these safety measures.

Special Disposal Concerns

Some facilities will reclaim computer equipment for salvage. Most of the companies will take all computer equipment. However, you should consult your state laws before dumping any computer equipment. Some computer components that are specifically regulated in various states include circuit boards, batteries, CRT screens, and laser printer toner.

Review

Cram Session

Following are some key points to remember:

- **Preventative maintenance is all about cleaning**   A system that has not been cleaned properly can build up dust. Dust can cause two major failures: heat buildup due to excessive insulation and blocked ventilation as well as the possibility of shorting out some circuits through impurities in the dust.

- **Cleaning supplies**   Common cleaning supplies include a standard cleaner, electrical contact cleaner, canned air, lint-free foam swabs, and a computer vacuum.

- **Keyboards and mice**   Keyboards and mice pick up the most dirt because these devices come into physical contact with the end user. Indeed, these devices convert these physical motions into data for the computer to process. Both keyboards and mice can exhibit erratic behavior when their surfaces and contacts are not clean.

- **Monitors**   Other than cleaning the exterior, monitors have little or no preventative maintenance procedures.

- **Printers**   Printers require different maintenance from one type to another. Dot matrix printers primarily require the removal of the paper dust from the perforated tractor-fed paper it uses. Inkjet printers have built-in maintenance cycles for the ink cartridges that are usually scheduled and run automatically, but they can be manually initiated if the print quality is suffering. Laser printers have little preventative maintenance to perform in the way of cleaning. Most maintenance can be performed with the replacement of the toner cartridge unit because this houses all the consumable parts and supplies in one convenient case.

- **Circuit boards**   Circuit boards are best cleaned with a can of compressed air, but they can also be cleaned with foam swabs and contact cleaner.

- **Floppy, tape, and optical drives**   Floppy drives, tape drives, and even optical drives have kits that can be purchased, although due to the abrasive nature of the procedure, these kits should be used sparingly.

- **Power supplies**   Power supplies require no PM procedures other than the occasional dusting with compressed air to remove the dust from the components, especially the fan.

- **Environmental hazards**   Environmental hazards include heat, humidity, water, food and drink, improper power, magnetic interference, static, and smoke.

- **Discharging CRTs**   Discharging a CRT requires a high voltage probe and an electrical ground point. After attaching the probe to ground and ensuring that you are not, simply touch the probe to the contact under the cup at the top of the tube. The meter will gradually return to zero, indicating a discharged state.

- **ESD**   ESD can destroy equipment and often does so without your notice. ESD charge equalization is the most common method and consists of an ESD wrist strap attaching your body to a common ground.

- **Backup power supply devices are often called uninterrubtible power supplies**   For some of these, this is incorrect. An SPS device provides backup power after a sensor switches from normal power to the battery-supplied power. A UPS device provides reliable, uninterrupted power from the battery at all times. The AC line into a true UPS device only charges the battery.

Review Questions

1. How does contact cleaner differ from a standard cleaner?

2. What is a common symptom of a dirty mouse?

3. Printers require differing preventative maintenance. What is a common problem among all types of printers?

4. In what container do laser printers house most consumables?

5. True or false: Floppy drives should have regularly scheduled maintenance run on them. Why or why not?

6. True or false: Tape drives should have regularly scheduled maintenance run on them. Why or why not?

7. Why should you wash toner from your hands and clothes with cold water?

8. Why is magnetic interference an environmental concern?

9. True or false: Touching a power supply before conducting PC repairs is an adequate ESD prevention technique. Why or why not?

10. What is a surge? What is a brownout?

11. Explain the differences between an SPS and a UPS.

Review Answers

1. Contact cleaner has an electrically conductive lubricating substance in it to protect the contacts from wear.

2. When a mouse is not cleaned well, the pointer might move erratically across and all around the screen, though the mouse is being moved in a single straight line. This erratic behavior is indicative of a dirty mouse.

3. All printers, regardless of the technology, have a problem with paper dust. Although this is more prevalent in tractor-fed paper, as in the dot matrix.

4. The toner cartridge houses all the consumables and most of the parts that require preventative care. Replacing this component is the first step to a preventative maintenance schedule for laser printers.

5. False. Floppy cleaning kits are abrasive and might damage the read/write heads after repeated use. This is especially true because floppy drives are used sparingly during the course of a common computer's use.

6. True. Although the process is somewhat abrasive, the tape drive is a scheduled device that has specific hours of use. This scheduling can easily predict the number of hours between cleanings and precedent a preventative maintenance schedule.

7. Toner is actually a fine plastic powder with a low melting point. In the same way that a fuser melts the toner to the page to form printed words, hot water will fuse the toner to your hands and clothes.

8. Magnetic interference, especially from electric motors, can induce a current in any conductor that the field passes through. This charge might be detrimental to the circuit or might simply cause the signal on that circuit to be canceled or become corrupt.

9. False. This process, although popular and better than nothing, is a myth. This is because simply moving your arm away from the power supply is enough to generate a potentially damaging charge, and the only place for it to discharge is into the next component you touch.

10. A surge is the opposite of a brownout. A surge is a temporary rise in the voltage level provided by the power station. A brownout is a temporary decrease in the voltage level provided by the power station. Both of these events can last from a few seconds to several hours.

11. An SPS device provides backup power after a sensor switches from normal power to the battery-supplied power. A UPS device provides reliable, uninterrupted power from the battery at all times. The AC line into a true UPS device only charges the battery.

Motherboards/ Processors/Memory

Motherboards

Without a doubt, the most important component in a PC system is the main board, or motherboard. Some companies refer to the motherboard as a system board or planar. The terms, *motherboard, main board, system board,* and *planar* are interchangeable. In this chapter, I will briefly examine the different types of motherboards available and those components usually contained on the motherboard and motherboard interface connectors as covered in the A+ exam objectives. For the definitive text on motherboards and bus structures, please consult Scott Mueller's *Upgrading and Repairing PCs, Eleventh Edition*, Chapter 4, "Motherboards and Buses."

Types

There are several common form factors used for PC motherboards. The form factor refers to the physical dimensions and size of the board and dictates what type of case the board will fit into. Some are true standards (meaning that all boards with that form factor are interchangeable), whereas others are not standardized enough to provide for true interchangeability. Unfortunately, these nonstandard form factors preclude any easy upgrade, which generally means they should be avoided. The more commonly known PC motherboard form factors that will be tested over include the AT and the newer ATX standards.

The easiest way to identify an AT form factor system without opening it is to look at the rear of the case. In an AT motherboard, the cards plug directly into the board at a 90-degree angle; in other words, the slots in the case for the cards are perpendicular to the motherboard. Also, the AT motherboard has only one visible connector directly attached to the board, which is the keyboard connector. Normally, this connector is the full-sized

5-pin DIN-type connector, although some Baby-AT systems will use the smaller 6-pin min-DIN connector (sometimes called a PS/2-type connector) and might even have a mouse connector. All other connectors will be mounted on the case or on card edge brackets and attached to the motherboard via cables.

Although the AT standard has been the old standby, the ATX form factor was the first of a dramatic evolution in motherboard form factors. The ATX form factor is essentially a Baby-AT motherboard turned sideways in the chassis, along with a modified power supply location and connector, relocated internal and external I/O connectors, and improved CPU cooling in its new location. The most important thing to know initially about the ATX form factor is that it is physically incompatible with either the previous Baby-AT or AT designs because of a completely redesigned system and port layout as shown in Figure 4.1. In other words, a different case and power supply are required to match the ATX motherboard. These new case and power supply designs have become common and can be found in many new systems.

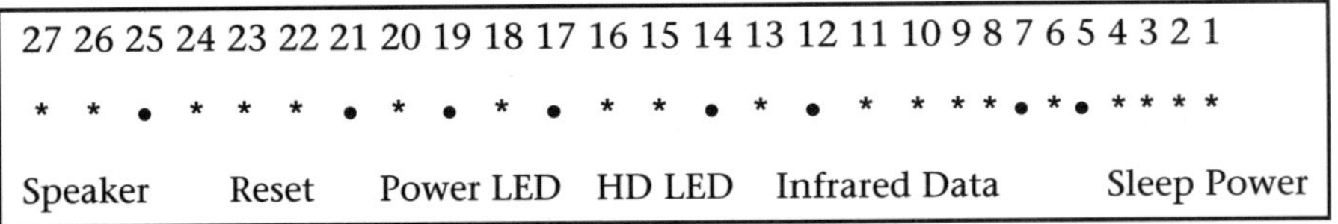

Figure 4.1 Typical ATX motherboard layout and rear panel connectors.

Components

A modern motherboard has several components built in, including various sockets, slots, connectors, chips, and so on. This section examines the components found on a typical motherboard.

Most modern motherboards have at least the following major components on them:

- Processor socket/slot
- Chipset (north and south bridges)
- Super I/O chip
- ROM BIOS (Flash ROM)
- SIMM/DIMM/RIMM sockets
- ISA/PCI/AGP bus slots
- CPU voltage regulator
- Battery

Some of these components have already been discussed in previous chapters, whereas others such as bus architectures, CMOS, processors, and memory will be discussed in the following sections.

Bus Architectures

At the heart of every motherboard are the buses that make it up. A *bus* is a common pathway across which data can travel within a computer. This pathway is used for communication and can be established between two or more computer elements.

The PC has a hierarchy of different buses. Most modern PCs have at least three different buses; some have four or more. They are hierarchical because each slower bus is connected to the faster one above it. Each device in the system is connected to one of the buses, and some devices (primarily the chipset) act as bridges between the various buses. The types of buses are as follows:

- **System bus**   This is the highest-speed bus in the system and is at the core of the chipset and motherboard. This bus is used primarily by the processor to pass information to and from cache, system RAM, and the chipset. The processor bus in Pentium II systems runs at either 66MHz or 100MHz and has the full 64-bit data path width of the processor.

Note

Notice that the main memory bus is always the same width as the processor bus. This will define the size of what is called a *bank* of memory. Memory banks and their width relative to processor buses are discussed in the "Memory Banks" section later in this chapter.

- **I/O bus**   The I/O bus or expansion slots are what enables your CPU to communicate with peripheral devices. The bus and its associated expansion slots are needed because basic systems cannot possibly satisfy all the needs of all the people who buy them. The I/O bus enables you to add devices to your computer to expand its capabilities. The most basic computer components, such as sound cards and video cards, can be plugged into expansion slots; you also can plug in more specialized devices, such as network interface cards, SCSI host adapters, and others.

Surprisingly, virtually all PC systems shipped today still incorporate the same basic I/O bus architecture as the 1984 vintage IBM PC/AT. However, most of these systems now also include a second high-speed local I/O bus, such as VL-Bus or PCI, which offers much greater performance for adapters that need it. Many of the newest systems also include a third high-speed bus called AGP for improved video performance beyond what PCI offers.

The A+ examination covers ISA and PCI buses heavily, but might touch on some of the older obsolete buses as well. For the definitive text on motherboards and bus structures, consult Scott Mueller's *Upgrading and Repairing PCs, Eleventh Edition*, Chapter 4.

ISA 8-bit (PC) and 16-bit (AT)

ISA, which is an acronym for *Industry Standard Architecture*, is the bus architecture that was introduced as an 8-bit bus with the original IBM PC in 1981; it was later expanded to 16 bits with the IBM PC/AT in 1984. IBM was forced to release the ISA specifications to public domain for industry standardization shortly thereafter. Because of this, ISA is the basis of the modern personal computer and the primary architecture used in the vast majority of PC systems on the market today. It might seem amazing that such a presumably antiquated architecture is used in today's high-performance systems, but this is true for reasons of reliability, affordability, and compatibility, plus this old bus is still faster than many of the peripherals that you connect to it!

The original 8-bit version ran at 4.77MHz in the PC and XT. The 16-bit version used in the AT ran at 6MHz and then 8MHz. Later, the industry as a whole agreed on an 8.33MHz maximum standard speed for 8/16-bit versions of the ISA bus for backward compatibility. Some systems have the capability to run the ISA bus faster than this, but some adapter cards will not function properly at higher speeds.

MCA

The introduction of 32-bit chips meant that the ISA bus could not handle the power of another new generation of CPUs. The 386DX chips can transfer 32 bits of data at a time, but the ISA bus can handle a maximum 16 bits. Rather than extend the ISA bus again, IBM decided to build a new bus; the result was the MCA bus. *MCA* (an acronym for *Micro Channel Architecture*) is completely different from the ISA bus and is technically superior in every way except standardization.

IBM not only wanted to replace the old ISA standard, but also to receive royalties on it; the company required vendors that licensed the new MCA bus to pay IBM royalties for using it in any system or expansion card design. This requirement led to the development of the competing EISA bus (see the following section on the EISA bus) and hindered acceptance of the MCA bus. Another reason why MCA has not been adopted universally for systems with 32-bit slots is that adapter cards designed for ISA systems do not work in MCA systems.

In the Real World

The MCA bus is not compatible with the older ISA bus, so cards designed for the ISA bus do not work in an MCA system. To avoid designing two different cards to go to market as MCA or ISA, some manufacturers designed cards that could insert into an MCA bus on one side or be flipped over to use the ISA connector on the other side.

An MCA system has no jumpers and switches on either the motherboard or any expansion adapter. This was the first software-based configuration of expansion cards. To configure, you do need the reference disk that goes with the particular system and the options disks that go with each of the cards installed in the system.

EISA

EISA is an acronym for *Extended Industry Standard Architecture*. This standard was announced in September 1988 as a response to IBM's introduction of the MCA bus—more specifically, to the way that IBM wanted to handle licensing of the MCA bus. Vendors did not feel obligated to pay retroactive royalties on the ISA bus, so they turned their backs on IBM and created their own buses. The EISA standard was developed primarily by Compaq, who formed the EISA committee, a nonprofit organization designed specifically to control development of the EISA bus. Very few EISA adapters were ever developed. Those that were developed centered mainly around disk-array controllers and server-type network cards.

At first glance, the 32-bit EISA slot looks a lot like the 16-bit ISA slot. The EISA adapter, however, has two rows of connectors. The first row is the same kind used in 16-bit ISA cards; the other, thinner row extends downward from the 16-bit connectors. This means that ISA cards can still be used in EISA bus slots because the connector doesn't extend all the way down into the slot.

EISA also mimicked the MCA design through the creation of a new software-based configuration called the EISA configurator. EISA setup software recognizes potential conflicts and automatically configures the system to avoid them. EISA does, however, enable you to do your own troubleshooting, as well as to configure the boards through jumpers and switches.

VESA-LB

The Video Electronics Standards Association (VESA) developed a standardized local bus specification known as *VESA local bus (VL-Bus)*. As in earlier local bus implementations, the VL-Bus slot offers direct access to system memory at the speed of the processor itself. The VL-Bus can move data 32 bits at a time, enabling data to flow between the CPU and a compatible video subsystem or hard drive at the full 32-bit data width of the 486 chip. The maximum rated throughput of the VL-Bus is 128MB to 132MBps. In other words, local bus went a long way toward removing the major bottlenecks that existed in earlier bus configurations.

Physically, the VL-Bus slot is simply an extension of the ISA slots in your system. Figure 4.2 shows how the VL-Bus slots can be situated in an ISA system.

Despite all the benefits of the VL-Bus (and, by extension, of all local buses), this technology has a few drawbacks, such as dependence on a 486 CPU, speed limitations, and electrical limitations. Despite the low cost, after a new bus called *PCI (Peripheral Component Interconnect)* appeared, VL-Bus fell into disfavor very quickly.

PCI

PCI redesigned the traditional PC bus by inserting another bus between the CPU and the native I/O bus by means of bridges. Rather than tap directly into the processor bus, with its delicate electrical timing (as was done in the VL-Bus), a new set of controller chips was developed to extend the bus. The PCI bus often is called a *mezzanine bus* because it adds another layer to the traditional bus configuration. PCI bypasses the standard I/O bus; it uses the system bus to increase the bus clock speed and take full advantage of the CPU's data path.

A PCI adapter card uses its own unique connector. This connector can be identified within a computer system because it typically is offset from the normal ISA, MCA, or EISA connectors. See Figure 4.3 for an example. The size of a PCI card can be the same as that of the cards used in the system's normal I/O bus.

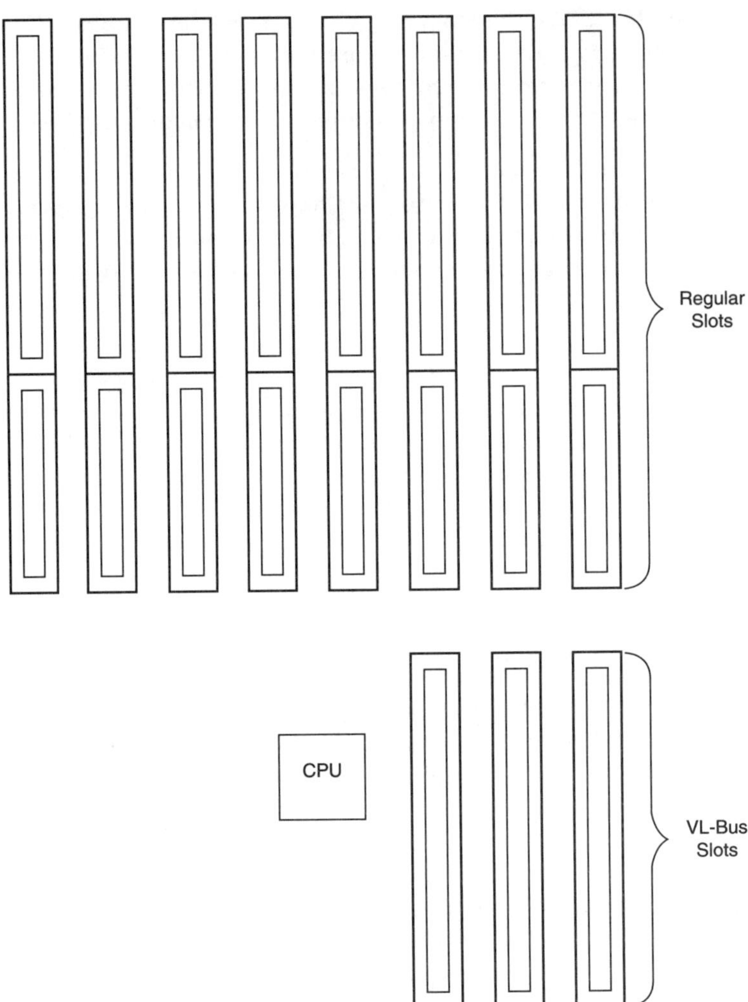

Figure 4.2 An example of VL-Bus slots in an ISA system.

Another important feature of PCI, now in version 2.1, is the fact that it was the model for the Intel PnP specification. This means that PCI cards do not have jumpers and switches and are instead configured through software. True PnP systems are capable of automatically configuring the adapters, whereas non-PnP systems with ISA slots have to configure the adapters through a program that is usually a part of the system CMOS configuration.

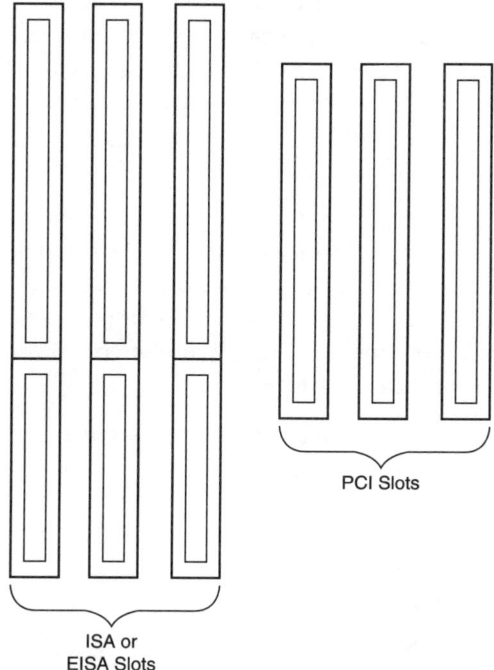

Figure 4.3 Possible configuration of PCI slots in relation to ISA or EISA slots.

AGP

The Accelerated Graphics Port (AGP) was created by Intel as a new bus specifically designed for high performance graphics and video support. AGP is based on PCI, but it contains a number of additions and enhancements and is physically, electrically, and logically independent of PCI. Unlike PCI, which is a true bus with multiple connectors (slots), AGP is more of a point-to-point high-performance connection designed specifically for a video card in a system, with only one AGP slot is allowed for a single video card.

Because AGP is independent of PCI, using an AGP video card will free up the PCI bus for more traditional input and output, such as for IDE/ATA or SCSI controllers, USB controllers, sound cards, and so on.

PCMCIA

In an effort to give notebook computers the kind of expandability that users have grown used to in desktop systems, the Personal Computer Memory Card International Association (PCMCIA) has established several standards for credit card–size expansion boards that fit into a small slot on laptops and notebooks.

Originally designed as a standard interface for memory cards, the PCMCIA document defines both the PC card hardware and the software support architecture used to run it. The PC cards in version 1 of the standard, called Type I, are credit card–size and 3.3mm thick. The standard has since been revised to support cards with many other functions. The third version, called PC Card Specification, defines three types of cards, with the only physical difference being their thickness. This was done to support the hardware for different card functions.

Most of the PC cards on the market today, such as modems and network interface adapters, are 5mm-thick Type II devices. Type III cards are 10.5mm thick and are typically used for PC card hard drives. All the card types are backward-compatible; you can insert a Type I card into a Type II or III slot. The standard PC card slot configuration for portable computers is two Type II slots, with one on top of the other. This way, you can also insert a single Type III card, taking up both slots but using only one of the connectors.

CardBus, a new version of PC cards, has a 32-bit interface that runs at 33MHz and provides 32-bit data paths to the computer's I/O and memory systems, as well as a new shielded connector that prevents CardBus devices from being inserted into slots that do not support the latest version of the standard. This is a vast improvement over the 8- or 16-bit bus width and 8MHz speed of the original PC Card–16 interface. If you connect your portable computer to a 100Mbps network, CardBus can provide the high-speed interface that, in a desktop system, would be provided by PCI.

For more information on PCMCIA, PC Cards, and card and socket services, please consult Chapter 23 "Portable PCs" of *Upgrading and Repairing PCs, Eleventh Edition.*

USB

USB ports are now found on most motherboards, and with Windows 98 there finally was an operating system that would properly support them. The big advantage of USB from an IRQ or resource perspective is that the USB bus uses only one IRQ no matter how many devices (up to 127) are attached. This means that you can freely add or remove devices from the USB without worrying about running out of resources or having resource conflicts.

The USB is a 12Mbps (1.5MBps) interface over a simple four-wire connection. The bus supports up to 127 devices and uses a tiered star topology built on expansion hubs that can reside in the PC, any USB peripheral, or even standalone hub boxes. Note that although the standard provides for up to 127 devices to be attached, they would all have to share the 1.5MBps bandwidth, meaning that for every device you add, the bus slows down some. In reality, few people will have more than eight devices attached at any one time.

If you aren't using any USB devices, you should turn off the port using your motherboard CMOS setup so that the IRQ it was using will be freed. In the future, as everything moves to USB-based keyboards, mice, modems, printers, and so on, the IRQ shortage will be less of a problem. The elimination of the ISA bus in systems will go a long way toward solving this problem as well.

FireWire

IEEE-1394 (or just 1394 for short) is a relatively new bus technology; it is the result of the large data-moving demands of today's audio and video multimedia devices. It is extremely fast, with data transfer rates up to an incredible 400Mbps, and even faster speeds are being developed.

Just as with USB, 1394 is fully PnP, including the capability for hot plugging (insertion and removal of components without powering down). Unlike the much more complicated parallel SCSI bus, 1394 does not require complicated termination, and devices that are connected to the bus can draw up to 1.5 amps of electrical power. 1394 is built on a daisy-chained and branched topology, and it provides for up to 63 nodes, with a chain of up to 16 devices on each node.

Expect the 1394 bus to be implemented in both desktop and portable computers as a replacement for other external high-speed buses such as SCSI and their devices. This includes all forms of disk drives, including hard disk, optical, floppy, CD-ROM, and the new DVD (Digital Video Disc) drives as well as digital cameras, tape drives, and many other high-speed peripherals.

For further information on USB and FireWire 1394, please consult Chapter 16 "Serial, Parallel, and Other I/O Interfaces" of *Upgrading and Repairing PCs, Eleventh Edition*.

CMOS

In the original AT system, a Motorola 146818 chip was used as the RTC (Real-Time Clock) and CMOS (Complementary Metal-Oxide Semiconductor) RAM chip. This is a special chip that had a simple digital clock that used 10 bytes of RAM and an additional 54 more bytes of leftover RAM in which you could store anything you wanted. The designers of the IBM AT used these extra 54 bytes to store the software-based system configuration, rather than using switch settings as in the XT.

Note that many newer systems have more than 64 bytes of CMOS RAM; in fact, in some systems they might have 2KB or 4KB. The extra room is used to store the PnP information detailing the configuration of adapter cards and other options in the system.

CMOS requires a constant charge to retain its data, so the CMOS battery was created. Originally, these were AA batteries connected to the system board, but they have evolved into the wafer-style watch batteries that you see on system boards today.

After you press the correct keystroke combination during startup (usually Delete or F1), you can add, change, or remove almost any hardware setting you want. At the very least, these devices can be configured: display, RAM, HDD, FDD, I/O devices and ports, and, of course, the system date and time.

Processors

The brain or engine of the PC is the processor (sometimes called microprocessor), or central processing unit (CPU). The CPU performs the system's calculating and processing. The processor is easily the most expensive single component in the system, costing up to four or more times the motherboard it plugs into. Intel is generally credited with creating the first microprocessor in 1971 and today they have almost total control over the processor market, at least for PC systems. This means that all PC-compatible systems use either Intel processors or Intel-compatible processors from a handful of competitors (such as AMD or Cyrix).

Tip

For the purposes of the A+ examination, I will discuss Intel chips exclusively and briefly. For information about the other processor manufacturers and their lines (such as AMD or Cyrix) and more in-depth information on Intel's line, please consult *Upgrading and Repairing PCs, Eleventh Edition*, Chapter 3, "Microprocessor Types and Specifications."

Processors can be identified by two main parameters: how wide (buses) they are and how fast (speed) they are.

Processor Speed Ratings

The speed of a processor is a fairly simple concept. Speed is counted in megahertz (MHz), which means millions of cycles per second, and faster is better! Still, a common misunderstanding about processors is regarding their different speed ratings. A computer system's clock speed is measured as a frequency, usually expressed as a number of cycles per second. A crystal oscillator controls clock speeds, using a sliver of quartz sometimes held in what looks like a small tin container. As voltage is applied to the quartz, it begins to vibrate (oscillate) at a harmonic rate dictated by the shape and size of the crystal (sliver). The oscillations emanate from the crystal in the form of an alternating current that alternates at the harmonic rate of the crystal. This alternating current is the clock signal, which forms the time base upon which the computer operates. A typical computer system runs millions of these cycles per second, so speed is measured in megahertz. (One hertz is equal to one cycle per second.)

Clock cycles aren't the only relevant speed measurement. Evaluating CPU performance can be tricky. CPUs with different internal architectures do things differently and can be relatively faster at certain things and slower at others.

Another confusing factor when comparing processor performance is that virtually all modern processors since the 486DX2 run at some multiple of the motherboard speed. For example, a Celeron 466 runs at a multiple of seven times the motherboard speed of 66MHz, whereas a Pentium III 550 runs at five and a half times the motherboard speed of 100MHz. Normally, you can set the motherboard speed and multiplier setting via jumpers or some other configuration mechanism (such as CMOS setup) on the motherboard.

Processor Buses

The width of a processor is a little more complicated to discuss because there are three main specifications in a processor that are expressed in width. They are as follows:

- **Data input and output bus**   The processor bus discussed most often is the external data bus—the pins used to send and receive data. The more signals that can be sent at the same time, the more data can be transmitted in a specified interval and, therefore, the faster (by capacity) the bus is. Having a wider data bus is like having a highway with more lanes, which allows for greater throughput.

- **Internal registers**   The size of the internal registers indicate how much information the processor can operate on at one time and how it moves data around internally within the chip. This is sometimes also referred to as the internal data bus. (A register is a holding cell within the processor; for example, the processor can add numbers in two different registers, storing the result in a third register.)

■ **Memory address bus**   The address bus is the set of wires that carry the addressing information used to describe the memory location to which the data is being sent or from which the data is being retrieved. As with the data bus, each wire in an address bus carries a single bit of information. This single bit is a single digit in the address. The more wires (digits) used in calculating these addresses, the greater the total number of address locations. The size (or width) of the address bus indicates the maximum amount of RAM that a chip can address.

On-board Processor Cache

Another factor of performance in processor chips is its cache sizes (L1 and L2). Cache is the memory placed directly on the processor die for immediate queuing of data and use by the processor whenever it is ready. This prevents the processor from having to wait for code and data from much slower main memory, therefore improving performance. If the processor doesn't have data ready to process, how efficient can it possibly be?

All modern processors starting with the 486 family include an integrated (Level 1) cache and controller. The integrated L1 cache size varies from processor to processor, starting at 8KB for the original 486DX and now up to 32KB, 64KB, or more in the latest processors. L1 cache runs at the full core speed of the processor internally, which means at the overclocked rate of the processor, not the slower system bus.

According to Intel, the L1 cache in most of their processors has approximately a 90-percent hit ratio. This means that the cache has the correct data 90 percent of the time. Consequently, the processor runs at full speed, 200MHz in this example, 90 percent of the time. However, 10 percent of the time, the cache controller guesses wrong, and the data has to be retrieved out of the significantly slower main memory. This means that the processor has to wait, which essentially throttles the system back to RAM speed, which in this example was 60ns or 16MHz.

To mitigate the dramatic slowdown every time there is a cache miss, a secondary or Level 2 (L2) cache can be employed.

Most L2 caches have a hit ratio also in the 90 percent range, which means that if you look at the system as a whole, 90 percent of the time, it will be running at full speed (200MHz in this example) by retrieving data out of the L1 cache, whereas 10 percent of the time, it will slow down to retrieve the data from the L2 cache. 90 percent of that time, the data will be in the L2, and 10 percent of the time, you will have to go all the way to the slow main memory to get the data due to an L2 cache miss. This means that the sample system runs at full processor speed 90 percent of the time (200MHz in this case), motherboard speed 9 percent of the time (66MHz in this case), and RAM speed about 1 percent of the time (16MHz in this case). You can clearly see the importance of both the L1 and L2 caches. Without them the system will be using main memory more often, which is significantly slower than the processor.

Processor Types

Table 4.1 lists the primary specifications for the Intel family of processors used in IBM and compatible PCs.

Table 4.1   Intel Processor Specifications

Processor	CPU Clock	CPU Speed In MHz	Voltage	Internal Register Size	Data Bus Width
8088	1x	4.77-12	5v	16-bit	8-bit
8086	1x	4.77-7.16	5v	16-bit	16-bit
286	1x	6-25	5v	16-bit	16-bit
386SX	1x	16-33	5v	32-bit	16-bit
386SL	1x	16-33	3.3v	32-bit	16-bit
386DX	1x	16-40	5v	32-bit	32-bit
486SX	1x	25-33	5v	32-bit	32-bit
486SX2	2x	25-66	5v	32-bit	32-bit
487SX	1x	25-33	5v	32-bit	32-bit
486DX	1x	25-50	5v	32-bit	32-bit
486SL2	1x	25-50	3.3v	32-bit	32-bit
486DX2	2x	50-66	5v	32-bit	32-bit
486DX4	2-3x	75-100	3.3v	32-bit	32-bit
486Pentium OD	2.5x	72.5	5v	32-bit	32-bit
Pentium 60/66	1x	60-66	5v	32-bit	64-bit
Pentium 75-200	1.5-3x	75-20	3.3-3.5v	32-bit	64-bit
Pentium MMX	1.5-4.5x	166-233	1.8-2.8v	32-bit	64-bit
Pentium Pro	2-3x	166-200	3.3v	32-bit	64-bit
Pentium II MMX	3.5-4.5x	233-300	1.8-2.8v	32-bit	64-bit
Pentium II Celeron	3.5-4.5x	233-300	1.8-2.8v	32-bit	64-bit
Pentium II Celeron	3.5-7x	233-466	1.8-2v	32-bit	64-bit
Pentium II PE3	3.5-6x	233-450	1.6v	32-bit	64-bit
Pentium II Xeon	4-4.5x	400-450	1.8-2.8v	32-bit	64-bit
Pentium III	4.5-6x	450-600	1.8-2v	32-bit	64-bit
Pentium III Xeon	5-6x	500-600	1.8-2v	32-bit	64-bit

FPU = Floating-Point Unit (internal math coprocessor)   WT = Write-Through cache (caches reads only)

WB = Write-Back cache (caches both reads and writes)   Bus = Processor external bus speed (motherboard speed)   Core = Processor internal core speed (CPU speed)   MMX = Multimedia extensions, 57 additional instructions for graphics and sound processing   3DNow = MMX plus 21 additional instructions for graphics and sound processing   SSE = Streaming SIMD (Single Instruction Multiple Data) Extensions, MMX plus 70

Max. Memory	Level 1 Cache	Level 2 Cache	L2 Cache Speed	Multi-media Instructions	No. of Transistors	Date Introduced
1MB	-	-	-	-	29,000	June '79
1MB	-	-	-	-	29,000	June '78
16MB	-	-	-	-	134,000	Feb. '82
16MB	-	-	Bus	-	275,000	June '88
16MB	OKB1	-	Bus	-	855,000	Oct. '90
4GB	-	-	Bus	-	275,000	Oct. '85
4GB	8KB	-	Bus	-	1.185M	April '91
4GB	8KB	-	Bus	-	1.185M	April '94
4GB	8KB	-	Bus	-	1.2M	April '91
4GB	8KB	-	Bus	-	1.2M	April '89
4GB	8KB	-	Bus	-	1.4M	Nov. '92
4GB	8KB	-	Bus	-	1.2M	March '92
4GB	16KB	-	Bus	-	1.6M	Feb. '94
4GB	2x16KB	-	Bus	-	3.1M	Jan. '95
4GB	2x8KB	-	Bus	-	3.1M	March '93
4GB	2x8KB	-	Bus	-	3.3M	Oct. '94
4GB	2x16KB	-	Bus	MMX	4.5M	Jan. '97
64GB	2x8KB	256KB 512KB 1MB	Core	-	5.5M	Nov. '95
64GB	2x16KB	512KB	_ Core	MMX	7.5M	May '97
64GB	2x16KB	OKB	-	MMX	7.5M	April '98
64GB	2x16KB	128KB	Core	MMX	19M	Aug. '98
64GB	2x16KB	256KB	Core	MMX	27.4M	Jan. '99
64GB	2x16KB	512KB 1MB 2MB	Core	MMX	7.5M	April '98
64GB	2x16KB	512KB	_ Core	SSE	9.5M	Feb. '99
64GB	2x16KB	512KB 1MB 2MB	Core	SSE	9.5M	March '99

additional instructions for graphics and sound processing but the cache memory must be provided outside the chip. [1] *The 386SL contains an integral-cache controller,* [2] *Intel later marketed SL Enhanced versions of the SX, DX, and DX2 processors. These processors were available in both 5v and 3.3v versions and included power-management capabilities.* [3] *The Enhanced mobile PII has on-die L2 cache similar to the Celeron.*

Memory

Memory is storage, plain and simple. People often call memory *RAM*, for *random access memory*. Main memory is called RAM because you can randomly (and quickly) access any location in memory. This designation is somewhat misleading and often misinterpreted. Read-only memory (ROM), for example, is also randomly accessible, yet it is normally differentiated from the system RAM because it cannot normally be written to. Also, disk memory is randomly accessible too, but it isn't considered RAM either.

To better understand physical memory in a system, you should see where and how it fits into the system. There are three main types of physical memory used in modern PCs:

- *ROM*—Read-only memory
- *DRAM*—Dynamic random access memory
- *SRAM*—Static random access memory

These and many other classifications of memory will be discussed in the following sections.

ROM

Read-only memory, or *ROM*, is a type of memory that can permanently or semipermanently hold data. It is called read-only because it is either impossible or difficult to write to. ROM is also often referred to as *nonvolatile memory* because any data stored in ROM remains there, even if the power is turned off. As such, ROM is an ideal place to put the PC's startup instructions—that is, the software that boots the system.

The main ROM BIOS is contained in a ROM chip on the motherboard, but there are also adapter cards with ROMs on them as well. ROMs on adapter cards contain auxiliary BIOS routines and drivers needed by the particular card, especially for those cards that must be active early in the boot process, such as video cards. Cards that don't need drivers active at boot time normally do not have a ROM because those drivers can be loaded from the hard disk later in the boot process.

The motherboard ROM normally contains four main programs, including the following in most systems:

- **POST (Power-On Self Test)**   A series of test routines that ensure the system components are operating properly.
- **CMOS Setup**   A menu-driven application that enables the user to set system configuration parameters, options, security settings, and preferences.
- **Bootstrap Loader**   The routine that first scans the floppy drive and then the hard disk, looking for an operating system to load.
- **BIOS (Basic Input/Output System)**   A series of device driver programs designed to present a standard interface to the basic system hardware, especially hardware that must be active during the boot process.

Because the BIOS is the main portion of the code stored in ROM, it is often called the *ROM BIOS*. In older PCs, the motherboard ROM BIOS could consist of up to five or six total chips, but most

PCs have required only a single chip for many years now. For more information on the motherboard ROM, see *Upgrading and Repairing PCs, Eleventh Edition*, Chapter 4.

RAM

RAM memory is the workspace for the computer's processor. It is a temporary storage area where the programs and data being operated on by the processor must reside. RAM storage is considered temporary because the data and programs remain there only as long as the computer has electrical power or is not reset. Before being shut down or reset, any data that has been changed should be saved to a more permanent storage device of some type (usually a hard disk) so it can be reloaded into memory again in the future.

Logical Types

The two categories of RAM, DRAM, and SRAM—are described in the following sections with some of their more common implementations.

DRAM

Dynamic RAM (DRAM) is the type of memory chip used for most of the main memory in a modern PC. The main advantages of DRAM are that it is very dense, meaning you can pack a lot of bits into a very small chip, and it is inexpensive, which makes it affordable for large amounts of memory.

The memory cells in a DRAM chip are tiny capacitors that retain a charge to indicate a bit. The problem with DRAM is that it is dynamic and because of the design must be constantly refreshed, or the electrical charges in the individual memory capacitors will drain, and the data will be lost.

EDO

Standard DRAM is accessed through a technique called *paging*. Normal memory access requires that a row and column address be selected, which takes time. Paging provides faster access to all the data within a given row of memory by keeping the row address the same and changing only the column. Memory that uses this technique is called *Page Mode* or *Fast Page Mode* memory.

EDO, a modified form of FPM memory, is also referred to as *Hyper Page Mode*. The name *Extended Data Out* refers specifically to the fact that unlike FPM, the data output drivers on the chip are not turned off when the memory controller removes the column address to begin the next cycle. This allows the next cycle to overlap the previous one, saving approximately 10ns per cycle.

SDRAM

SDRAM stands for *Synchronous DRAM*, a type of DRAM that runs in synchronization with the memory bus. SDRAM delivers information in very high-speed bursts using a high-speed, clocked interface. SDRAM removes most of the latency involved in asynchronous DRAM because the signals are already in synchronization with the motherboard clock. Because of this, SDRAM's performance is dramatically improved over FPM or EDO RAM. However, SDRAM is still a type of DRAM, and the initial latency is the same, but overall cycle times are much faster than with FPM or EDO.

VRAM

VRAM is another form of DRAM exclusively used for video controllers. Because video is a one-way data path (from the controller to the monitor) the VRAM chip can have two "doors," one for data coming in and one for data going out. Rather than all data entering and leaving through one access point, the data from the controller goes into the chip at one access point, is queued for the monitor, and leaves out the other access point. This provides faster RAM buffering and therefore faster video card processing.

SRAM

SRAM stands for *Static RAM*, which is so named because it does not need the periodic refresh rates like DRAM (Dynamic RAM). Because of SRAM's design, not only are refresh rates unnecessary, but SRAM is much faster than DRAM and fully able to keep pace with modern processors. With these attributes, why don't people use SRAM for all system memory?

Compared to DRAM, SRAM is much faster, but it is also much lower in density and much more expensive. The lower density means that SRAM chips are physically larger and store fewer bits overall. The high number of transistors and the clustered design means that SRAM chips are both physically larger and much more expensive to produce than DRAM chips.

SRAM is normally used for CACHE as described in the previous section "On-board Processor Cache."

Physical Characteristics

The physical characteristics are described in the following sections.

DIP

Originally, systemshad memory installed via individual chips. They are often referred to as *DIP* (*Dual Inline Package*) chips because of their design. DIP chips had to be installed in banks of 9 chips to make as little as 64KB of 300ns memory! Besides being a time-consuming and labor-intensive way to deal with memory, DIP chips had one notorious problem: They crept out of their sockets over time as the system went through thermal cycles.

What was needed was a chip that was both soldered yet removable, and that is exactly what was found in the chip called a SIMM.

SIMM

For memory storage, most modern systems have adopted the Single Inline Memory Module (SIMM) or Dual Inline Memory Module (DIMM) as an alternative to individual memory chips. These small boards plugin to special connectors on a motherboard or memory card. The individual memory chips are soldered to the SIMM/DIMM, so removing and replacing them is impossible. Instead, you must replace the entire module if any part of it fails. The SIMM/DIMM is treated as though it were one large memory chip.

PC systems use two main physical types of SIMMs—30-pin (8 bits plus 1 optional parity bit) and

72-pin (32 bits plus 4 optional parity bits)—with various capacities and other specifications. The 30-pin SIMMs are smaller than the 72-pin versions and can have chips on one or both sides. The 30-pin SIMMs are basically obsolete and are being followed rapidly by the 72-pin versions. This is true primarily because the 64-bit systems, which are now the industry standard, would require eight 30-pin SIMMs or two 72-pin SIMMs per bank.

SIPP

Single inline pinned packages, sometimes called *SIPPs*, really are SIMMs with pins, not contacts. The pins are designed to be installed in a long connector socket that is much cheaper than the standard SIMM socket. SIPPs are inferior to SIMMs because they lack the positive latching mechanism that retains the module, and the connector lacks the high-force wiping contacts that resist corrosion. SIPPs are rarely used today.

DIMM

DIMMs, which are popular on Pentium-MMX, Pentium Pro, and Pentium II–based systems, are 168-pin units with 64-bit (nonparity) or 72-bit (parity or ECC) data paths. A 168-pin DIMM is physically one inch longer than a 72-pin SIMM and can be recognized by having a secondary keying notch, but the main physical difference is that DIMMs have different signal pins on each side of the module. That is why they are called Dual Inline Memory Modules and why with only an inch of additional length, they have many more pins than a SIMM.

Figures 4.4, 4.5, and 4.6 show typical 30-pin (8-bit) and 72-pin (32-bit) SIMMs and a 168-pin (64-bit) DIMM, respectively.

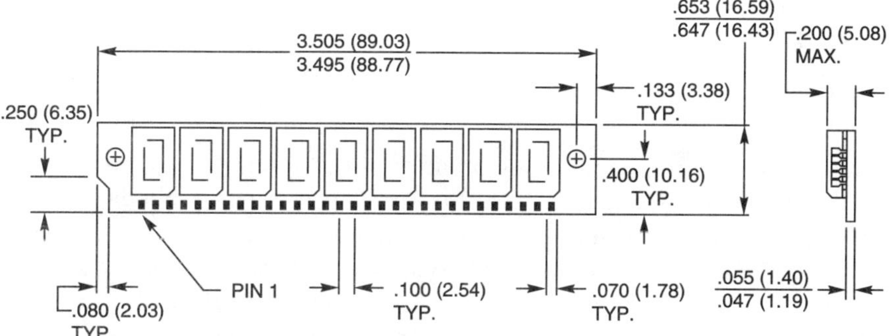

Figure 4.4 A typical 30-pin SIMM. The one shown here is 9-bit, although the dimensions would be the same for 8-bit.

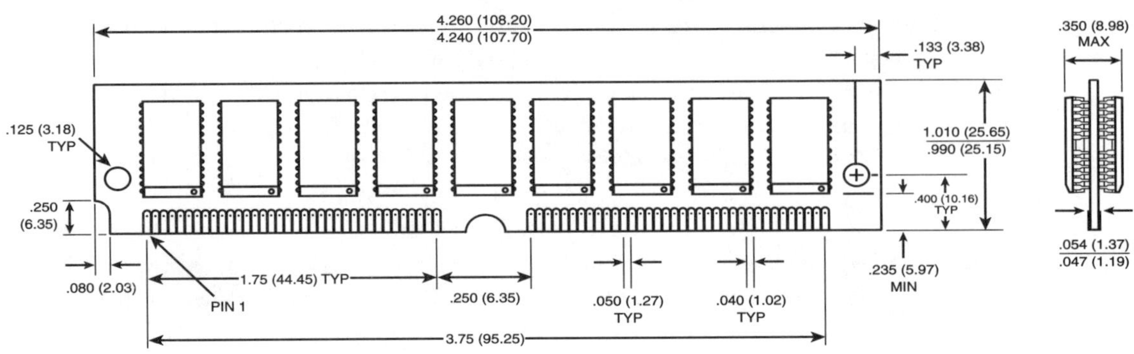

Figure 4.5 A typical 72-pin SIMM, although the dimensions would be the same for 32-bit.

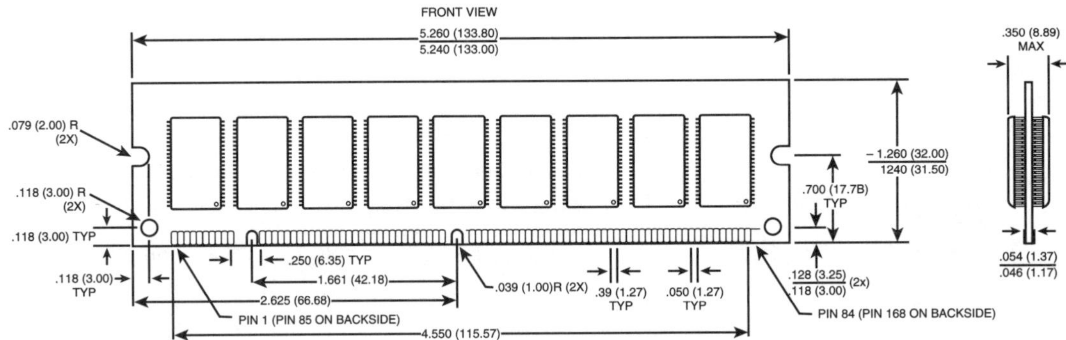

Figure 4.6 A typical 168-pin DIMM. The one shown here is 72-bit, although the dimensions would be the same for 64-bit.

Memory Banks

Perhaps the most important ramification of the data bus in a chip is that the width of the data bus also defines the size of a bank of memory. A bank is the smallest amount of memory that can be addressed by the processor at one time. This means that a 32-bit processor, such as the 486-class chips, reads and writes memory 32 bits at a time. Pentium-class processors, including the Pentium II, read and write memory 64 bits at a time. Because standard 72-pin SIMMs (Single Inline Memory Modules) are only 32 bits wide, they must be installed one at a time in most 486-class systems; they're installed two at a time in most Pentium-class systems. Newer DIMMs (Dual Inline Memory Modules) are 64 bits wide, so they are installed one at a time in Pentium class systems. Each DIMM is equal to a complete bank of memory in Pentium systems, which makes system configuration easy: They can then be installed or removed one at a time.

In the Real World

Some systems required more memory than the data width of the processor to form a bank. These systems used memory interleaving to speed access to the memory. If the memory is interleaved, a virtual bank can be twice the absolute data bus width of the processor.

Parity

One standard IBM set for the industry is that the memory chips in a bank of nine each handle 1 bit of data: 8 bits per character plus 1 extra bit called the *parity bit*. The parity bit enables memory-control circuitry to keep tabs on the other 8 bits—a built-in cross-check for the integrity of each byte in the system. If the circuitry detects an error, the computer stops and displays a message informing you of the malfunction.

This has two basic benefits:

- Parity guards against the consequences of faulty calculations based on incorrect data.
- Parity pinpoints the source of errors, which helps with problem resolution, thus improving system serviceability.

Now look at how parity checking works, and then examine in more detail the successor to parity checking, called *ECC (Error Correcting Code)*, which cannot only detect but correct memory errors on-the-fly.

IBM originally established the odd parity standard for error checking. The following explanation might help you understand what is meant by odd parity. As the 8 individual bits in a byte are stored in memory, a parity generator/checker, which is either part of the CPU or is located in a special chip on the motherboard, evaluates the data bits by adding up the number of 1s in the byte. If an even number of 1s is found, the parity generator/checker then creates a 1 and stores it as the ninth bit (parity bit) in the parity memory chip. That makes the sum for all 9 bits (including the parity bit) an odd number. If the original sum of the 8 data bits were an odd number, the parity bit created would be a 0, keeping the sum for all 9 bits an odd number. The basic rule is that the value of the parity bit is always chosen so that the sum of all 9 bits (8 data bits plus 1 parity bit) is stored as an odd number. If the system used even parity, then the example would be the same except the parity bit would be created to ensure an even sum. It doesn't matter whether even or odd parity is used; the system will use one or the other, and it is completely transparent to the memory chips involved. Remember that the 8 data bits in a byte are numbered 0 1 2 3 4 5 6 7. To give a quick reference chart for this, refer to Table 4.2.

Table 4.2 Parity Calculation Chart

If the parity scheme is...	And the first eight bits are...	The parity bit should be:
Even	Even	Even
Even	Odd	Odd
Odd	Even	Odd
Odd	Odd	Even

For more examples on parity and error-correcting code RAM, please consult Chapter 6, "Memory," in *Upgrading and Repairing PCs, Eleventh Edition.*

Review

Cram Session

- Motherboards are the heart of the system. The two main classifications covered on the exam are AT and ATX. System boards commonly contain the CPU, chipset, ROM BIOS, CMOS, memory sockets, expansion bus, system bus, and some I/O ports.

- Expansion bus architectures today are commonly ISA, PCI, and AGP, although other bus structures are covered on the exam and are discussed in the chapter including MCA, EISA, and VESA-LB.

- ISA bus structures are, as the name suggests, the industry standard and provide 8-bit and 16-bit connections.

- MCA is IBM's obsolete 32-bit expansion bus. Due to the high cost and lack of backward compatibility, the MCA bus never caught on. It was, however, the first bus-mastering, software-configurable expansion bus.

- EISA was the industry standard competition for MCA. Also a 32-bit, bus-mastering, software-configurable design, EISA provided backward compatibility with existing ISA structures. EISA is also now obsolete.

- VESA local bus was a backward-compatible attempt at placing devices on the system bus directly. This created some problems for the doomed bus, but it did provide a much faster design than anything previously available.

- PCI is also a local bus design, but by redesigning everything and providing PCI slots in combination with ISA slots on a system board, it became the most popular expansion bus shortly after introduction. PCI is still the most common expansion bus used in today's faster computers, along with a few ISA slots for compatibility.

- AGP is an enhancement to PCI, but it does not replace PCI as the new expansion bus. AGP is designed for one fast slot for today's more demanding video cards. This slot gives the video cards direct access at system bus speeds to the system RAM to eliminate the need for ever increasing memory sizes on the video cards themselves.

- PC Card, or its older name PCMCIA, defines a standardized bus structure for portable systems. Developed originally as a memory card standard, this bus now supports 32-bit Cardbus designs as well as the older PCMCIA Type 1, 2, and 3 16-bit designs.

- CMOS replaced switch settings in the IBM AT and has provided a place to store system configuration ever since. This chip can retain system settings as long as the its battery supplies power.

- CPU, or central processing unit, is the brain of the computer. The processor is measured in MHz, or millions of cycles per second. Many other measurements for CPUs exist, such as internal data path width, external data path width, address bus, L1 and L2 cache, clock multiplier, and voltage required. Many of these comparisons are listed in Table 4.1, Intel Processor Specifications.

- RAM is random access memory. This is generally known as the system memory and can be dynamic (slower, requires refreshing) or static (faster, does not require refreshing).

- ROM is read-only memory and is usually burned into a chip. There are versions of ROM that are electrically erasable and programmable (EEPROM) and are known as FlashROMs.

- Memory can come in several different packages. These include DIP, SIMM, SIPP, and DIMM. The only RAM modules used today are SIMM and DIMM.

- Memory banks are the smallest accessible amount of memory. A bank is the same width as the external data path of the CPU. A 32-bit CPU requires 32-bits of RAM to be delivered simultaneously.

- Parity is a memory fault-tolerance algorithm. By adding the bits (adding up the number of 1's in the byte), you can determine the bit value that should be recorded in the parity bit. These values can be used to determine whether any single bit becomes corrupted during use and to halt the system with a parity error.

Review Questions

1. What are the changes that were made in the layout of the ATX system board?

2. The ISA bus standard supported what speed?

3. Why did Micro-channel never catch on?

4. What advantages do MCA, EISA, and PCI all have in common?

5. What was VESA originally developed as?

6. PCI inherently supports one feature that no other adapter cards did when they were created. What is it?

7. Will a PC Card Cardbus device work in a PCMCIA slot? Why or why not?

8. What is the bandwidth of a Universal Serial Bus? Why will the 127 possible devices never be reached on a single bus?

9. What is clock multiplication?

10. Why is L1 cache so important to the concept described in Question 9?

11. What are the differences between RAM and ROM?

12. What are the differences between static RAM and dynamic RAM?

13. Why are DIMMs the standard for today's Pentium class and higher machines?

14. If you have a byte "10110010" and the parity scheme is set to even, what is the value of the parity bit?

Review Answers

1. The ATX form factor is essentially a Baby-AT motherboard turned sideways in the chassis, along with a modified power supply location and connector, relocated internal and external I/O connectors, and improved CPU cooling in its new location.

2. The original IBM 8-bit ISA bus (also called PC bus) ran at the same as the system bus which was 4.77MHz. The industry later standardized on 8.33MHz for the final revisions of the 8-bit and 16-bit bus structures.

3. Even though MCA is technically superior in every way—except standardization—MCA did not catch on because IBM required vendors that licensed the new MCA bus to pay IBM royalties for using it in any system or card design.

4. MCA, EISA, and PCI are all 32-bit, bus-mastering, and software-configurable expansion bus structures.

5. The Video Electronic Standards Association was founded by NEC to create a high speed video port.

6. Plug and Play support. This has since been added to some ISA cards designs.

7. No. The faster, wider CardBus card will not even plug into the PCMCIA slot due to the raised keyed metal tabs on the connector. This is a good thing because the CardBus cards have different power and data requirements that would be electrically incompatible.

8. USB has a bandwidth of 12 Megabits per second (Mbps). If 127 devices were connected, this would give each device fewer than 94.5Kbps each on the shared bus, which is too little data path for most USB devices.

9. Clock multiplication is the practice of running the processor internally at some factor faster than the system bus.

10. If the souped up CPU cannot acquire data to process at the internal CPU speed of two to seven times faster than the system bus, the CPU is really only running at system bus speed. This means that a 550MHz Pentium III would only run at 100MHz! L1 cache runs at the same speed as the processor internally and provides 90 percent of the data the processor wants.

11. RAM is random access memory, whereas ROM is read-only memory. Other than the ability to write to RAM, the main difference between these two is that RAM requires power to maintain its data, whereas ROM retains its data even with the power off.

12. Dynamic RAM uses capacitors to store data values. These capacitors will lose their charge after two microseconds and must be refreshed. This refresh cycle takes time away from memory access time and is less efficient. Static RAM uses transistors to store data value. Because these do not require the refresh cycle, static RAM is much faster and more efficient. Unfortunately, it is also larger because of the transistor size and is much more expensive.

13. DIMMs are 64-bit memory banks. SIMMs—even 72-pin SIMMS—would require at least two chips to make one bank or memory. Keep in mind that one bank of memory is the smallest size that the CPU can access.

14. The answer is 0 because in the parity example given, even+even=even.

Chapter 5

Printers

Printer Concepts

The capability to produce a printed version (often called a hard copy) of a document is a primary function of a PC, and along with modems, printers have become a required accessory. There are a wide variety of printers on the market supporting a multitude of features and speeds. This chapter examines the underlying concepts of all printer technology, the basic types of printers available today and how they function, and how to install and troubleshoot a printer on your PC.

Note

For more information on printers, please consult Scott Mueller's *Upgrading and Repairing PCs, Eleventh Edition*, Chapter 22, "Printers and Scanners."

Bit-Image Versus Full-Character

There are two types of methods in which a printed character is formed on the page. The first and oldest method is fully formed characters. In this method, a precut die is inked and pressed against the page—printing-press style. Although this method certainly has had the best output historically, the bit-image method has become the most common method. Bit-image is the process of forming a complete character using overlapping dots in a particular pattern.

The fully formed character is common in typewriters and older printers known as daisywheel style printers. These printers had a very high print quality, but they could not print graphics.

The bit-image printer is best shown in the dot-matrix printer. In this printer, a lower quality image is exchanged for some graphics capability. Today's bit-image printers include dot-matrix, inkjet, and, to some degree, laser printers (although these are more a hybrid between the two technologies). These bit-image printers have almost completely replaced full-character printers and have the quality to support such a change in technology. Because of this, bit-image printing is all that will be covered in this chapter.

Bit-Image Resolution

The term *resolution* is used to describe the sharpness and clarity of the printed output. All these printer technologies create images by laying down a series of dots on the page. The size and number of these dots determine the printer's resolution and the quality of the output. If you look at a page of text produced by a low-resolution dot-matrix printer, for example, the pattern of dots that forms the individual characters is immediately obvious to the naked eye (see Figure 5.1). This is because the dots are relatively large and of a uniform size. On high-resolution laser printer output, however, the characters look solid because the dots are much smaller and often can be of different sizes.

Figure 5.1 Because printed characters are composed of individual dots, lower-resolution images can contain diagonal lines in which a jagged effect is quite obvious.

Printer resolution is usually measured in dots per inch (dpi). This refers to the number of separate dots that the printer can produce in a straight line one inch long. Most printers function at the same resolution both horizontally and vertically, so a specification such as 300dpi implies a 300×300-dot one-inch square.

Feed Mechanisms

There are several different types of feeder mechanisms, but the two most common types are tractor feed and automatic sheet feed.

Tractor feed is most commonly used in dot-matrix printing, although some old inkjets had tractor mechanisms. This feeder uses rotating wheels of pins that push the perforated edges of the paper forward into the printer.

Automatic sheet feed is what most Xerox machines use. A cartridge of some type is loaded with a stack of letter- or legal-sized paper, and rubber feed rollers take the top page and feed it into the printer. Most inkjets and all laser printers use this method.

Consumables

The cost of consumables can vary greatly, depending on the kind of printer you choose. The printer's consumables include the paper, the color medium (either toner cartridges, ink cartridges, or inked ribbons), and even the electricity the printer uses.

In the Real World

Often, larger printer problems can be eliminated by replacing a consumable. The laser printer is notorious for this. The consumable toner cartridge in it is so complex that many things are resolved by replacing this component. This is not only a Real World tip, but an exam tip as well.

Printers that require special papers add to the cost of consumables because these papers are inevitably more expensive than standard stock. These printers also limit your selection of papers. There are many grades of laser printer paper; you can switch from inexpensive copier paper to more luxurious stock as the need arises. There is also a wide range of colored and textured papers that can add distinction to your documents. Specialized papers for use in inkjet and other printers that require them are not available in anywhere near the same variety.

Types of Printers

There are three basic types of printer technologies used with PCs, which are defined by the method in which the image is produced on the paper. These three technologies are as follows:

- **Laser**   Laser printers function by creating an electrostatic image of an entire page on a photosensitive drum with a laser beam. When an ultrafine colored plastic powder called toner is applied to the drum, it adheres only to the sensitized areas corresponding to the letters or images on the page. The drum spins and is pressed against a sheet of paper, transferring the toner to the page and creating the image. This is the same basic technology used by copiers.

- **Inkjet**   Inkjet printers, as their name implies, have tiny nozzles that spray ink onto a page in the proper pattern to form letters and images.

- **Dot-matrix**   Dot-matrix printers use an array of round-headed pins to press an inked ribbon against a page. The pins are arranged in a rectangular grid (called a matrix); different combinations of pins form the various characters and images.

In the Real World

There is a fourth type of technology that you probably won't encounter on the exam but is in widespread use today. This type is called a thermal printer and is used on most cash registers and point-of-sale devices. This printer uses a heating element as the print head and special, heat-sensitive paper that turns a dark color when subjected to high temperatures.

In general, laser printers provide the best quality output, followed closely by inkjet, with dot-matrix printers coming in a distant third. As with most computer equipment, the prices of printers have dropped tremendously in recent years, making the laser printers that used to be a high-ticket item accessible to users at almost every level. Dot-matrix printers have become largely relegated to commercial applications requiring continuous feed and multipart forms. Inkjet printers have become important parts of SOHO (small office-home office) printing because of their high print quality (rivaling less-expensive lasers for text), color capabilities, and versatility.

Each of the three main printer types uses a different method to create images on a page, as well as a different substance: powdered toner, liquid ink, or a fabric ribbon. The following sections examine how each type of printer creates images on the page and other technologies that are used.

Dot-Matrix

Dot-matrix printers were, at one time, the most popular type of printer on the market because they were small, inexpensive to buy and to run, and fairly reliable. With all the advancements in printing over the years, although they continue to perform certain tasks quite well, dot-matrix printers generally are too noisy, offer mediocre print quality, and have poor paper-handling abilities.

Print and Feed Mechanisms

Dot-matrix printers are different from inkjet and laser printers in several fundamental ways. Most importantly, dot-matrix printers do not process an entire page's worth of data at a time as lasers do, but rather work with streams of characters. As a result, their speed is measured in characters per second (cps) instead of pages per minute.

Dot-matrix printers work by advancing paper vertically around a rubberized roller, called a *platen*, one line at a time. At the same time, a print head travels back and forth horizontally on a metal bar. The print head contains a matrix of metal pins (usually either 9 or 24) that it extends in various combinations to make a physical impression on the paper. Between the pins and the paper is an inked ribbon, much like that used in a typewriter. The pins pressing through the ribbon onto the page make a series of small dots, forming typographic characters on the page (see Figure 5.2). Dot-matrix printers also usually have rudimentary graphical capabilities, enabling them to produce low-resolution bitmaps using their limited memory as a band buffer.

Dot-matrix printers are usually associated with continuous sheet paper, driven by pinholes on the edges. Most models can also handle single sheets, although rarely with the accuracy found in most laser or inkjet printers. Because they are impact printers, meaning that there is actual physical contact between the print head and the paper, dot-matrix printers can do one thing that lasers and inkjets can't: print multipart forms and carbon copies. Many printers enable you to adjust the pressure of the impact to support various numbers of copies.

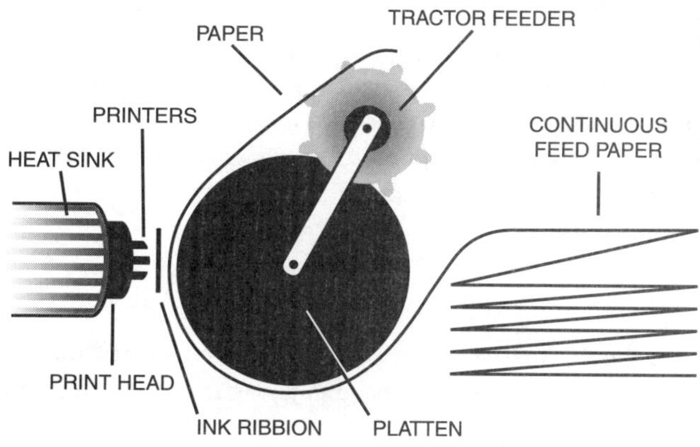

Figure 5.2 Dot-matrix print head configuration.

Print Quality

The print resolution of a dot-matrix printer is based not on its memory or its processing power, but rather on its mechanical capabilities. The grid of dots that a dot-matrix printer uses to create characters is not a data set in a memory array or a pattern on a photosensitive drum; rather, the grid is formed by a set of metal pins that physically strike the page in various combinations. The resolution of the printer is therefore determined by the quantity of its pins, which is usually either 9 or 24. Because it uses more pins to create characters of the same size, a 24-pin printer has pins that are necessarily smaller than those of a 9-pin printer, and the dots they create are smaller as well. As with the other printer types, smaller dots result in fewer jagged edges to the printed characters and a better appearance to the document overall.

Twenty-four–pin dot-matrix printers are often described by manufacturers as producing "near letter quality" output. In a literal sense, I suppose this is true because the output that these printers produce is near (but not quite) what you would want to send to a correspondent. Dot-matrix printers still have their place in the professional world, such as for printing multipart forms and carbon copies, but when it comes to printing letters and other general office documents, they lack the resolution needed to produce a professional-looking product.

Preventative Maintenance

Dot-matrix printers are more prone to collecting dirt and dust than any other type of printer. This is due both to the physical contact between the inked ribbon and the print head and to the use of continuous feed paper. As the printer runs, a fabric ribbon turns within its cartridge to keep a freshly inked surface in front of the print head. This lateral movement of the ribbon, combined with the continuous high-speed back-and-forth motion of the pins within the print head, tends to produce an ink-saturated lint that can clog the print heads and smudge the printed characters. Film ribbons can help reduce these problems and provide better print quality, but at the cost of a shorter ribbon life.

Continuous feed paper presents another problem. This paper has perforated borders on both edges with holes that the printer uses to pull the paper through the printer. Depending on the quality of the paper you purchase, some of the dots punched out to produce the holes might be left in the pad of paper. As the paper passes through the printer, these dots can be left behind and can eventually interfere with the paper-handling mechanism. Keep dot-matrix printers clean by removing the dots and dust with canned air or a vacuum cleaner and swabbing the print heads regularly with alcohol.

Inkjet

Inkjet printers, like the dot-matrix, are also bit-image printers, but they tend to be full-page printers. That is, you must wait for the entire page to advance out of the printer (and dry!) before using it.

Print and Feed Mechanisms

There are two basic types of inkjet printing in use today: thermal and piezo (discussed in the following sections). These terms describe the technology used to force the ink out of the cartridge through the nozzles. The inkjet cartridge typically consists of a reservoir for the liquid ink and the tiny (as small as one micron) nozzles through which the ink is expelled onto the page. The number of nozzles is dependent on the printer's resolution; configurations using anywhere from 21 to 128 nozzles per color are common. Color inkjet printers use four reservoirs with different color inks (cyan, magenta, yellow, and black). By mixing the four inks, the printer can produce virtually any color. (Most inkjets use one replaceable cartridge to hold the reservoirs for the three colors: cyan, magenta, and yellow.)

Thermal Inkjet Printing

Thermal inkjet printers function by superheating the ink in the cartridge to approximately 400 degrees. This causes vapor bubbles to form inside the cartridge that rise to the top of the reservoir. The pressure from the vapor forces ink out of the cartridge through the nozzles in tiny droplets that form the dots on the page. The vacuum caused by the expelled ink draws more ink down into the nozzles, making a constant stream of droplets as needed.

The thermal type of inkjet printing was the first to be developed and is still the most popular. Because of the vapor bubbles that form in the cartridge, Canon began calling its inkjet printers "BubbleJets," a name that has become almost synonymous with this technology.

Piezo Inkjet Printing

Piezo inkjet printing is a newer technology than thermal printing, and it presents distinct advantages. Instead of heat, these printers apply an electric charge to piezoelectric crystals inside the cartridge nozzles. These crystals change their shape as a result of the electric current, forcing the ink out through the nozzles.

Removing the high temperatures from the inkjet printing process presents two important advantages. First, the selection of inks that can withstand 400 degree heat is very limited; piezo technology enables printers to use ink formulations that are better suited to the printing process and less prone to smearing, which is a traditional problem with inkjet printing. Second, spray nozzles that are not exposed to extreme heat can last far longer than those traditional thermal cartridges. Epson pioneered the use of piezo inkjet printing.

Print Quality

Whereas laser printers produce their images by fusing toner to the paper, inkjet printers place the ink on top of the paper. Although many general purpose papers supposedly suitable for laser, copier, and inkjet printers are sold, using anything less than true inkjet paper will degrade the actual print resolution. This is because inkjet paper should be smoother than laser/copier paper and should promote rapid drying of ink. Paper that lacks these features will have loose fibers, causing the ink to "wick," creating a fuzzy appearance to inkjet printing. Photo-realistic printing at resolutions above 720dpi require the use of photo-quality paper that is heavy, very smooth, and very fast-drying. Many users' disappointments with inkjet print quality stem from improper paper choices.

Inkjet printers tend to have lower resolutions than lasers and are also quite a bit slower than laser printing. Although it is possible to build high-end laser printers that can produce 16 pages per minute (ppm) or more, inkjets are limited in how fast they can actually dispense liquid ink and rarely go above a maximum of eight pages per minute, if that.

The biggest problem with most inkjet printers, however, is that the ink they use has a tendency to smear on standard paper stock. There are special inkjet papers that prevent this problem, but they are more expensive and offer far less variety than the laser printer papers on the market.

Consumables

Inkjet printer users who are concerned about the high cost of consumables can go one of two routes: purchasing third-party ink cartridges (available for the most popular brands and models) or ink refill kits. The ink refill kits are the most cost-effective way to save money, but you need to check availability for your brand and model of printer, compare the quality, and do your refills with regard for the mess that squeezing bottles of liquid ink can cause. Check printer warranties also before you try these.

In the Real World

Many manufacturers no longer repair inkjet printers. It is far easier to replace a faulty printer with a new device than to troubleshoot and repair a device that only costs $200. I guess that you could consider the entire printer to be a consumable!

Preventative Maintenance

To avoid inkjet problems, make sure that you turn off the printer with its own power switch, not the surge protector or power director! The printer's own power switch initiates a controlled shutdown of the printer, including capping the print heads to keep them from drying out. If you turn off the power externally (with a surge protector, for example), the print heads might dry out because they're exposed to the air, which eventually clogs them beyond user adjustment.

Minor clogging of inkjet cartridges can sometimes be cured by using the printer's diagnostics routines, accessible either through pushbuttons on the printer or through the printer's property sheets in Windows 9x.

Laser Printers

Laser printers are the highest quality, most prevalent printers today. As their costs decrease, they can even be found with home computer systems. Lasers range from $500 to $5000, but their print quality is second to none. Using the electrophotostatic (EP) process like a copy machine, these devices are an interesting hybrid of bit-image formation and full-character creation in a multiple page printer.

Printer Components

There are several components that are unique to laser printer technologies. These components are explained better in the appropriate printing stage under print mechanisms, but they are briefly discussed here to provide a familiarity with them:

- **EP Cartridge**   The electrophotostatic cartridge, or what is commonly called the toner cartridge, is actually the heart of the laser-printing process. This cartridge contains all the consumable components in a laser printer in one neat unit. These consumable components are involved in five of the six print stages that will be discussed in the next section. These components include the photosensitive drum, toner, cleaning blade, and charging roller (see Figure 5.3).

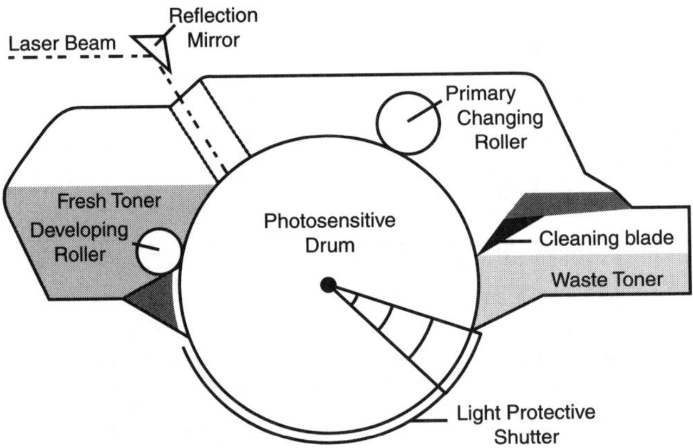

Figure 5.3 An EP cartridge.

- **Charging roller**   This component is part of the conditioning phase and places a uniform negative charge on the drum—preparing it for the writing process.

- **Photosensitive drum**   This component is a metal cylinder that is coated with a substance that can hold a charge while in the absence of light. When the laser light strikes the surface, the charge is dissipated to the electrically grounded drum core. Because the image is created and developed on this component, it is used in the first five stages of the EP process.

- **Toner**   This is an ultrafine black plastic powder that can hold an electrical charge. Toner is the "ink" in a laser printer.

- **Cleaning blade**   This component is used in the cleaning phase and simply removes the excess toner from the drum.

- **Laser**   The laser turns the digital signal from the processor into pulses of laser light directed at the photosensitive drum.

- **Fuser**   The fuser is the core component of the fusing or fixing stage of the EP process. This unit houses both the superheated Teflon-coated fusing roller and the pressure roller.

Print Mechanisms

The electro-photostatic process of printing a document on a laser printer consists of the following cyclical stages (see Figure 5.4):

- **Cleaning**   Residual toner is scraped off the photosensitive drum and into the waste bin in the cartridge.

- **Conditioning**   The charging roller places a uniform negative charge on the surface of the photosensitive drum.

- **Writing**   The laser-scanning assembly pulses a laser beam across the drum to form a latent image where the surface charge dissipates to the drum core. The non-exposed surface of the drum maintains its negative charge.

- **Developing**   The drum passes by the toner supply and developing roller, allowing the negatively charged toner to adhere to the previously created latent image. (The negatively charged toner is repulsed from the negatively charged non-exposed drum surfaces).

- **Transferring**   The negatively charged, developed image of toner is attracted to the positively charged, blank page and is transferred to the paper.

- **Fusing**   The heated fusing roller melts the toner and the pressure roller literally bonds the cooling toner to the paper fibers (see Figure 5.4).

Consumables

With laser printers, the price of toner can vary widely from printer to printer, depending on what other components are included in the cartridge. Clearly, a toner cartridge that includes a new photoreceptor drum and developer assembly will cost significantly more than a cartridge containing toner alone. However, in terms of printer maintenance and output quality, the extra expense might be justified.

Depending on the printer you select, there might be a competitive market for ink, toner, or ribbon cartridges. If you choose to try various brands, it's a good idea to record how many pages you get from each cartridge. It is often the case that cheaper cartridges are actually less economical because they produce fewer pages.

There also is a large, even more volatile market for refilled toner and inkjet cartridges. Some vendors of toner cartridges for laser printers, for example, completely rebuild old cartridges by cleaning and repairing (or replacing) the photoreceptor and developer assemblies in addition to adding new toner. This can save you an enormous amount of money over the years and help the environment as well. Less reputable vendors, however, simply drill a hole into the cartridge, pour in some toner, and ship it out the door, which can result in a leaky cartridge and more problems than the savings are worth. If you're not using rebuilt toner cartridges, ask any vendor you're considering for referrals. Also, be aware that HP and Canon, the major vendors in the laser-printer toner cartridge business, encourage recycling empty toners with postage-paid envelopes in every "new" cartridge box.

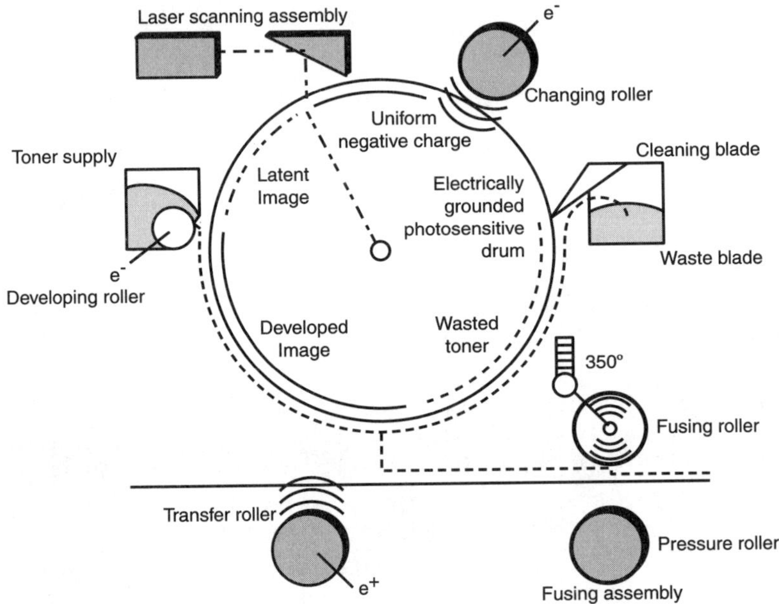

Figure 5.4 The electro-photostatic process.

Preventative Maintenance

For laser printers, the best preventative maintenance regimen results from purchasing a printer that uses toner cartridges with photoreceptor and developer assemblies. These are the components that regularly come in contact with the toner, so replacing them on a regular basis ensures that these vital parts are clean and undamaged. If your printer does not use this type of cartridge, you should take extra care to clean the inside of the printer whenever you replenish the toner, following the manufacturer's recommendations. Some printers include a special brush or other tool for this purpose.

Troubleshooting Printers

You can avoid many printing problems with regular preventative maintenance procedures, but there are still likely to be occasions when you find that the output from your printer is not up to its usual standards or that the printer is not functioning at all. When you are faced with a printing problem, it can sometimes be difficult to determine whether the problem originates in your application, in the computer's printer driver, or in the printer hardware.

In many cases, you can apply standard troubleshooting methodology to printing problems. For example, if you experience the same printing problem when you generate a test page from the printer's control panel as when you print a document from your PC, you can rule out the computer, the driver, and the printer connection as the source of the problem and begin examining the printer. If you experience the same printing problem with different drivers, you can probably rule out the driver as the cause (unless the manufacturer produced several versions of the driver with the same bug).

Consistency is also an important factor when troubleshooting printer problems. If one page in ten exhibits the problem, you can generally rule out software as the cause and begin looking at the hardware, such as the connecting cable and the printer.

The following sections examine some of the most commonly seen printer problems, categorizing them according to the source of the problem. However, these categories must be taken loosely because some of the problems can have several different causes.

It's important to understand that none of the procedures described in the following sections should take the place of the maintenance and troubleshooting instructions provided with your printer. Your printer might use components and designs that differ substantially from those described in this chapter, and the manufacturer should always be the ultimate authority for hardware maintenance and problem-solving procedures.

Printer Hardware Problems

Problems with the printer usually result from the consumables, such as toner and paper. If the toner cartridge is nearly empty or if the printer's internal components become encrusted with loose toner, the quality of the print output can degrade in various ways. In the same way, paper that is damp, bent, wrinkled, or inserted into the tray improperly can cause myriad problems. You should always check these elements before assuming that printer's internal hardware is at fault:

- **Fuzzy print**   On a laser printer, characters that are suddenly fuzzy or unclear are probably the result of using paper that is slightly damp. On an inkjet printer, fuzzy or smeary characters can result when you use various types of paper not specifically intended for inkjet printing. This can also occur if there is a problem with the connection between the print cartridge and the cradle. Try reinstalling the print cartridge.

- **Variable print density**   If you find that some areas of the page are darker than others when using a laser printer, the problem is probably due to the distribution of the toner on the photoreceptor. The most common cause for this is uneven dispensation of the toner as its container empties. Removing the toner cartridge and shaking it from side to side redistributes the toner and should cause it to flow evenly. You can also use this technique to get a few more pages out of a toner cartridge after the printer has registered a "toner low" error. If your printer consistently produces pages with the same varied print density, the problem could be the printer's location. If the unit is not resting on a level surface, the toner can shift to one side of the cartridge, affecting the distribution of the toner on the page. It is also possible that your printer might have a light leak that is causing one area of the photoreceptor to be exposed to more ambient light than others. Moving the printer away from a bright light source can sometimes remedy this problem.

- **Dirty or damaged corotrons**   A laser printer's corotrons (also called corona wires) apply electrostatic charges to the photoreceptor and the paper. If the transfer corotron (which charges the paper) has clumps of toner or paper fragments on it, it can apply an uneven charge to the paper, and you might see faint or fuzzy white lines running vertically down your printed pages. All-black or all-white pages can be caused by a broken charger or transfer corotron (respectively). A toner cartridge that contains the photoreceptor drum typically includes the charger corotron as well, so replacing the cartridge can remedy some of these problems. You can also (gently!) clean a dirty corotron with a foam swab or other material as recommended by the manufacturer. The transfer corotron is usually built in to the printer (and not the cartridge) and will require professional servicing if it is broken. These components are made of fragile wires, so be very careful when you clean them.

In the Real World

These corotrons are more commonly known as corona wires. Corona wires have been replaced in recent years with a conductive foam charging roller. These rollers should never be cleaned. They should never even be touched because the oil from your hands will destroy the electrical conductivity in the foam, rendering the part useless.

- **Sharp vertical white lines**   A sharp white line extending vertically down the entire length of your laser-printed pages that does not go away when you shake the toner cartridge is probably caused by dirt or debris in the developer unit that is preventing the unit from evenly distributing the toner onto the photoreceptor. Again, if the toner cartridge includes the developer unit, replacing it is the simplest fix. If not, your printer might have a mechanism that enables you to remove the developer roller for cleaning or even a tool designed to remove dirt from the roller while it is in place. It might also be possible to clean the roller by slipping the corner of a sheet of paper down the slots between the roller and the metal blades on either side of it.

- **Regularly spaced spots**   If your laser-printed pages have a spot or spots that are consistently left unprinted, the cause might be a scratch or other flaw in the photoreceptor drum or a buildup of toner on the fusing roller. You can often tell the difference between these two problems by the distance between the spots on the page. If the spots occur less than three inches apart (vertically), the problem is probably caused by the fusing roller. Because the photoreceptor drum has a larger diameter than the fusing roller, the spots it produces would be farther apart or perhaps only one on a page. Replacing a toner cartridge that contains the photoreceptor drum and the fuser cleaning pad (an oil-impregnated pad that presses against the fuser roller to remove excess toner) should solve either of these problems. Otherwise, you will probably have to replace the drum assembly or the fuser cleaning pad separately. Some printers require professional servicing to replace the photoreceptor drum.

- **Gray print or gray background**   As the photoreceptor drum in a laser printer wears, it begins to hold less of a charge, and less toner adheres to the drum, resulting in printing that is gray rather than black. On printers that include the drum as part of the toner cartridge, this is not usually a problem because the drum is changed frequently. Printers that use the drum for longer periods of time often have a print-density control that enables you to gradually increase the amount of toner dispensed by the developer unit as the drum wears. Eventually, however, you will have to replace the drum; at that point, you must lower the print density back to its original setting, or you might find that your prints have a gray background because the developer is applying too much toner to the photoreceptor drum.

- **Loose toner**   If the pages emerging from your laser printer have toner on them that you can rub or brush off, they have not been properly fused. Usually, this means that the fuser is not reaching the temperature needed to completely melt the toner and fuse it to the page. A problem of this type nearly always requires professional service.

- **Solid vertical black line**   A vertical black line running down the entire length of several consecutive pages is a sign that your laser printer's toner cartridge might be nearly empty. Shaking the cartridge can usually eliminate the problem, but eventually you will have to replace it.

- **Frequent paper jams**   Paper handling can be a delicate part of the printer mechanism that is affected by several elements. Printer jams can result when paper is loaded incorrectly into the feed tray, when the paper is damp or wrinkled, or when you use the wrong kind of paper. Occasional jams are normal, but frequent jamming can indicate that you are using paper stock that is too heavy or textured in such a way as to be improper for laser printing. Jams can also result when the printer is not resting on a level surface or when the printer feed mechanisms aren't clean.

  Envelope handling is often the weak spot in paper handling, especially with older laser printers or low-cost inkjet printers. Because of their uneven thickness, they tend to produce a high percentage of jams. Even if your printer is designed to handle multiple envelopes, consider feeding them one at a time if you have problems, or use alternative addressing means such as clear labels.

- **Blank pages appear between printed pages**   Paper that is damp, wrinkled, or too tightly compressed can cause two or more sheets to run through the printer at one time. To prevent this, store your paper in a cool, dry place, don't stack the reams too high, and riffle through the stack of paper before you insert it in the feed tray. This can also be caused by different paper types or sizes loaded in the IN tray at the same time.

in the Real World

Before you look for a paper problem, be sure to check the printer setup. Some printers, especially on networks, are set to use a blank page to separate print jobs.

- **Memory overflow/printer overrun errors**   These errors indicate that the job you sent to the printer was too complex or consisted of more data than its buffers could handle. This can be caused by the use of too many fonts, text that is too dense, or graphics that are too complex. You can resolve this problem by simplifying your document or installing more memory in the printer. You can also try adjusting the page-protection setting in your printer driver (see the previous option).

Connection Problems

Some connection problems include:

- **Gibberish**   If your page printer produces page after page of seemingly random "garbage" characters, the problem is probably that the printer has failed to recognize the PDL used by the print job. For example, a PostScript print job must begin with the two characters %!. If the printer fails to receive these characters, all the remaining data in the job prints as

ASCII. This kind of problem is usually the result of some sort of communications failure between the PC and the printer. Check that the cable connections are secure and the cable is not damaged. If the problem occurs consistently, it might be the result of an improperly configured port in the PC, particularly if you are using a serial port. Check the port's parameters in the operating system. A serial port should be configured to use 8 data bits, 1 stop bit, and no parity (N-8-1).

Using the wrong printer driver will also cause gibberish printing. If you had an inkjet printer as your default, then switch to a laser printer but fail to set the laser printer as the default, your print jobs will produce garbage printing unless you specifically send jobs to the laser printer. Similarly, failing to flip a switchbox to use the intended printer will also cause this type of printing error. Thus, many of these printing problems are due to operator error. Whenever you change to a new printer, make sure you set it as the default. Also, to avoid printer-switch errors, consider adding a second parallel port for the other printer or use the new USB-compatible printers if your system is compatible with them.

- **Printer not available error**   When Windows 9x does not receive a response from a printer over the designated port, it switches the driver to offline mode, which enables you to print jobs and store them in the print spooler until the printer is available. The printer might be unavailable because the parallel or serial port is incorrectly configured, the printer cable is faulty, or the printer is turned off, offline, or malfunctioning. A malfunctioning port can be caused by an IRQ conflict (LPT1 uses IRQ 7, and COM 1 and COM 2 use IRQs 4 and 3, by default) or in the case of a serial port, incorrect start/stop/parity bit settings could be the culprit. A switchbox that is supposed to automatically scan for print jobs but has been set to manual mode or has been turned off can also cause this error.

- **Printer does not notify Windows when it is out of paper, jammed, or has another problem**   This is usually indicative of a communications problem between the printer and the PC. Check the printer cable and its connections at both ends. Some manufacturers recommend that you use a cable that is compliant with the IEEE-1284 standard.

In the Real World

IEEE-1284 cables don't work in their advanced EPP/ECP modes unless your printer port is also set for an IEEE-1284 mode. Check your system documentation for details.

- **Intermittent or failed communications or a partial print job followed by gibberish**   Interruptions in the communication between the computer and the printer can cause data to be lost in transit, resulting in partial print jobs or no print output at all. Aside from a faulty cable, these problems can result from the use of additional hardware between the printer port and the printer. Switchboxes used to share a printer among several computers and peripherals that share the parallel port with the printer (such as CD-ROM drives) are particularly prone to causing problems such as this.

- **Port is busy error or printer goes offline**   These errors can occur when an ECP sends data to a printer at a rate faster than it can handle. You can remedy the problem by using the Windows 9x System Control Panel to load the standard printer port driver instead of the ECP driver.

Driver Problems

The best way to determine whether a printer driver is causing a particular problem is to stop using it. If a problem printing from a Windows application disappears when you print a directory listing by issuing the DIR > LPT1 command from the DOS prompt, you can safely say that you need to install a new printer driver. Other driver problems include the following:

- **Form feed light comes on but nothing prints**   This indicates that the printer has less than a full page of data in its buffer and that the computer has failed to send a form feed command to eject the page. This is a common occurrence when you print from a DOS prompt or application without the benefit of a printer driver or use the Print-Screen key from DOS or within your BIOS setup screens, but it can also be the result of a malfunctioning driver. Some drivers (particularly PostScript drivers) provide an option to send an extra form feed at the end of every print job. Otherwise, you must eject the page manually from the printer's control panel.

- **Incorrect fonts printing**   Virtually all laser printers have a selection of fonts built in to the printer, and by default, most drivers use these fonts in place of similar TrueType or PostScript Type 1 fonts installed on the computer. There can be noticeable differences between the two fonts, however, and the printed text might not look exactly like that on the screen. Slight size discrepancies between the fonts can also cause the page breaks in the printed output to differ from those on the screen.

In the Real World

Because different printers will use TrueType or Type 1 fonts differently, you should select the printer your document will be printed with before you save the document. After you select the printer, scroll through the document and check for problems due to page breaks being shifted, margins changing, or other problems.

You should also perform this procedure before you fax your document using a fax modem. Because fax resolution is a maximum of 200dpi in most cases, this lower resolution can cause major layout changes, even with scalable fonts such as TrueType or PostScript Type 1.

Application Problems

Some application problems can include:

- **Margins out of range error**   Most laser printers have a border around all four sides of the page of approximately one third of an inch where the toner cannot reach. If you configure an application to use margins smaller than this border, some drivers can generate this error message, whereas others simply truncate the output to fit the maximum printable page size. If your application or driver does not generate an error message and does not give you an opportunity to enter a correct margin setting, be sure to check your printer manual to find the possible margin settings before printing.

In the Real World

Some applications offer a "print-to-fit" option that automatically adjusts the document to fit on the page in case you've made a margin-setting mistake. These options work by changing the font size or by readjusting line and page breaks. This option can be useful, but preview it before you use it.

Printer Connections

The first step in the printing process is to get the print job data from the PC to the printer. PCs traditionally use the parallel port to communicate with a printer, although many printers can use a serial port. Some devices can even use both types of ports at the same time to connect to two different computers. Network printers often bypass these ports entirely and use an internal adapter to connect directly to the network cable. The newest SOHO and office printers offer USB connections, either as their only port or along with a parallel port. The commonly used connections are discussed in the following sections.

Parallel

Parallel printer communications provide the closest connection to plug-and-play possible, with the notable exception of USB. Parallel is the single most common printer connection used today for end users (see Figure 5.5).

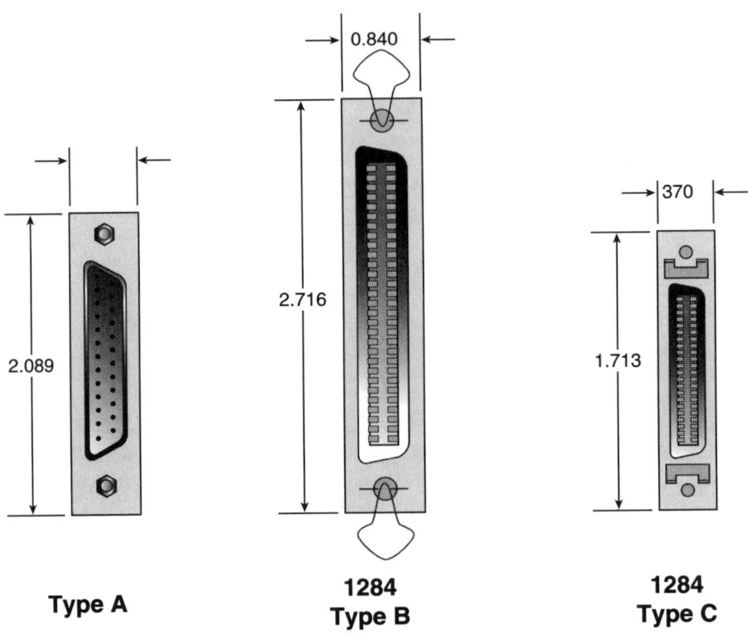

Figure 5.5 Three different parallel port connections.

Many printers today support even more advanced communications with a PC, enabling a user to interrogate the printer for its current status using a software application and even to configure parameters that previously were accessible only from the control panel on the printer. This type of communication requires that the PC have a bidirectional, ECP, or EPP port.

Serial

Serial printer communication has fallen out of favor with today's computing community because of the configuration headache that it requires. Serial printers often require specialized cables in addition to nonstandard configuration parameters (see Figure 5.6).

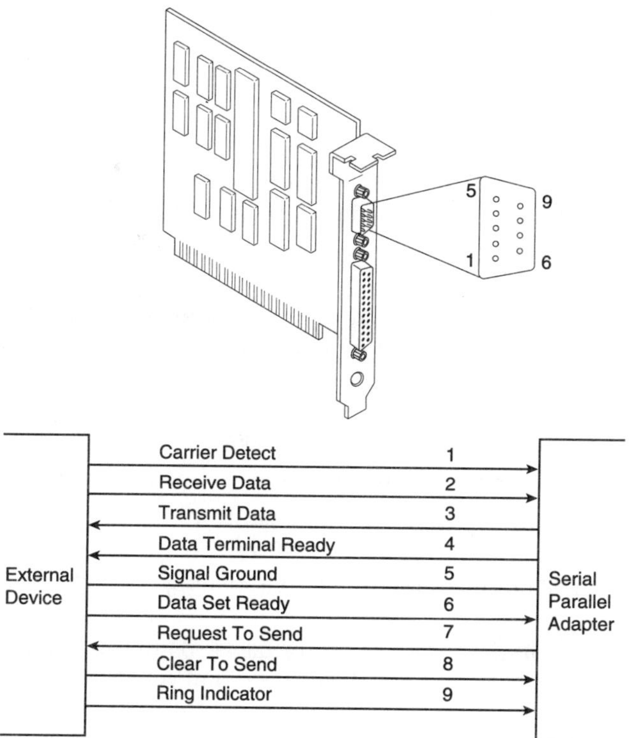

Figure 5.6 AT style 9-pin serial port connection.

Network

Network printing is quickly replacing even parallel printer connections in corporate and work-group environments. This can assuredly provide a cost savings over having a stand-alone printer on every desktop. These network printer resources will be covered in Chapter 7, "Basic Networking."

Review

Cram Session

Following are some key points you should keep in mind when readying yourself for the exam:

- Fully formed character printers are obsolete. Their replacement, bit-image printers, create images by placing patterns of closely packed dots on the page.

- Printer resolution is much better than screen resolution—often 300dpi (dots per inch) or better.

- The two predominate feed mechanisms today are continuous (or tractor) feed paper and automatic sheet feed paper. Of the two, automatic sheet feeder is by far the most prevalent in new printers.

- The most common printers used today are the dot-matrix, the inkjet, and the laser printer. These printers vary in technologies and are important for the exam.

- Consumables include paper, ink, disposable printer components, and electricity.

- Review the sections on printer troubleshooting earlier in this chapter. This will be a significant part of the 10 percent of the exam covering printers.

- The six stages of the EP process are cleaning, conditioning, writing, developing, transferring, and fusing.

- Printers have several built-in self-tests that can enable you to better provide troubleshooting services. One tests the hardware, one tests the logic, and yet another might test the process itself.

Review Questions

1. What is a bit image?

2. Which printers use bit-image printing?

3. What is a tractor feeder?

4. What is one advantage that dot-matrix printers have over most other printers on the market today?

5. What are consumables for a dot-matrix printer?

6. You are printing on a dot-matrix printer and getting long jagged tears in the paper horizontally. What is the most likely cause?

7. What are consumables for an inkjet?

8. What do solid black lines through the text on the printed page from a laser printer indicate?

9. What do solid black lines through the text on the printed page from an inkjet printer indicate?

10. What does a repeating defect usually indicate?

11. If your printer seems to be printing gibberish in Windows 95, what steps should you take to troubleshoot?

12. What are some of the methods you can use to connect a printer?

13. What are the three most common ways to connect a printer today?

14. If you have removed a paper jam and the printer still will not respond, what could be wrong?

15. What is the fourth type of printer commonly in use today?

16. What are the six stages of the EP process?

17. How does the EP process work?

Review Answers

1. A bit image is any character or graphic formed by overlapping or adjacent dots.

2. Dot-matrix, inkjet, and laser all use this technology. Only older daisy-wheel printers do not. A laser printer is something of a hybrid because the actual transfer to the page from the drum is a full-character transfer, but the initial creation of the character on the drum by the laser is bit-image.

3. A tractor, or continuous, paper feeder provides a drive mechanism with rotating pins to advance the paper through the printer.

4. Dot-matrix printers are the only impact printer commonly used today. The largest benefit from this is the capability to print multi-part forms.

5. Dot-matrix consumables include paper, the ink ribbon cartridge, and even the print head.

6. The print head is damaged and has one pin that did not retract. The carriage-return motion of the print head causes the jammed, and now bent, pin to tear all paper under the print head.

7. Inkjets include the paper, ink cartridge, and jets in the cartridge as consumables, although some manufacturers refuse to repair inkjet printers, which makes the entire printer consumable eventually.

8. Solid dark lines indicate that there is a scratch on the surface of the drum or fusing assembly.

9. The inkjets are clogged. A standard maintenance cycle should fix this problem.

10. A repeating defect can be used to determine which cyclical component needs repair.

11. First, try to print from a generic application such as Wordpad. If it all functions, continue on. Second, try to print from a DOS window. This should avoid the ever present Windows driver model. If this still fails, run the self tests on the printer.

12. USB, FireWire, SCSI, Parallel, Serial, and Network are some of the ways that you can connect a printer.

13. The three most common ways are parallel, serial, and network interface connections.

14. Printer jams can result when paper is loaded incorrectly into the feed tray, when the paper is damp or wrinkled, or when you use the wrong kind of paper. You also could be using paper stock that is too heavy or textured in such a way as to be improper for laser printing. Also, check to be sure that the printer is not resting on a level surface.

15. Thermal printers are the fourth style of printers that were not discussed greatly and are not covered on the exam.

16. The six stages of the EP process are cleaning, conditioning, writing, developing, transferring, and fusing.

17. In the EP process, the cleaning blade cleans the excess toner off of the drum from the previous print cycle; the charging roller lays a charge on the drum; the laser writes to the drum, dissipating the charge; the developing roller places toner onto the weakly charged areas on the drum; the transfer roller charges the paper to attract the toner; and the fusing roller melts the toner into the paper.

Chapter 6

Portable Systems

Portable Systems Components

Portable computers, like their desktop counterparts, have evolved enormously since the days when the word "portable" could refer to a desktop-sized case with a handle on it. Today, portable systems can rival the performance of their desktop counterparts in nearly every way. It is to the point that many systems are now being marketed as "desktop replacements," which companies are providing to traveling employees as their primary systems. Laptops with 15" screens, 384MB of RAM, 400MHz processors, and 14GB hard drives are now available, and advancements are being made every day. This chapter examines the types of portable computers available and the technologies designed specifically for use in mobile systems.

Note

Additional information on portable systems can be found in Chapter 23, "Portable PCs," in Scott Mueller's *Upgrading and Repairing PCs, Eleventh Edition*.

From a technical standpoint, some of the components used in portable systems are very similar to those in desktop computers, whereas others are completely different. The following sections examine the various subsystems found in portable computers and how they differ from their desktop counterparts.

Batteries

Most portable systems today use one of three battery types:

- **Nickel Cadmium (NiCad)**   As the oldest of the three technologies, nickel cadmium batteries are rarely used in portable systems today because of their shorter life and sensitivity to improper charging and discharging. The life of the battery's charge can be shortened significantly if the battery is not fully discharged before recharging or if it is overcharged. Despite this memory effect, however, NiCad batteries hold a charge well when not in use and can be recharged 1,500 times or more.

- **Nickel Metal-Hydride (NiMH)**   More expensive than NiCads, NiMH batteries have a longer life than NiCads, are less sensitive to the memory effect caused by improper charging and discharging, and do not use the environmentally dangerous substances found in NiCads. They can be recharged as many as 500 times. NiMH batteries also require nearly twice as long to recharge as NiCads. Although they are still used in many portable systems, NiMH batteries are now found mostly in computers at the lower end of the price range.

- **Lithium-Ion (Li-ion)**   As the current industry standard, Li-ion batteries are longer-lived than either NiCad or NiMH technologies, cannot be overcharged, and hold a charge well when not in use. Li-ion batteries can also support the heavy-duty power requirements of today's high-end systems. But beware—Li-ion batteries can only be used in systems specifically designed for them. Inserting a Li-ion battery into a system designed for a NiCad or NiMH can result in a fire. Although the most expensive of the three technologies, Li-ion batteries have come to be used in all but the very low end of the portable system market.

In the Real World

Lithium is an unstable substance, and some battery explosions resulted in a large number of pure lithium battery recalls in the early 1990s. Subsequent models were manufactured using lithium ions from chemicals such as lithium-cobalt dioxide (LiCoO2). Despite a slightly lower energy density, Li-ion batteries are much safer than the lithium designs.

LCD Panels

An LCD consists of two sheets of a flexible, polarizing material with a layer of liquid crystal solution between them. If you press gently on an LCD screen while it is lit, you can see how it gives slightly, displacing the liquid inside. When an electric current is passed through the liquid, the crystals align and become semipermeable to light.

There are two different technologies that are used in LCD panels that you might encounter: passive matrix and active matrix.

Passive Matrix

The passive-matrix display has an array of transistors running down the x- and y-axes of two sides of the screen (as shown in Figure 6.1). The number of transistors determines the screen's resolution. For example, a dual-scan display with 640 transistors along the x-axis and 480 along the y-axis creates a grid. Each pixel on the screen is controlled by the two transistors representing its coordinates on the x- and y-axes.

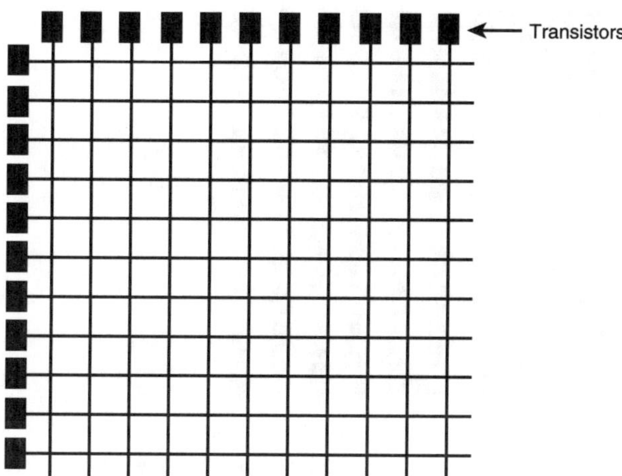

Figure 6.1 Dual-scan LCD displays use a combination of two transistors on intersecting axes to control the color of each pixel.

Dual-scan displays are generally inferior to active-matrix screens. Dual-scan displays tend to be dimmer because the pixels work by modifying the properties of reflected light (either room light or, more likely, a white light source behind the screen), rather than by generating their own light. Dual-scan panels are also prone to ghost images and are difficult to view from an angle, making it hard for two or more people to view the same screen.

Of course, passive-matrix displays are also far less expensive than active-matrix screens. The drawbacks of a passive-matrix display are most noticeable during video-intensive applications, such as presentations, full-color graphics, video, or fast-moving games, or under bright lighting conditions, such as in a window seat on an airplane, outdoors, or in offices with a lot of window lighting. For computing tasks that consist largely of reading words on the screen, such as word processing and email, the passive matrix display is quite serviceable, even for long periods of time.

Active Matrix

An active-matrix display differs from a dual-scan in that it contains at least one transistor for every pixel onscreen, rather than just at the edges. The transistors are arranged on a grid of conductive material, with each connected to a horizontal and a vertical member as shown in Figure 6.2.

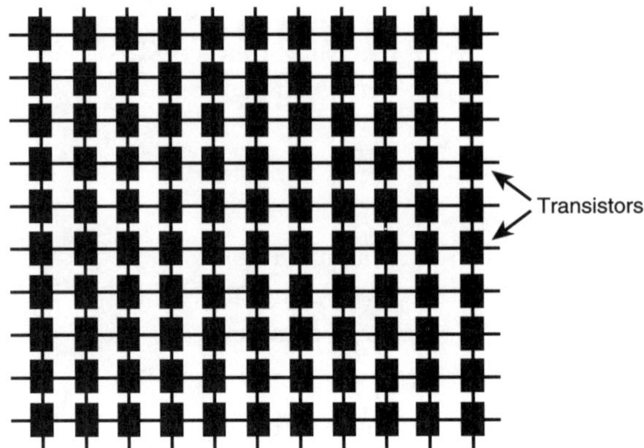

Figure 6.2 Active-matrix LCD displays contain a transistor for each pixel on the screen. The pixels generate their own light for a brighter display.

Most active-matrix displays use a thin film transistor (TFT) array. TFT is a method for packaging one to four transistors per pixel within a flexible material that is the same size and shape as the display, so the transistors for each pixel lie directly behind the liquid crystal cells they control.

Because every pixel is individually powered, each one generates its own light of the appropriate color, creating a display that is much brighter and more vivid than a dual-scan panel. The viewing angle is also greater, enabling multiple viewers to gather around the screen, and refreshes are faster and crisper, without the fuzziness of the dual scans, even in the case of games or full-motion video.

On the downside, it should be no surprise that with 480,000 or more transistors rather than 1,400 (on an 800×600 screen), an active-matrix display requires a lot more power than a dual scan. It drains batteries faster and costs a great deal more, as well.

In the Real World

In any LCD display, caution should be taken that the display not be abused. Cracks in the display will destroy it and are not covered by any manufacturer's warranty. A common cause of a cracked LCD display (other than physically dropping it) is leaving the laptop in the car in extremely cold temperatures overnight and then turning on the PC as soon as it is taken inside.

AC Adapters

Most portable computers have a split power supply. Rather than have an AC-DC converter and the proper DC output circuits in the same housing, the AC-DC transformer is located in a "brick" on the power cable itself. This is due to the lack of space and ventilation inside the portable PC case itself.

As with all other AC-DC transformers, these cables cannot be interchanged with other electronic devices. The exact range of voltage and current output on an AC adapter can vary greatly from laptop to laptop, even if they are from the same manufacturer. Always use the adapter that was made for it by the manufacturer.

Docking Stations

A *docking station* is a desktop unit to which you attach (or dock) your portable system when you are at your home or office. At the very least, a docking station provides an AC power connection, a full-size keyboard, a standard desktop mouse, a complete set of input and output ports, and a VGA jack for a standard external monitor.

When docked, the keyboard and display in the portable system are deactivated, but the other components—particularly the processor, memory, and hard drive—remain active. You are essentially running the same computer but using a standard full-size desktop interface. Docking stations can also contain a wide array of other features, such as a network interface adapter, external speakers, additional hard disk or CD-ROM drives, additional PC card slots, and a spare battery charger.

The use of a docking station eliminates much of the tedium involved in maintaining separate desktop and portable systems. With two machines, you must install your applications twice and continually keep the data between the two systems synchronized. With a docking station and a suitably equipped portable, you can achieve the best of both worlds.

PCMCIA Expansion Cards

In an effort to give notebook computers the kind of expandability that users have grown used to in desktop systems, the Personal Computer Memory Card Industry Association (PCMCIA) has established several standards for credit card–size expansion boards that fit into a small slot on laptops and notebooks. The development of the PC card interface is one of the few successful feats of hardware standardization in a market full of proprietary designs.

Note

PC-Cards are covered in more depth in Chapter 4, "Motherboards/Processors/Memory" and in Chapter 23 of Scott Mueller's *Upgrading and Repairing PCs, Eleventh Edition.*

Pointing Devices

Most portable systems have pointing devices that conform to one of the three following types:

- **Trackball**   A small ball (usually about 1/2-inch) partially embedded in the keyboard below the spacebar, which is rolled by the user. While serviceable and accurate, trackballs have become unpopular, primarily due to their tendency to gather dust and dirt in the well that holds the ball, causing degraded performance.

- **Trackpoint**   Developed by IBM and adopted by many other manufacturers, the trackpoint is a small, rubberized button located between the G, H, and B keys of the keyboard as shown in Figure 6.3. It looks like a pencil eraser and can be nudged in any direction to move the cursor around the screen. The trackpoint is very convenient because you can manipulate it without taking your hands off of the keyboard. On some earlier models, the rubber cover tended to wear off after heavy use. Newer versions are made of sturdier materials.

Figure 6.3 Location of a trackpoint device.

- **Trackpad** The most recent development of the three, the trackpad, also known as a *glidepoint*, uses one of two technologies. Either it is an electromagnetically sensitive pad that senses pressure on the surface, or it is a heat-sensitive pad that senses the heat in the user's finger. With either technology, it is usually about 1×2 inches across and responds to the movement of a finger across its surface. Mouse clicks can be simulated by tapping the pad in designated tap zones. Trackpads have great potential but tend to be overly sensitive to accidental touches, causing undesired cursor movements and especially unwanted mouse clicks. Newer pads can adjust the sensitivity as well as disable all the additional features such as tap zones. Trackpads can also be sensitive to humidity and moist or cold fingers, resulting in unpredictable performance.

Review

The following sections should help you quickly review for the exam objectives after you have completely studied the chapter material.

Cram Session

- Portable systems can rival the performance of their desktop counterparts in nearly every way. With the addition of a docking station and external monitor/keyboard, even the ergonomic problems of a miniaturized PC fall away.

- There are three different types of common batteries for laptops. They are from worst to best (and least used to most used today) Nickel-Cadmium (NiCad), Nickel-Metal-Hydride (NiMH), and Lithium-Ion (Li-ion).

- Displays on laptops are primarily the province of Liquid-Crystal Displays (LCD). The technology behind these displays can be segregated into two categories: active and passive. Active-matrix screens are clearer, brighter, and, consequently, more expensive than their passive-matrix counterparts.

- PCMCIA, or PC-cards, provide standardized expandability in a completely proprietary market. Type II cards are the most common today, although most laptops will support the double-height Type III cards as well.

- Relative-positioning pointing devices commonly come in three distinct types on various portable computers: trackball, trackpoint, and trackpad. External mice are also commonly supported, but the internal pointing device should be disabled prior to external use.

Review Questions

1. Which battery can provide power to a laptop for the longest time?

2. What does the acronym PCMCIA stand for? What major problem do these cards solve for the laptop industry?

3. Why are trackballs falling into disfavor?

4. What are the minimum ports available on a docking station?

5. Which LCD technology provides the brightest, clearest display? Why?

6. What is a "memory effect," and which battery experiences this?

7. What is a tap zone?

Review Answers

1. Li-ion batteries provide the most uptime. These batteries are the successors to the NiCad- and NiMH-style batteries and are used in most higher-end portables today.

2. PCMCIA is the acronym for the Personal Computer Memory Card Industry Association. These PC-Cards provide an industry standard for expansion previously unavailable to the proprietary portable market.

3. Trackballs collect dirt in the well in which the ball sits. In addition, the skin oils pick up this dirt and transfer it directly to the rollers that sense the motion of the trackball. This causes the pointer to behave erratically, often causing extreme frustration to the user.

4. A docking station usually has a power connection, external VGA port, keyboard and mouse ports, as well as parallel and serial ports. Other functions might be available as well. A port replicator might have all of these same ports, minus the power connection.

5. Active-matrix displays have the best and brightest display because each pixel is provided its own power and signal rather than the grid method used in the passive-matrix display.

6. The nickel-cadmium (NiCad) battery fails to charge to full capacity after repeated misuse and improper discharging of the battery. This can occur simply because the user only uses the battery for 20 minutes at a time and then recharges it.

7. A tap zone is a specific area on a touchpad, although it might be defined in the driver for the entire pad to be one "zone." In this zone, a finger tap on the pad is translated to the operating system as a mouse click.

Chapter 7

Basic Networking

Basic Network Concepts and Components

A local area network (LAN) enables you to share files, applications, print-ers, disk space, modems, faxes, tape backup drives, and CD-ROM drives among different systems; use client/server software products; send elec-tronic mail; and otherwise make a collection of computers work as a team.

In today's world, there are many ways to construct a LAN. As you have seen, a LAN can be as simple as two computers connected via either their serial or parallel ports. Although the term network is not often used for this sort of arrangement, it does satisfy the definition.

In most cases, however, computers are connected to a network using a net-work interface adapter that either takes the form of an expansion card (called a network interface card, or NIC) or is integrated into the com-puter's motherboard. The adapter in each computer then connects to a cable or wireless installation in such a way as to permit any computer on the network to communicate with any other.

Unless the computers that are connected together know that they are con-nected together and agree on a common means of communications and what resources are to be shared, they cannot work together. Networking software is just as important as networking hardware because it establishes the logical connections that make the physical connections work.

At a minimum, each network requires the following:

- Physical (cable) or wireless (IRDA or radio-frequency) connections between computers

- A common set of communications rules, known as a network protocol

- A well-defined security model that matches the business structure
- Software that allows resources to be shared with other PCs, known as a network operating system
- Resources that can be shared, such as printers, disk drives, and CD-ROMs
- Software that allows computers to access the computer(s) with shared resources, provide some level of access control, and some means of distinguishing which computers are active on the network—a network client, which allows a workstation to access the shared resources on the network

These rules apply to the simplest networks, the most powerful networks, and all networks in-between, regardless of their nature.

Clients

Client PCs are usually operated by users on their individual desktops, whereas servers are usually located in a secured area. On a client/server network, the client PC is used only by the person sitting in front of it, whereas a server enables many people to share its resources.

On a peer-to-peer network, however, the distinction begins to blur. Because client PCs can also function as servers, it can be necessary to equip them with more powerful components. Technically, there is no reason why you cannot buy a PC marketed as a client PC or a standalone system and use it as a server, as long as it has sufficient resources to run the server software.

Servers

A network server is far more likely to be a top-of-the-line PC, with the fastest processor available, a lot of RAM, and a large amount of hard disk space. Servers must be high-quality, heavy-duty machines because, in serving the whole network, they do many times the work of an ordinary workstation computer. You might type on the server's keyboard only a couple of times a day, and you might glance at its monitor only infrequently. The server's CPU and hard disk drives, however, take the brunt of responding to the file-service requests of all the workstations on the LAN.

The processor in a server should be the most advanced and the fastest that you can afford. Servers often require large amounts of memory, much more than workstations, and both Windows NT and NetWare run better when they have more than the minimum required amount of memory.

Hard disk drives are often the most important components in a server. File sharing is one of the primary reasons for networking computers, and the server's hard drives need to be durable, reliable, and geared to the task of serving multiple users simultaneously. For this reason, SCSI hard drives in a fault-tolerant RAID array are preferred over IDE drives in today's servers.

Fault Tolerance

RAID (Redundant Array of Inexpensive Disks or Redundant Array of Independent Drives) technologies automatically store multiple copies of the server data on various hard drives, so in the event of a drive failure, all the data remains available to users. Table 7.1 summarizes the major levels of RAID available.

Table 7.1   RAID Levels Summary

RAID Level	Features	Notes
0	Data transferred in parallel across several drives; no redundancy.	Creates a single logical drive from several drives without any failure recovery capabilities; useful for high-bandwidth data handling such as video and image editing.
1	Disk mirroring; data written to one drive is duplicated on another. Disk Duplexing is the same, but uses two redundant interface cards.	Has been implemented on EIDE as well as SCSI-based drive pairs; requires only two identical drives and special interface card; duplexing uses one interface card per drive to eliminate adapter failure concern; can be implemented on client PCs as well as servers; hardware implementation more reliable and faster than software implementation.
2	Bit interleaving across 32(!) drives with parity information created on 7 (!) drives.	Very expensive in hardware costs, but offers fast performance; suitable for enterprise-level servers.
3	Data striping across multiple drives; parity information stored on a dedicated drive; implemented at byte level.	Popular choice for data integrity at a relatively low hardware cost; 3 drive minimum.
4	Data striping across multiple drives; parity information stored on a dedicated drive; implemented at block level.	Not widely supported on PC servers; difficult to rebuild lost data in case of drive replacement; poor performance.
5	Error-correction data striped across all drives in the array; concurrent read/write.	Most powerful form of RAID; allows easy "hot swapping" of any failed drive with appropriate server hardware; 3 drive minimum.

In the Real World

RAID levels 2, 3, and 4 are closer to exercises in academia than any real RAID device. In today's servers, RAID levels 0, 1, and 5 are common.

Most PC manufacturers sell computers that are specifically designed to function as servers. These machines can have specialized components designed for heavy use and fault tolerance, and you pay more as a result.

Network Interface Adapters

The network interface adapter is the PC's link to all the other computers on the network. All file requests and other network communications enter and leave the computer through the network adapter. Figure 7.1 shows a typical network interface adapter card that you might install in a server or workstation. Although servers for small networks might well use the same network interface card (NIC) as the client PCs do, there are increasingly popular NICs designed for server use. It serves no purpose to install a high-speed adapter in a server if the network clients do not also support that same speed. The only difference that you might find is that a server might have more than one adapter to connect to multiple networks.

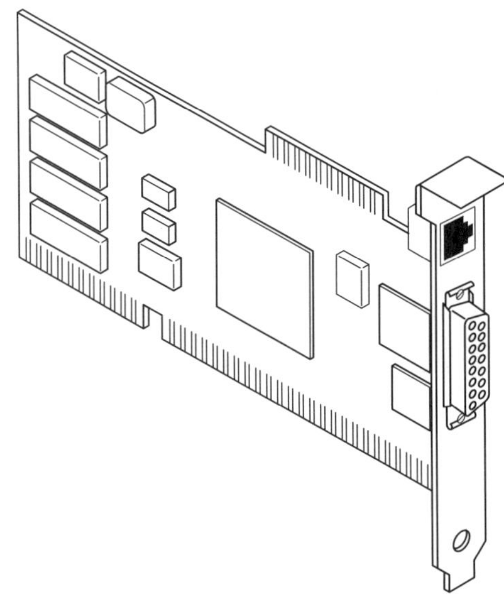

Figure 7.1 The network interface adapter sends and receives messages to and from all the computers on the LAN.

All the network interface adapters on a LAN are designed to use Ethernet, Token Ring, or some other data-link–layer protocol. Before you purchase adapter cards (or network cables, for that matter), you must decide which data link protocol you want to use. You can find network interface adapters for each of these protocols, however, that perform better than others. A particular network adapter might be faster at processing messages because it has a large amount of onboard memory (RAM); because it contains its own microprocessor; or perhaps because the adapter uses a PCI bus rather than ISA, and thus can transfer more data to and from the CPU at one time.

Client/Server Security Versus Peer-to-Peer Security

Although every computer on a LAN is connected to every other, they do not necessarily all communicate with each other. There are two basic types of LANs, based on the communication patterns between the machines, called client/server networks and peer-to-peer networks.

On a client/server network, every computer has a distinct role, either that of a client or a server. A server is designed to share its resources among the client computers on the network and provide a single security database with which it ensures that the users are who they say they are and only allows access to the resources to which they have permissions.

Typically, servers are located in secured areas, such as locked closets and data centers, because they hold the organization's most valuable data and do not have to be accessed by operators on a continual basis. The rest of the computers on the network function as clients (see Figure 7.2).

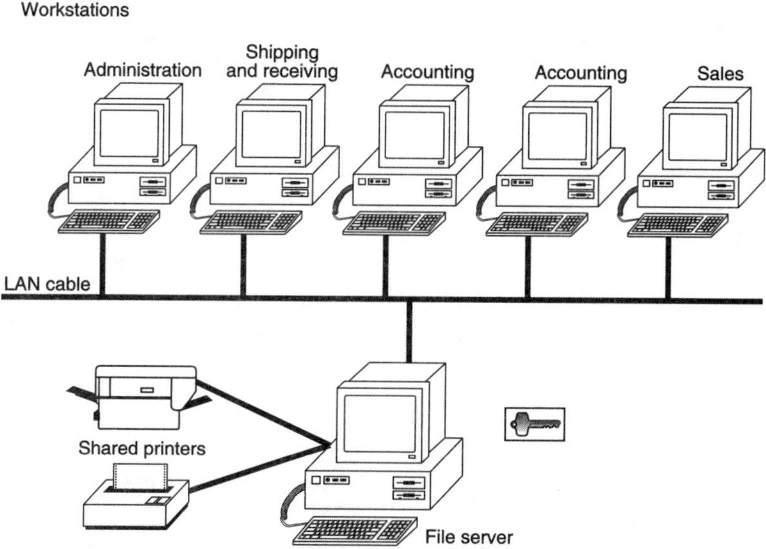

Figure 7.2 The components of a client/server LAN.

By contrast, on a peer-to-peer network, every computer is equal and can communicate with any other computer on the network to which it has been granted access rights (see Figure 7.3). Essentially, every computer on a peer-to-peer network functions as both a server and a client. This is why you might hear about client and server activities, even when the discussion is about a peer-to-peer network. Each peer has its own security database that is not the same as the security database on the other peers. Because of this, the user at the sales computer might have one password to access the accounting computer and a completely different password to access the shipping and receiving computer. Administrative tasks increase exponentially with each user added to the network. Peer-to-peer networks can be as small as two computers or as large as hundreds of units, although Microsoft recommends having no more than 25 in a single workgroup for these exact administrative reasons.

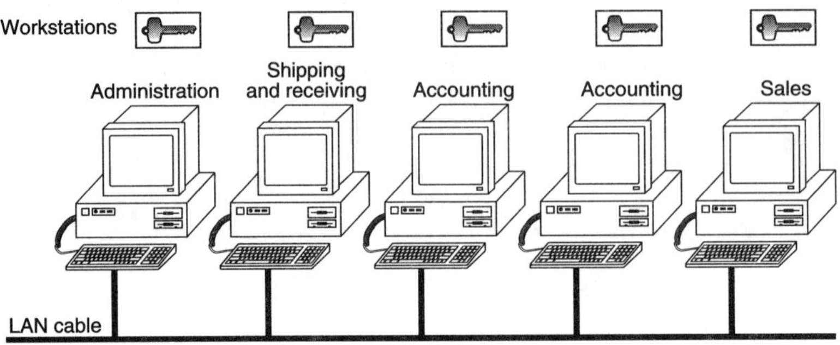

Figure 7.3 The security of a typical peer-to-peer network.

Peer-to-peer networks are more common in small offices or within a single department of a larger organization. The advantage of a peer-to-peer network is that you don't have to dedicate a computer to function as a file server. Instead, every computer can share its resources with any other. The potential disadvantages to a peer-to-peer network are that there is typically less security and less control because users normally administer their own systems, whereas client/server networks have the advantage of centralized administration.

Table 7.2 provides a comparison of various aspects of the client/server and peer-to-peer networking models.

Table 7.2   Comparing Client/Server and Peer-to-Peer Networking

Item	Client/Server	Peer-to-Peer
Access control	Via user/group lists of permissions; single password provides user access to only the resources on his/her list; users can be given several different levels of access.	Via password lists by resource; each resource requires a separate password; access varies with password; no centralized user list.
Security	High because access is controlled by user or by group identity.	Low because knowing the password gives anybody access to a shared resource.

Item	Client/Server	Peer-to-Peer
Performance	High because server doesn't waste time or resources handling workstation tasks.	Low because <u>Aservers@</u> often act as workstations.
Hardware Cost	High, due to specialized design of server, high-performance nature of hardware, and redundancy features.	Low because any workstation can become a server by sharing resources.
Software Cost	License fees per workstation user are part of the cost of the Network Operating System server software (Windows NT and Windows 2000 Server, Novell NetWare).	Free; all client software is included with any release of Windows 9x and Windows NT Workstation and Windows 2000 Professional.
Backup	Centralized when data is stored on server; allows use of high-speed, high-capacity tape backups with advanced cataloging.	Left to user decision; usually mixture of backup devices and practices at each workstation.
Redundancy	Duplicate power supplies, hot-swappable drive arrays, and even redundant servers are common; network OS normally capable of using redundant devices automatically.	No true redundancy among either peer "servers" or clients; failures require manual intervention to correct with high possibility of data loss.

Communication

The network client software operates at many levels within each computer. It is the top portion of a protocol stack, that is, a series of modules and services layered atop one another. Later in this chapter, you will learn about the different types of protocols that modems use to communicate with one another. Networked computers use protocols, too, and for the same reason. For two systems to communicate, they must be speaking the same language.

A LAN connection is more complicated than a modem connection, however, and there are many more protocols involved at every layer of the networking interface. For this reason, the network client and other protocols are sometimes called the *protocol stack*. When designing a LAN, there are different communication protocols available at the various layers of the stack that a network administrator can select to suit a particular environment.

The OSI Model

One of the most commonly used teaching and reference tools in local area networking is called the OSI (Open Systems Interconnection) Reference Model. Developed by the International Organization for Standardization (abbreviated as the ISO) in the 1980s, the OSI model splits a computer's networking stack into seven discrete layers (see Figure 7.4). Each layer provides specific services to the layers above and below it.

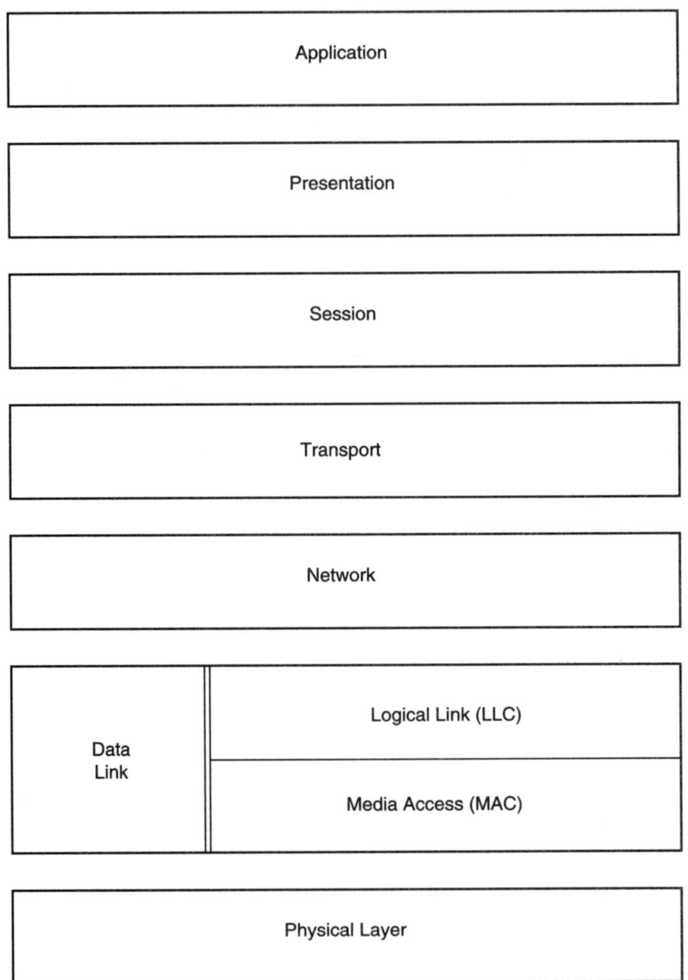

Figure 7.4 The OSI reference model.

At the bottom of the model is the physical side of the network, including cables, NICs, and other hardware. At the top of the model is the application interface that enables you to use your word processor to open a file on a network drive as easily as you can open one on your local drive. In between are layers describing additional services, all which combine to make network communications possible. Descriptions of the seven layers follow:

- **Physical**   This part of the OSI model specifies the physical and electrical characteristics of the connections that make up the network (twisted-pair cables, fiber-optic cables, coaxial cables, connectors, repeaters, and other hardware). You can think of this layer as the hardware layer. Although the rest of the layers might be implemented as firmware (that is, chip-level functions on the network adapter) rather than actual software, the other layers are software in relation to this first layer.

- **Data link**   This layer controls how the electrical impulses enter or leave the network cable. The network's electrical representation of your data (bit patterns, encoding methods, and tokens) is known to this layer and only to this layer. It is here that most errors are detected and corrected (by requesting retransmissions of corrupted packets). In some networking systems, the data link layer is subdivided into a Media Access Control (MAC) layer and a Logical Link Control (LLC) layer. The MAC layer deals with network access (token-passing or collision-sensing) and network control. The LLC layer, operating just above the MAC layer, is concerned with sending and receiving the user data messages. Ethernet and Token Ring are data link–layer protocols.

- **Network**   This layer switches and routes the packets as necessary to get them to their destinations and is responsible for addressing and delivering message packets. Although the data link layer is conscious only of the immediately adjacent computers on the network, the network layer is responsible for the entire route of a packet from source to destination. IP and IPX are examples of network-layer protocols.

- **Transport**   When more than one packet is in process at any time, such as when a large file must be split into multiple packets for transmission, the transport layer controls the sequencing of the message components and regulates inbound traffic flow. If a duplicate packet arrives, this layer recognizes it as a duplicate and discards it. TCP and SPX are transport-layer protocols.

- **Session**   The functions in this layer enable applications running at two workstations to coordinate their communications into a single session (which you can think of in terms of a highly structured dialogue). The session layer supports the creation of the session, the management of the packets sent back and forth during the session, and the termination of the session.

- **Presentation**   When IBM, Apple, DEC, NeXT, and Linux-based computers want to one another, a certain amount of translation and byte reordering obviously needs to be done. The presentation layer converts data into an interim format for transmission over the network and back into the machine's native format afterward.

- **Application**   This layer defines the interface to the applications running on a networked computer. Application-layer protocols can be programs in themselves (such as FTP), or they can be used by other programs (as SMTP, the Simple Mail Transfer Protocol, is used by most email applications) to redirect data to the network.

It is important to understand that although the OSI model was designed to be a model for the development of actual networking software, the products used on today's LANs do not exactly correspond to these layers. Although you might find that certain protocols fall neatly within the boundaries between the layers, others might overlap or provide services that span several layers. As mentioned earlier, the model is primarily used as a tool for teaching networking and as a reference tool for networking professionals.

Note

Further information on the OSI model can be found in *Upgrading and Repairing PCs, Eleventh Edition* Chapter 19, "Local Area Networking," and in the latest edition of Que's *Upgrading and Repairing Networks, Second Edition.*

Network Topologies

Each computer on the network is connected to the other computers with cable (or some other medium). Sometimes a single piece of cable winds from station to station, visiting all of the network's computers along the way. This cabling arrangement is in Figure 7.5. (A physical topology is simply a description of the way the workstations and servers are physically connected.) The potential disadvantage to this type of wiring is that if one computer or cable connection malfunctions, it can cause all the stations beyond it on the bus to lose their network connections. Thin and thick Ethernet coaxial cables are typically installed using a bus topology.

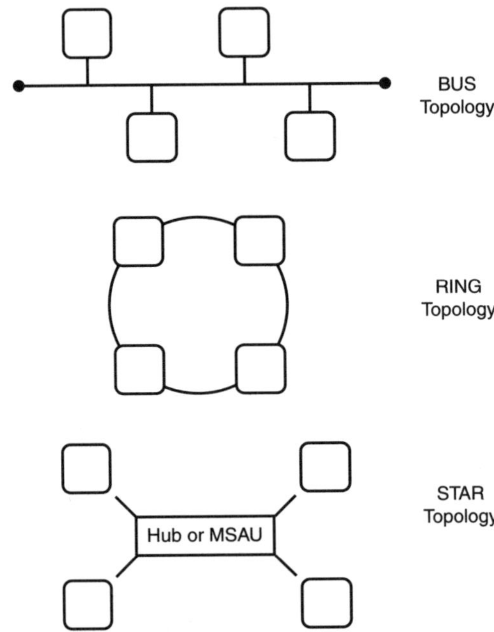

Figure 7.5 The bus, ring, and star physical topologies.

The second topology often listed in discussions of this type is a *ring*, in which each workstation is connected to the next, and the last workstation is connected to the first again (essentially a bus topology with the two ends connected). Data travels around a Token Ring network in this fashion, for example.

Another type of topology uses separate cables to connect each computer to a central wiring nexus, often called a hub or a concentrator. Figure 7.6 shows this arrangement, which is called a *star topology*. Because each computer uses a separate cable, the failure of a network connection affects only the single machine involved. The other computers can continue to function normally. Bus cabling schemes use less cable than star, but are harder to diagnose or bypass when problems occur. Inside the hub or concentrator, however, the signals still proceed in a bus or ring fashion. This is known as the logical topology. An Ethernet network or a Token Ring network can have the outward appearances of a star topology but logically are still a bus Ethernet or a Token Ring inside. At this time, Ethernet using 10BaseT cable in a star topology is the most commonly implemented type of LAN.

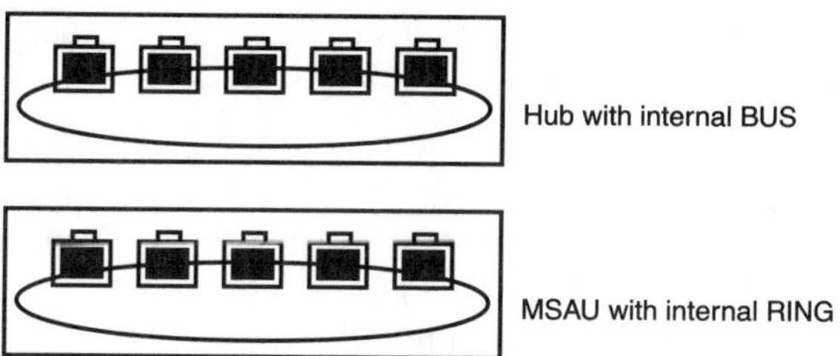

Figure 7.6 The inner logical paths of a central hub and MSAU.

Access Methods

Access methods are a function of the physical and data link layers of the OSI model. These include Ethernet's Carrier Sense-Multiple Access/Collision Detection (CSMA/CD) and Token Ring's Token-Passing methods.

Some of the more important network access protocols are listed in Table 7.3.

Table 7.3   Network Protocol Summary

Network Type	Speed	Max Number of Stations	Cable Types	Notes
ARCnet	2.5Mbps	255 stations	RG-62 coax UTP/ Type 1 STP	Obsolete for new installations; was used to replace IBM 3270 terminals (which used the same coax cable).
Ethernet	10Mbps	Per segment: 10BaseT-2 10Base2-30 10Base5-100 10BaseFL-2	UTP Cat 3 (10BaseT), Thicknet (coax; 10Base5), Thinnet (RG-58 coax; 10Base2), Fiber optic 10BaseF)	Being replaced by Fast Ethernet; can be interconnected with Fast Ethernet by use of dual-speed hubs and switches; use switches and routers to overcome "5-4-3" rule in building very large networks.

(continues)

Table 7.3   Continued

Network Type	Speed	Max Number of Stations	Cable Types	Notes
Fast Ethernet	100Mbps	Per segment: 2	Cat 5 UTP	Fast Ethernet can be interconnected with standard Ethernet through use of dual-speed hubs, switches, and routers.
Token Ring	4Mbps or 16Mbps	72 on UTP 250-260 on type 1 STP	UTP, Type 1 STP, and Fiber Optic	High price for NICs and MAUs to interconnect clients; primarily used with IBM mid-size and mainframe systems.

Ethernet

Ethernet-based LANs enable you to interconnect a wide variety of equipment, including UNIX workstations, Apple computers, printers, and PCs. You can buy Ethernet adapters from dozens of competing manufacturers, supporting all three cable types defined in the standard: Thinnet, Thicknet, and UTP. Traditional Ethernet operates at a speed of 10Mbps, but the more recent "Fast Ethernet" standards push this speed to 100Mbps.

Because computers on a LAN share a common network medium (usually a cable), there must be a scheme to arbitrate each system's access to the network. If two computers transmit a packet at the same time, a collision can result, garbling both packets and causing data loss. This arbitration scheme is called a media access control (or MAC) mechanism, and Ethernet networks use a MAC mechanism called Carrier Sense, Multiple Access with Collision Detection (CSMA/CD).

When a computer on an Ethernet network wants to transmit, it first listens to the network to see if the network is currently in use. If another computer is transmitting, the system waits for a while and then listens again. If the network is clear, the system transmits its data. This is not a foolproof method, however, as it is possible for two computers to detect a clear network and transmit at the same time, causing a collision.

Collisions are a regular and accepted occurrence on an Ethernet LAN, and a good deal of the technology is devoted to detecting them. When a computer realizes that its transmission has collided with another packet, it waits for a random period of time (called a backoff interval) and transmits the same packet again.

Token Ring

Token Ring networks differ substantially from Ethernet. Originally designed by IBM to run at 4Mbps over STP or UTP cable in a logical ring topology, the standard was revised to include a 16Mbps version, which is what most installations use today. Token Ring adapters and hubs (MSAUs) are considerably more expensive than their Ethernet counterparts, but this cost can often be justified by the protocol's greater speed and its excellent performance even at high traffic levels.

Token Ring networks use a different type of MAC mechanism than Ethernet LANs, called *token passing.* On a Token Ring network, computers continually pass a special packet called a token among themselves. The token is just a short message indicating that the computer possessing it is allowed to transmit. If a computer has no data to send, it passes the token on to the next downstream computer as soon as it receives it. Only the computer holding the token can transmit data onto the LAN. Every packet transmitted on the network circulates through all the computers on the ring, including its intended destination, and eventually ends up back at the computer that sent it. The sender is then responsible for removing the packet from the network and generating a new token, thus releasing control of the network to the next system.

Because it is not possible for two computers to transmit at the same time on a properly functioning Token Ring network, there are no collisions, and because every computer has an equal opportunity to transmit, network performance does not degrade at high traffic levels. In special situations, it is also possible to assign priorities to certain computers so they get more frequent access to the LAN.

Network Protocols

When you add network client software to a PC, the first step is to install a driver for the network interface adapter in the machine. This driver not only identifies the adapter hardware, but it implements the data link–layer protocol. The next step is to install support for the protocols running above the data link layer. There are usually several different protocols operating at the upper layers, but for the purposes of a client installation, they are treated as a single entity.

For example, after installing a driver for the Ethernet adapter in your PC, you can select a protocol suite such as TCP/IP or IPX to work at the upper layers. Both TCP/IP and IPX actually consist of several different protocols, but you install them as one module that operating systems such as Windows 9x and Windows NT somewhat confusingly refer to by the term protocol.

In nearly all cases, you can also install multiple protocol suites to support different networking clients on the same computer. For example, a single Ethernet adapter can use IPX to access NetWare servers and TCP/IP to share Windows NT resources, both at the same time.

The following sections examine the upper-layer protocols most commonly used on today's LANs.

TCP/IP

TCP/IP stands for Transmission Control Protocol/Internet Protocol. TCP and IP are separate transport- and network-layer protocols, respectively, but TCP/IP is the colloquial name given to the entire suite of networking protocols developed for use by the Internet, of which TCP and IP are only two. Later, the TCP/IP protocols were adopted by the UNIX operating systems, and they have now become the most commonly used protocol suite on PC LANs. Virtually every operating system with networking capabilities supports TCP/IP, and it is well on its way to displacing all the other competing protocols.

Operating at the network layer, IP is the main protocol of the TCP/IP suite. It supplies network data with addressing and routing information, and it splits packets into smaller fragments as needed during the trip to their destination. This is the level at which your IP address is stored to logically identify your computer on the LAN and even the Internet.

IPX

The IPX protocol suite is the collective term for the proprietary protocols created by Novell for their NetWare operating system. IPX protocol standards are privately held by Novell; however, this has not prevented Microsoft from creating its own IPX-compatible protocol for the Windows operating systems.

IPX (Internetwork Packet Exchange) is a connectionless, network-layer protocol that is equivalent in function to IP. The suite's equivalent to TCP is the Sequenced Packet Exchange (SPX) protocol, which provides connection-oriented, reliable service at the transport layer.

The IPX protocols are typically used today only on networks with NetWare servers, and they are often installed along with another protocol suite such as TCP/IP. Even NetWare, however, is phasing out its use of IPX and making the move over to TCP/IP, along with the rest of the networking industry.

NetBEUI

NetBEUI (NetBIOS Extended User Interface) is a protocol used primarily on small Windows NT networks. It was the default protocol in Windows NT 3.1, the first version of that operating system. Later versions, however, use the TCP/IP protocols as their default.

NetBEUI is a simple protocol that lacks many of the features that enable protocol suites such as TCP/IP to support networks of almost any size. NetBEUI is not routable, so it cannot be used on large internetworks. It is suitable for small peer-to-peer networks, but any serious Windows NT network installation should use TCP/IP.

Cabling

Generally speaking, the cabling systems described in the next few sections use one of three distinct cable types. These are twisted-pair (in shielded and unshielded varieties known as STP, UTP, 10BaseT, or 100BaseT), coaxial in thin and thick varieties (known as 10Base2 and 10Base5, respectively), and fiber-optic. The kind of cable you use depends mostly on the data link–layer protocol that you elect to use, the conditions at the network site, and, of course, your budget. All the major data link–layer protocols used on LANs (such as Ethernet and Token Ring) include highly specific guidelines for the installation of the network cable as part of their specifications. Technically, these guidelines are part of the physical layer, but this is one example of how protocols in the real world do not conform exactly to the OSI model.

LANs are local because the network adapters and other hardware components typically cannot send LAN messages more than a few hundred feet. Table 7.4 lists the distance limitations of different kinds of LAN cable. In addition to the limitations shown in the table, keep in mind that you cannot connect more than 30 computers on a single Thinnet Ethernet segment, 100 computers on a Thicknet Ethernet segment, 72 computers on a UTP Token Ring cable, or 260 computers on an STP Token Ring cable.

Table 7.4   Network Distance Limitations

Network Adapter	Cable Type	Maximum	Minimum
Ethernet	Thin	607 ft.	20 in.
	Thick (drop cable)	164 ft.	8 ft.
	Thick (backbone)	1,640 ft.	8 ft.
	UTP	328 ft.	8 ft.
Token Ring	STP	328 ft.	8 ft.
	UTP	148 ft.	8 ft.

Twisted-Pair Cable

Twisted-pair cable is just what its name implies: insulated wires within a protective casing, with a specified number of twists per foot. Twisting the wires reduces the effect of electromagnetic interference (that can be generated by nearby cables, electric motors, and fluorescent lighting) on the signals being transmitted. Shielded twisted pair (STP) refers to the amount of insulation around the cluster of wires and therefore its immunity to noise. You are probably familiar with unshielded twisted-pair (UTP) cable; it is often used for telephone wiring. Figure 7.7 shows unshielded twisted-pair cable; Figure 7.8 illustrates shielded twisted-pair cable.

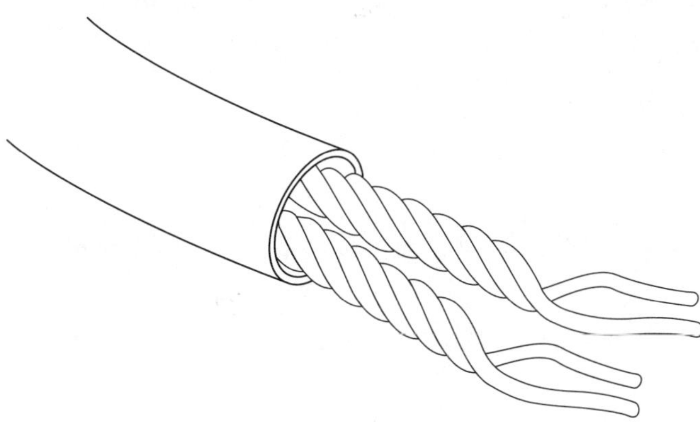

Figure 7.7 An unshielded twisted-pair cable.

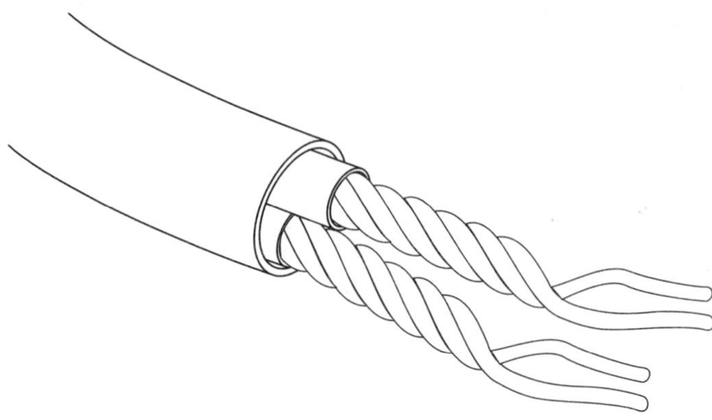

Figure 7.8 A shielded twisted-pair cable.

Coaxial Cable

Coaxial cable is fairly prevalent in your everyday life, as it is the standard medium used by cable TV networks and for antenna connections. Thin and thick, of course, refer to the diameter of the coaxial cable itself. Standard Ethernet cable (Thick Ethernet), rarely used for networking today, is as thick as your thumb. Thin Ethernet cable (sometimes called Thinnet or CheaperNet; RG-58) is slightly narrower than your little finger. The thick cable has a greater degree of noise immunity, is more difficult to damage, and requires a vampire tap (a connector with teeth that pierce the tough outer insulation) and a drop cable to connect to a workstation. Although thin coaxial cable carries the signal over shorter distances than the thick cable, it is lower in cost (hence the name CheaperNet) and uses a simple, bayonet-locking connector called a BNC (Bayonet-Neill-Concelman) connector to attach to workstations. Thin Ethernet was at one time the standard for Ethernet networking, but it has since been replaced by 10BaseT (unshielded twisted pair). Thinnet is wired directly to the back of each computer on the network and generally installs much more easily than Thicknet, but it is more prone to signal interference and physical connection problems.

Figure 7.9 shows an Ethernet BNC coaxial T-connector, and Figure 7.10 illustrates the design of coaxial cable.

Fiber-Optic Cable

Fiber-optic cable uses pulses of light rather than electrical signals to carry information. It is therefore completely resistant to the electromagnetic interference that limits the length of copper cables. Attenuation (the weakening of a signal as it traverses the cable) is also less of a problem, enabling fiber to send data over huge distances at high speeds. It is, however, very expensive and difficult to install and maintain. Splicing the cable, installing connectors, and using the few available diagnostic tools for finding cable faults are skills that very few people have.

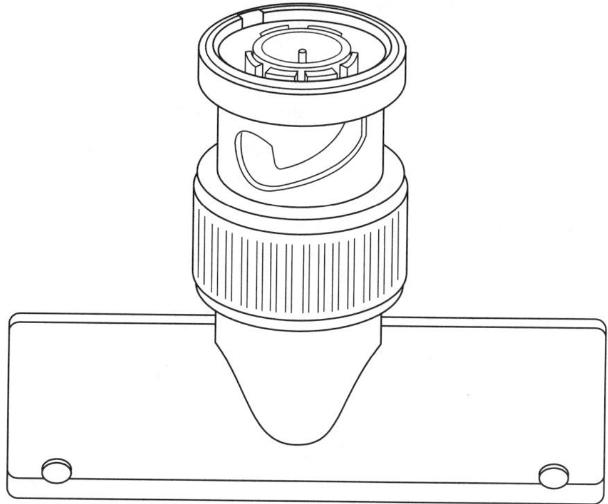

Figure 7.9 An Ethernet coaxial cable T-connector.

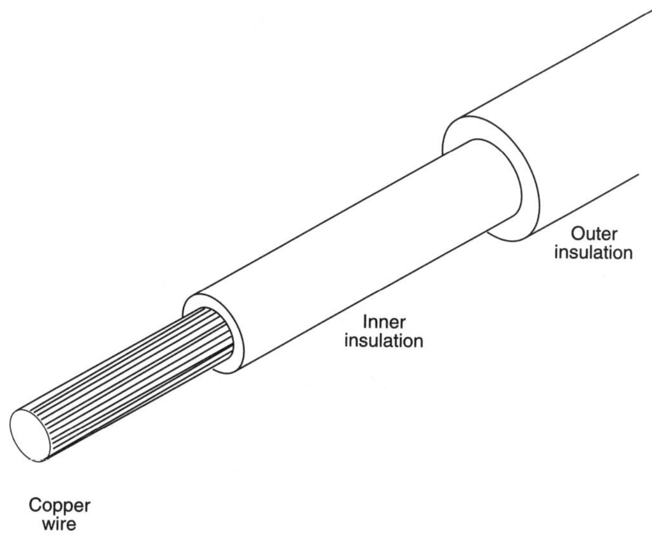

Figure 7.10 Coaxial cable.

In the Real World

Fiber-optic cable is often used to connect buildings in a campus network environment for two very important reasons. One is that fiber can travel over 2km, whereas copper-based technologies are significantly more restricted. The other reason is that because fiber does not use electrical signals, it eliminates the problems with differing ground sources.

Fiber-optic cable is simply designed but unforgiving of bad connections. It usually consists of a core of glass thread with a diameter measured in microns (millionths of a meter), surrounded by a solid glass cladding. This, in turn, is covered by a protective sheath. The first fiber-optic cables were made of glass, but plastic fibers also have been developed. The light source for fiber-optic cable is a light-emitting diode (LED); information usually is encoded by varying the intensity of the light. A detector at the other end of the cable converts the incoming signal back into electrical impulses. Two types of fiber-optic cable exist: single mode and multimode. Single mode has a smaller diameter, is more expensive, and can carry signals over a greater distance.

Figure 7.11 illustrates fiber-optic cables and their connectors. Multimode has a diameter five to ten times greater than single mode, making it easier to connect. This ease of use makes it the most commonly used fiber. However, multimode suffers from higher distortion and lower bandwidth.

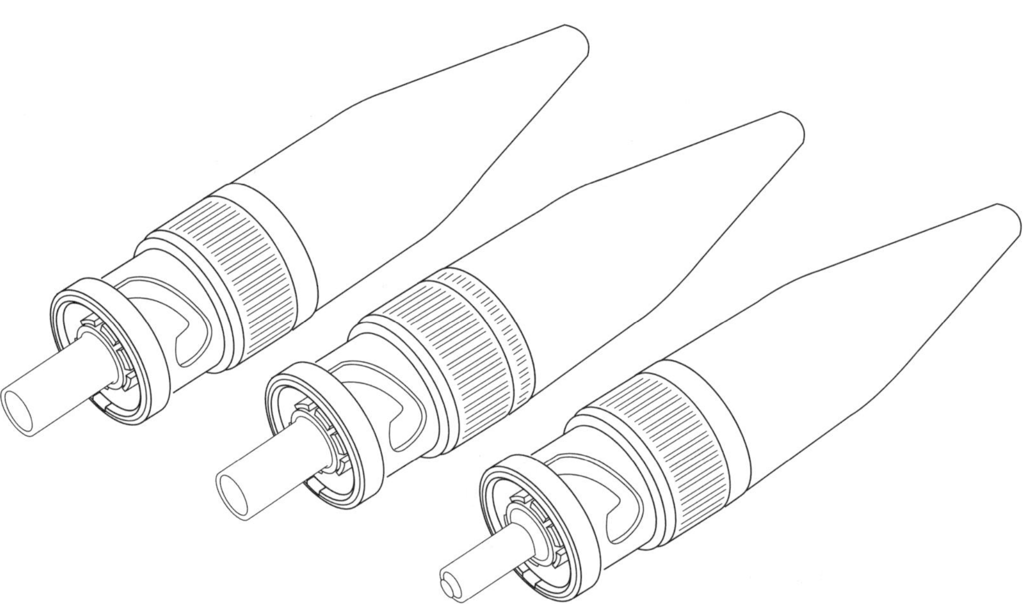

Figure 7.11 Fiber-optic cables use light to carry LAN messages. The ST connector is commonly used with fiber-optic cables.

Configuring NICs

With a network interface card, configuration is relatively simple after you have picked out the card that matches your network access method. Perform the same steps as necessary for installing any expansion card as indicated in Chapter 1, "Installation, Configuration, and Upgrading," assigning it DMA, I/O addresses, and IRQs as necessary.

Once this is complete, some additional configuration is necessary. This includes client, logical address, and protocol configuration as covered in Chapter 13, "Networks."

Network Repairs

Network repairs are best left to networking professionals. If you are interested in this, CompTIA has a new certification called Network+ that is designed to test your skills in the networking field. For more information, please review Que's *Upgrading and Repairing Networks*.

In general, working on a network requires the same logical steps that repairing a PC does. You must be careful, however, because a downed network affects many, many more people that a single downed computer.

Bandwidth

Particularly a problem with Ethernet networks, *bandwidth* is the size of the pipe through which you pass data. There will come a time when you cannot pass data due to the amount of data already occupying the bandwidth. When this happens, many things can resolve it. You can segment the network, increase your bandwidth, or decrease the traffic.

If nothing is done, packets can be lost in the traffic. When this happens, two computers sitting side by side might not be able to communicate reliably over the saturated network link. Most NICs have buffering and other recovery procedures. However, if the data sent across the link no longer exists on the source computer, as in the case of real-time data, and never reaches the destination, that information is irretrievably lost.

These are just some of the issues that affect network performance. All these issues and many more are covered in the *Upgrading and Repairing Networks* text and future Network+ Exam Guides by Que.

Review

Cram Session

- Networking is all about communications between computers. This communication enables users to primarily share files and print on shared devices.

- Clients are the creators of data and the recipients of network server services. Servers are the repository for client data and the provider of network services and security.

- RAID, Redundant Array of Independent Drives, provides fault tolerance to the network server. RAID 1, mirroring, and RAID 5, striping with parity, are the most common schemes.

- NICs provide the transceiving of digital signals to and from the physical wire and the expansion bus.

- Client/server provides a single, centralized point for security, data repository, and other network services. Although more expensive, this is also a far more robust and secure network model.

- Peer-to-peer creates more administrative overhead while providing more flexibility for the users. Peer-to-peer is often implemented because of the cost savings by eliminating the server.

- The seven-layered OSI model is a blueprint for network communications. The layers from bottom to top are physical, data link, network, transport, session, presentation, and application.

- Physical network topologies are a picture of the physical wiring layout. These include bus, ring, and star, or some combination of them.

- Logical topologies are the logical path that the data takes inside of the central hub or MSAU in a physical star.

- Access methods vary between Ethernet and Token Ring. Ethernet uses CSMA/CD, whereas Token Ring uses a token-passing method.

- Common network layer protocols include TCP/IP (typically used for the Internet and Windows NT), IPX/SPX (typically used only for Novell), and NetBEUI (typically used only for peer-to-peer workgroups), although NetBEUI is not a true networking protocol because it cannot be routed.

- The three common cabling types are coaxial (Thinnet and Thicknet), twisted pair (unshielded and shielded), and fiber optic (multimode and single mode).

- Network repair information can be found in both Scott Mueller's *Upgrading and Repairing PCs, Eleventh Edition* and in more depth in *Upgrading and Repairing Networks, Second Edition*.

Review Questions

1. Which network model provides the most security? Why?

2. What are the two primary services a network server provides?

3. What is disk duplexing?

4. What does RAID stand for?

5. What OSI layers are fixed in the NIC?

6. Which networking model is the least expensive?

7. IP is a sample protocol for which of the OSI layers?

8. Which topology does Ethernet use?

9. What is a logical topology?

10. What does CSMA/CD stand for? What network type uses it?

11. How far can a node be from an Ethernet hub using UTP cabling?

Review Answers

1. Client/Server provides more security because to access any resources, each user must use an individually assigned login ID and password. Peer-to-peer assigns a single password to a resource, and anyone with that password can access it.

2. File and print sharing are the most common. Other common services include email and Internet access.

3. Duplexing is a modification of RAID 1 that uses two adapter cards, one for each hard drive in the mirror set. This eliminates the possibility of one controller failing and taking down both hard disk drives. This is a high-availability enhancement to a fault tolerant solution.

4. Redundant Array of Inexpensive Disks was the original acronym definition, but with the costs of some hard drives in the $2,000–$3,000 range, the acronym was changed to Redundant Array of Independent Drives.

5. To purchase a NIC, you must know what type of cabling you have (Layer 1—Physical) and what type of access method you will use (Layer 2—Data Link).

6. Peer-to-peer networking is the least expensive due to the absence of an expensive network server. However, this is a shortsighted viewpoint because the long-term costs of supporting a peer-to-peer workgroup model far outweigh the initial cost of a file server.

7. Internet Protocol, the second part of TCP/IP, is a network layer protocol. It communicates your logical network address and is responsible for routing packets around you network.

8. Ethernet uses a physical bus or star with a hub, but even with a physical star topology, it always logically uses a bus topology inside the hub.

9. A logical topology is the path that the data takes in its transmission through the center of a star network.

10. Carrier Sense, Multiple Access, Collision Detection. Ethernet uses this as its DataLink-MAC sublayer access method.

11. UTP can stretch 328 feet or 100 meters before signal attenuation reaches a point that the data cannot be interpreted correctly.

Chapter 8

Customer Satisfaction

Communication

Customer satisfaction is an extremely important part of your everyday service career. It is also one of the most difficult subjects to test over. For this reason, CTIA has included customer service questions on the exam, *but they are not figured into your final score*. Regardless of your answers, this objective will not be applied to your score. Because of this, customer service basics will be covered in broad strokes.

That said, customer service is key to competing in today's ruthless business environment. This means that in the real world, customer service is a part of a much more complex system.

What is customer service or satisfaction? It is many different things to many different people, but in this section, I will try to put some definition to it.

Customer service is all about good people skills in terms of communication and the ability to avoid a conflict. It is one part common courtesy and one part common sense. As my father always told me, "common sense" isn't very common, and most people (myself included) have to work harder at putting someone else first than they do at learning the technical skills. Although you will need good technical skills to be able to solve the problem and satisfy the customer, the rest of this book is devoted to that aspect of your career, so I will bypass that topic here.

Customer service is interacting positively with the customer, through good listening skills and the ability to "read" the customer. You will also need to use these skills to determine on which level you will need to talk to the user.

Note

For supplemental reading, I highly recommend Dale Carnegie's *How to Win Friends and Influence People*. This book will take you beyond customer service to a whole new level of personal insight and people skills.

Listening

You have heard the old saying "God gave you two ears and one mouth so you listen twice as much as you talk." This is the truth in basic communication. However, communication is not just listening to the user and him listening to you. Communication is what happens when one person runs a thought through his own personal understanding (which might or might not be correct) and expresses it in his version of a common language and the other person interprets the spoken language through his own understanding (which might or might not be correct) and comes up with the same general thought. Because of this, just listening will not do: Active listening and real communication are necessary.

Active listening is the practice of using affirming and confirming questions about what the user is saying and interpreting the spoken words to find the real meaning. Active listening will put you into the customer's mindset because you are trying to interpret what he says into something you understand and can empathize with.

Verbal and Nonverbal Clues

Spoken language is not the only means of communication, certainly. In fact, some studies show that what people say only conveys 20 percent of their meaning. The other 80 percent comes from how they say it and other nonverbal clues.

First, be aware of the message you are sending to the user. Use positive body language and maintain eye contact when communicating. Then concern yourself with using the customer's body language to help interpret her meaning.

Jargon

After you understand what the customer is saying, it will be your turn to talk. Make sure that you understand at what technical level the user is and try to speak at that level. Try to avoid using technical jargon to puff up your own image because chances are that you will actually degrade your image because the customer cannot understand you.

When a person cannot understand another individual, that person is more likely to assume it is because the person talking is wrong, rather than assume that it is their own fault. Again, keep in mind that the basis for communication is a common language.

Above all else, do not talk down to the user. Avoid the use of patronizing tones and attitudes. Although it might seem like it at times, these are not your children; they are your customers.

Conflict Avoidance

Much of the previous topic on communication will help avoid conflicts. To prove the point, try to think of any war where the people on both sides spoke the same native language. To be sure, there are a few but certainly not very many.

If you are communicating with one another and a conflict still is inevitable, don't worry: It happens to the best of us. You work in an industry and occupation where people only call if something is broken and their stress levels are high.

Conflict Resolution and Professional Conduct

If you already have a rapport established with the customer, things will not often escalate to this level. If you do not, establish one immediately by "dressing for success" and maintaining a positive (but not fake!) mental attitude. When first impressions are out of the way, you can attempt to diffuse the situation.

First, become a Boy Scout. Their motto is to always "be prepared." Being prepared for the high emotional levels can help you maintain your own composure and being prepared for the situation technically can aid you in getting the job completed quickly (which is the ultimate tranquilizer).

Second, don't argue with him. Ever.

Third, be understanding and try to empathize with the customer (beware of patronizing tones and attitudes).

Fourth, set realistic expectations on how long it will take and what you might need to do or need the user to do.

And lastly, be appreciative of him trying to work with you and taking time out to answer your questions. You will be surprised what exuding confidence and kindness can do for a bad situation.

Review

Cram Session

Customer service is not scored on the exam. It is, however, tested and rated in everyday life. Here are a few things you should keep in mind:

- Customer service is all about good people skills in terms of communication and the ability to avoid a conflict. It is interacting positively with the customer through good listening skills and the ability to "read" the customer.

- Communication is what happens when one person runs a thought through his own personal understanding (which might or might not be correct) and expresses it in his version of a common language and the other person interprets the spoken language through his own understanding (which might or might not be correct) and comes up with the same general thought.

- Active listening is the practice of affirming and confirming using questions about what the user is saying and interpreting the spoken words to find the real meaning.

- Make sure that you understand at what technical level the user is and try to speak at that level. Try to avoid technical jargon.

- To resolve conflicts, you can establish a rapport, be prepared, don't argue, be understanding, set realistic expectations, and be appreciative.

Review Questions

1. What is customer satisfaction?

2. What is active listening?

3. Why should you avoid jargon?

4. What is the last thing that you should do after repairing the problem?

Review Answers

1. Customer satisfaction is many things. What is it to you? It is the soft skills necessary to satisfy the customer, even in the face of a problem.

2. Active listening is the practice of affirming and confirming using questions about what the user is saying and interpreting the spoken words to find the real meaning.

3. Because the use of jargon in some cases talks down to the user and seems to show off that you know something that he doesn't. Don't bother—he already knows that you know more than him about computers. He wouldn't call you if you didn't know something that he didn't.

4. "Thank you." Thank the user for answering your questions and also for his time spent answering those questions.

Part II

Computing and Technology Industry A+ Operating Systems Exam #220-102

Chapter 9

Function, Structure, Operation, and File Management

Brief Overview of Operating Systems and Major Components

This chapter focuses on the operating systems most commonly used on PCs today and their relationships to the PC hardware. The qualified A+ candidate will know about the entire system—hardware and software.

Most of the PCs in use today run a version of Windows, with Windows 9x being the most popular, followed by NT or older DOS/Windows 3.x versions. Windows NT is a more advanced alternative that is constantly growing in popularity, mostly in networked or corporate environments. Other non-Microsoft operating systems are available, such as Linux, which offer a great deal of power and flexibility. This chapter will examine the basic structure of the three operating systems covered by the A+ Operating Systems Exam; DOS, Windows 3.x, and Windows 95. I will cover their basic components, the system boot process, and their file structures.

Note

For additional information on operating systems and their basic concepts and components, please consult the eleventh edition of *Upgrading and Repairing PCs*, Chapter 26, "Operating System Software and Troubleshooting."

An operating system (OS) is made up of several components. It attaches to the BIOS so that part of the OS actually becomes an extension of the BIOS, providing more interrupts and services for other programs to use. The OS provides a communication buffer between the BIOS and software running at higher layers in the system hierarchy (such as applications). Because an OS provides the application programmer with interrupts and services she can use in addition to those provided by the BIOS, a lot of "reinventing the wheel" in programming routines is eliminated. For example, Windows provides a rich set of functions that can open, close, find, delete, create, rename files, and perform other file-handling tasks. When programmers want to include these functions in their programs, they can rely on Windows to do most of the work, rather than have to develop routines that perform these functions themselves.

DOS

DOS consists of two primary components: the input/output (I/O) system and the shell. The I/O system consists of the underlying programs that reside in memory while the system is running; these programs load when DOS first boots. The I/O system is stored in the `IO.SYS` and `MSDOS.SYS` (or `IBMBIO.COM` and `IBMDOS.COM`) files that are flagged with the hidden attribute on a bootable DOS disk. No matter what the exact names are, the function of these two files is basically the same for all versions of DOS.

The user interface program, or shell, is stored in the `COMMAND.COM` file, which also loads during a normal DOS boot sequence. The shell is the portion of DOS that the user employs to communicate with the system, providing the DOS prompt and internal commands such as `COPY` and `DIR`.

Windows 3.x

The 16-bit Windows platforms—Windows 3.1, Windows 3.11, and Windows for Workgroups—cannot strictly be called operating systems. They are instead graphical environments that operate on top of DOS, using much of the same technology described under the DOS sections in this chapter. Windows, however, takes advantage of protected-mode microprocessor capabilities and extended memory-addressing in ways that DOS cannot.

The environment that is commonly referred to as 16-bit Windows or Windows 3.x can actually be any one of three products. The differences between the versions are rather slight, and the three are largely indistinguishable in terms of the user interface. In general, when this chapter refers to Windows 3.x, any one of the three products can be inferred; however, there were a few differences.

Both Windows 3.1 and 3.11 contain no networking support whatsoever. At the time they were released, NetWare was the dominant networking platform in the business world and supplied the client software needed to connect a DOS or Windows system to NetWare servers. At the same time, however, Microsoft began to promote their own server-based networking environment, Windows NT, and a workgroup-based one called Windows for Workgroups in 1993.

Windows for Workgroups is an environment almost identical to Windows 3.1, except that it includes a Windows network client that enables the system to connect either to Windows NT servers or to other Windows for Workgroup systems on a peer-to-peer basis. Windows for Workgroups also supports external clients such as those for NetWare, making it possible to run a heterogeneous network containing both Microsoft and Novell network resources.

Windows 3.x also introduced a new feature to PCs commonly called multitasking, although it was really only time-slicing the processor and relied on the cooperation of the applications running to relinquish control of the processor. This form of multitasking is referred to as *cooperative multitasking*.

Internal and External DOS Commands

Internal commands are built in to COMMAND.COM and are available whenever the DOS prompt is present. They are generally the simpler, frequently used commands such as COPY, CLS, and DIR. Internal (or resident) commands execute rapidly because the instructions for them are already loaded into memory inside of COMMAND.COM; they are memory-resident. A partial list of internal DOS commands follows:

- CD   This command is used to change the directory in which you are located. CHDIR is the same command with a different syntax.
- CLS   This clears the screen. It is suspected that it used to stand for clear local screen.
- COPY   This is the most functional command of the group and one that is the closest to being a utility and requiring an external .COM file to load from.
- DEL   Erases the file specified after the prompt.
- DIR   Displays the files in the current directory.
- MD   Makes a subdirectory one level below the current directory that you are in.
- PATH   Creates a search path for the OS to stroll through when a command or file that is not in the current directory is executed.
- REN   Renames files specified after the command to a second name specified after the first.
- RD   Removes a subdirectory one level below the current directory when it is empty.
- TYPE   Displays the contents of any text file. Editing is a completely different task and cannot be done from the type command.

External commands are not resident in the computer's memory; the instructions to execute these commands must be located on a disk. Because the instructions are loaded into memory only for the execution of the command and then are overwritten in memory after they are used, they are often called transient commands. Most DOS commands are transient; otherwise, the memory requirements for DOS would be much larger than they are. External commands are used less frequently than resident commands and take longer to execute because their disk files must be found and loaded before they can run. DOS' external commands take the form of individual executable files, such as FORMAT.COM and XCOPY.COM, that are located in the DOS home directory (typically C:\DOS, or C:\WINDOWS\COMMAND in Windows 9x).

When you look up a command in a DOS manual, you generally find some indication of whether the command is internal or external. Most executable files operate like transient DOS commands. The instructions to execute the command must be located on a disk. The instructions are loaded into memory only for execution and are overwritten in memory after the program is no longer being used.

CONFIG.SYS

CONFIG.SYS is a configuration file that provides a modifiable text file for the user to add device drivers and memory managers. The CONFIG.SYS is loaded only once during startup; any changes to the file require a reboot to reload it. An example of a CONFIG.SYS file follows:

```
DEVICE=C:\DOS\HIMEM.SYS
DEVICE=C:\DOS\EMM386.EXEX /NOEMS
DOS=HIGH
DEVICEHIGH=C:\ANSI.SYS
FILES=30
BUFFERS=20
^Z
```

Many of these commands will be discussed in Chapter 10, "Memory Management."

AUTOEXEC.BAT

AUTOEXEC.BAT is another text-based configuration file. This file is loaded after the CONFIG.SYS and allows batch commands to be run during startup. As a batch file, any DOS command-line executable is able to be added to AUTOEXEC.BAT. Unlike CONFIG.SYS, AUTOEXEC.BAT can be loaded from the command prompt in the same way any other batch file can be run as if it were an executable. Commonly used to configure the user environment, a sample AUTOEXEC.BAT is listed as follows:

```
PROMPT $P $G
SET TEMP=C:\WINDOWS\TEMP
PATH=C:\;C:\DOS;C:\WINDOWS;C:\WP51
CHKDSK C:
CLS
DIR /W
^Z
```

All these commands are internal DOS commands and need no executable to run except CHKDSK.COM. This file is an external DOS command and requires the path statement so it knows where to look for the executable.

ANSI.SYS

ANSI.SYS loads a device driver to provide support for the ANSI BBS character set. This is most commonly used to configure your DOS environment for color and attach to one of the few bulletin board systems (BBS) that are left.

Windows 3.x

When starting, Windows loads the core components that provide the basic functions of the environment. These components are as follows:

WIN.COM

When you load Windows 3.1 by typing WIN at the DOS prompt, the system executes the WIN.COM program that examines the capabilities of the hardware in the system and loads Windows in the appropriate mode to support that hardware.

Windows required access to XMS (extended memory specification) memory, as provided by an extended Memory Manager such as HIMEM.SYS, that is loaded by the CONFIG.SYS file during the system boot sequence. To access XMS, WIN.COM shifts the processor from real mode to protected mode, something that DOS cannot do. In protected mode, a program can be allotted a specific area of memory that is protected from interference by other programs.

KRNL

This is `KRNL286.EXE` or `KRNL386.EXE`, depending on whether Windows is loading into standard mode or 386-enhanced mode, respectively. The kernel file is responsible for managing system resources such as memory and processor cycles, as well as for loading applications and scheduling system events.

Note

The 286 kernel is obsolete and no longer used in today's computers. The 1998 revisions of the A+ examination take this into account and will not include questions about `KRNL286.EXE`.

USER.EXE

`USER` is responsible for the manipulation of the windows, icons, and other elements that make up the Windows user interface. When you use the mouse or the keyboard to open, close, move, or resize a window, `USER.EXE` passes the input to the application associated with the window.

GDI.EXE

The graphical device interface is responsible for the generation of screen images and other graphics operations.

PROGMAN.EXE

This is the core navigation and desktop interface application for Windows 3.x systems. The Windows 9x equivalent is called the Explorer. It has its own configuration file called `PROGMAN.INI`, which provides settings on groups and windows sizes or colors.

SYSTEM.INI

The `SYSTEM.INI` contains the system information necessary for configuring the computer and its device drivers. This file, as with all these in a Windows 3.x driver, is extremely important and can be found in the Windows subdirectory.

WIN.INI

The `WIN.INI` contains the system configuration information necessary for users logging in to the computer. This file, as with all these in a Windows 3.x format, is extremely important and can be found in the Windows subdirectory.

Windows 95

Much of Windows 9x is based on the same concepts as DOS and Windows 3.1 but was developed to the next logical stage. Since the initial release of Windows 95, quite a few patches and feature updates have been released by Microsoft, as well as two major releases. The Windows 95 OEM

Service Release 2 (OSR2) and OSR 2.5 (also called Windows 95 versions B and C) were available only with the purchase of a new computer or hard drive from an authorized Microsoft OEM (original equipment manufacturer). OSR 2.5 adds integrated USB support to OSR2. USB support could be added to OSR2, and the result was often called OSR 2.1. Besides optional or integral USB support, the most important feature in these upgrades was a new file system called FAT32 that is designed to support with greater efficiency the larger hard disk drives now being put in PCs.

In the Real World

There were several released versions of Windows 95 as designated by its build number and version numbers found in the System Properties. The original release was version 4.00.950 and was called version A. Later, a service pack was released for Windows 95 version A only. OSR2 was released as Windows 95 B. An additional release of version B was released as OSR2.1 with an updated file set. OSR2.5 was released as version C and contained USB support as well as updated drivers and driver models.

IO.SYS and *MSDOS.SYS*

The same two system files, IO.SYS and MSDOS.SYS, still exist in Windows 9x, except that all the system-file code is now located in IO.SYS. The MSDOS.SYS file is now an ASCII text file that contains configuration settings for the system's boot behavior.

During the system startup process, the initial procedures are very similar to those of a DOS system, as outlined earlier in this chapter. In Windows 9x, however, IO.SYS automatically loads the equivalents of HIMEM.SYS, IFSHLP.SYS, and SETVER.EXE into memory.

The Registry

You can still use CONFIG.SYS and AUTOEXEC.BAT files to load real-mode device drivers and memory-resident programs, but the 32-bit device drivers designed specifically for use with Windows 9x, as well as most of its configuration settings, are loaded from entries in the Windows 9x Registry.

The Registry is a database of reference information, configuration settings, and application parameters that is continuously available to all Windows 9x modules. It replaces not only the functionality of the CONFIG.SYS and AUTOEXEC.BAT files, but the Windows 3.1 WIN.INI and SYSTEM.INI files as well.

The Registry takes the form of two disk files called SYSTEM.DAT and USER.DAT. SYSTEM.DAT contains machine-specific settings; USER.DAT contains the settings specific to the user who logs into the system. By maintaining multiple USER.DAT files, different people can share the same computer, with each user maintaining her own system configuration and desktop preferences. Registry files can be imported, exported, modified, backed up, and restored to maintain, modify, and protect the settings for a particular user or machine.

REGEDIT.EXE

One way in which this hierarchical Registry database can be modified is through the use of the REGEDIT command. As shown in Figure 9.1, REGEDIT opens the Registry database and gives you the option to modify, print, or export/save the Registry or any portion of it.

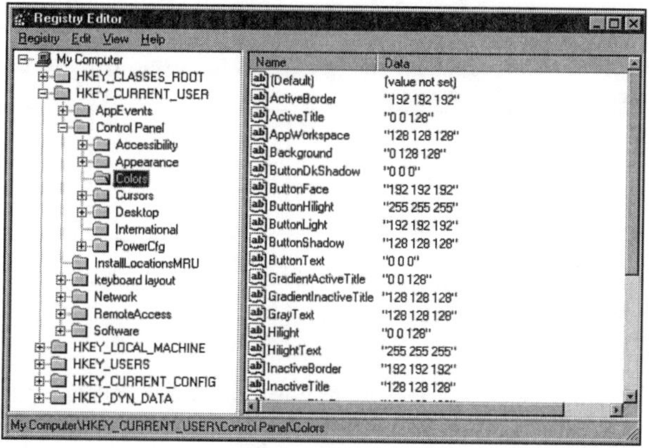

Figure 9.1 An example of the *REGEDIT* command in Windows 95.

Kernel, GDI, and USER

Much of the Windows 9x system architecture is similar to that of Windows 3.1, but it is rewritten in 32-bit code. The core elements of the operating system are still the kernel, the user, and the GDI, but all three now exist in both 32-bit and 16-bit versions. The 32-bit versions generally provide better performance and support for 32-bit applications, whereas the 16-bit versions are retained for backward compatibility.

Multitasking

Single-processor multitasking is the process of time-slicing the processor. This allows multiple programs to share the processor—slowing all programs somewhat, but giving the illusion of true multi-tasking. Each application has one or more "threads" or excecutable code that the CPU must process. To appear as multitasking, the CPU works on one thread for a certain number of cycles and then places it on hold while another thread is serviced. Both Windows 3.x and Windows 95 use time-slicing to simulate multitasking. Windows 3.x uses a process called cooperative multitasking, whereas Windows 9x uses a much more reliable process called preemptive multitasking.

Cooperative Multitasking

Cooperative multitasking can be described as three 16-bit programs sharing the processor like children sharing a toy, as in Figure 9.2. In this example, each of the applications know about the other applications because they use the same shared memory space and work together on sharing the CPU. This design allows some poorly written and badly behaving applications to use the CPU and never allow it to be given to another application. If the application in question fails, the CPU has no way of knowing which application it should service next, locking up the system.

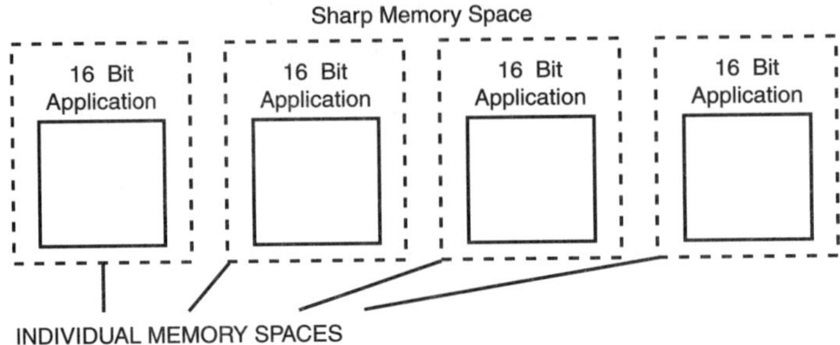

Figure 9.2 The CPU services each application in turn; applications have control over the length of the turns and must remain aware of all other applications.

Preemptive Multitasking

Preemptive multitasking is better described as three 32-bit programs, each loaded in their own memory space, that do not know about each other, as shown in Figure 9.3. Each application believes that it is the only application running on its system. Time-slicing is still used to access the CPU, but Windows 9x (or Windows NT) decides who gets processing time and when. Because Windows 9x maintains control of the sharing, when one program refuses to share and attempts to lock up the system, Windows 9x can pull the service from the errant software package and provide it to the next application.

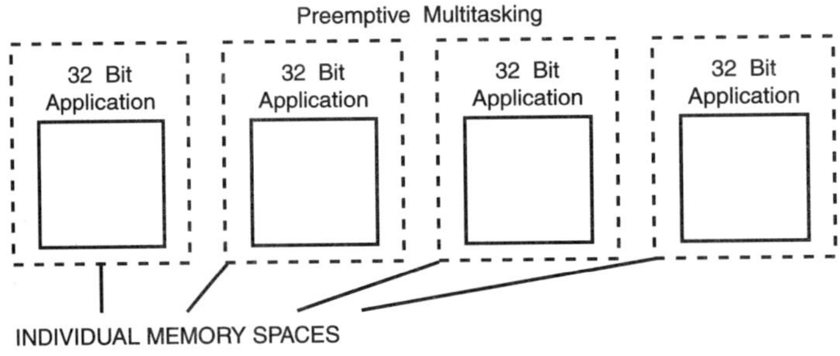

Figure 9.3 The CPU services each application in turn; the operating system has control over the length of turns, and 32-bit applications are unaware of each other.

Note

For more information on mutitasking and multithreading, please consult *Platinum Edition Using Microsoft Windows 95*, published by Que. If you are in the process of upgrading to the newest Windows flavor—Windows 2000—consider picking up a copy of *Special Edition Using Microsoft Windows 2000 Professional*, also published by Que.

File and Directory Structures

Physically, it is the hard disks and other media that provide the basic technology for storing data. Logically, however, it is the file system that provides the hierarchical structure of volumes and directories in which you store individual files and the organizational model that makes it possible for the system to locate data anywhere on a given disk or drive.

Directory Trees

This organizational model is best explained by using a file cabinet as an example:

- The entire cabinet is representative of the computer.
- Each drawer you are working with represents a different drive letter you are currently working with, say drive C in this case.
- Each hanging folder represents a subdirectory, or "folder" in Windows 9x lingo. (You can worry about nested folders, or folders within folders, at a later time.)
- Each manila file within the hanging folder is a "file."
- Obviously, each piece of paper in the file represents your data—for example, the four pages of one of your Microsoft Word documents.

To find your data, organize your hard disk like a well-ordered file cabinet. Using the commands to change directories, you enter **CD\My Documents** and follow this by listing the files in the subdirectory by using the DIR command and finally loading the data file that you were looking for called *Mydocument*.doc.

Attributes

File attributes are part of the properties of each file. In DOS, these attributes are visible when using the ATTRIB.EXE command. There are four separate types of attributes. These are Archive (a), Read Only (r), Hidden (h), and System (s). Each of these attributes specifies security at a fundamental level. In Windows 3.x, these can only be changed by selecting a file in FileManager, choosing Properties, and following the selections in the dialog box. Windows 95, as a more object-friendly environment, provides access to a similar property sheet by right-clicking the object in question and choosing properties as shown in the Figure 9.4.

Naming Conventions

As with file attributes, the true operating systems DOS and Win95 each have their own method to maintain their filenames. Files in either system must be unique to their subdirectory, that is, no two files in one subdirectory can have the same name. Because both systems use FAT partitions, both must use the FAT naming scheme limitations.

DOS uses the FAT naming standard of 8.3. That is, eight characters, a period, and three more characters. The characters cannot contain any of the following characters:

    < > = + / \ " , : ; ? *

The three characters at the end are used to identify the type of file it is and are associated with the applications in Windows so that double-clicking the file launches the associated application and opens the selected file within it.

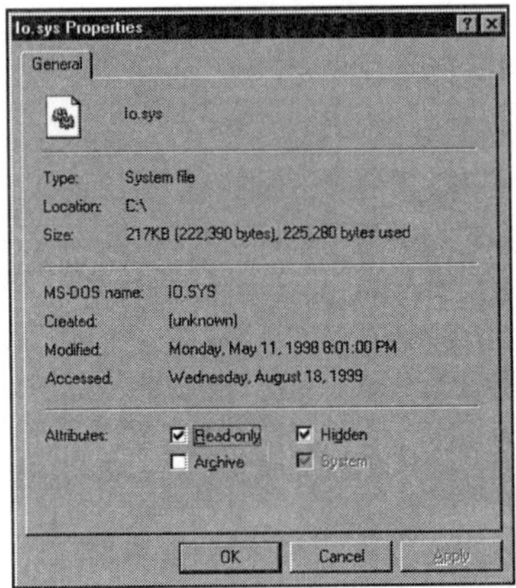

Figure 9.4 File attributes as displayed on the object's Properties dialog box.

Windows 3.x uses the same DOS standards because it is not a true operating system.

Windows 95 uses a similar standard as a basis, but it has developed a workaround to provide for 255-character filenames. Windows 95 creates at least two separate file entries in the file allocation table for each long filename. One entry provides backward compatibility for any 16-bit applications still in use on Windows 95, the other provides a location to store the long filename. The long filename is broken into separate 11-character pieces and is placed as separate entries within the FAT. Thus, a 250-character name would take 24 separate entries into the FAT—one for the backward-compatible filename in 8.3 format and the other 23 for saving the long filename.

Disk Preparation and Management

Low-Level Formatting

The low-level format is not used by most technicians today due to the overwhelming popularity of IDE hard disks. The hard disk manufacturer performs the low level format for you, essentially introducing the hard disk to its attached IDE controller. Some SCSI devices still require a low-level format, but do not perform this format on an IDE drive unless the drive has failed miserably.

Partitioning

Partitioning a hard disk is the act of defining areas of the disk for an operating system to use as a volume.

When you partition a disk, the partitioning software writes a master partition boot sector at the first sector on the hard disk. This sector contains data that describes the partitions by their starting and ending locations. The partition table also indicates to the ROM BIOS which of the partitions is bootable and, therefore, where to look for an operating system to load.

Multiple partitions are necessary because today's drives are far larger than had ever been planned for when the disk preparation tools were created. This means that you must find a way of dividing up a larger hard disk into separate logical drives if you use a drive larger than the partition size limitation.

The FDISK program is the accepted standard for partitioning hard disk drives for use with all versions of Windows 9x and DOS (see Figure 9.5). Partitioning prepares the boot sector of the disk in such a way that the FORMAT.COM program or the Windows GUI format utility can operate correctly.

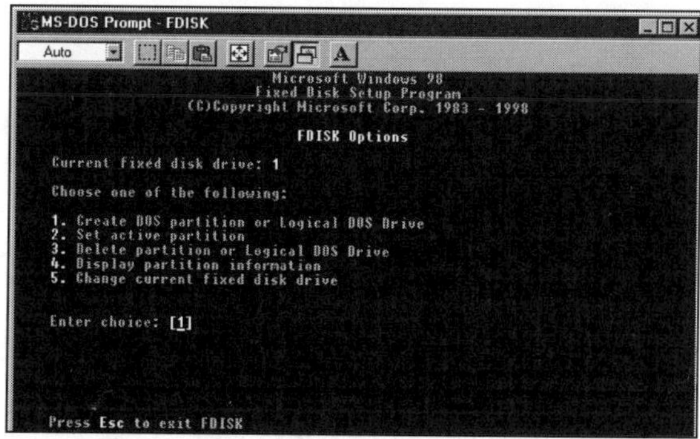

Figure 9.5 The FDISK main menu.

With any version of Windows 95 or 98, as with MS-DOS, FDISK enables you to create two different types of disk partitions: primary and extended. A primary partition can be bootable, but an extended partition cannot. If you have only a single hard disk in your system, at least part of the drive must be prepared as a primary partition if you want to start your computer from the hard disk (and who doesn't?). A primary partition equals a single drive letter (C: on one-drive systems), whereas an extended partition acts as a sort of logical container for additional drive letters (D: and beyond). A single extended partition can contain a single drive letter (also referred to as a *logical DOS drive*) or more than one logical DOS drive of different sizes.

Depending on the version of Windows in use (and with any version of MS-DOS), it might be necessary to subdivide a hard drive through the use of FDISK. The original release of Windows 95 and MS-DOS supports FAT16, which provides no more than 2GB per logical drive letter. Thus, a 10GB hard disk prepared with MS-DOS or the original Windows 95 must have a minimum of five drive letters and could have more.

FAT

File systems are normally an integrated part of an operating system (OS), and many of the newer operating systems provide support for several file systems from which you can choose.

The most commonly used file systems today are based on a file allocation table (FAT), which keeps track of the data stored in each cluster on a disk. There are several varieties of the FAT system, called FAT12, FAT16, and FAT32, all which are differentiated by the number of digits used in the allocation table numbers:

- **FAT12**   Used on all volumes less than 16MB (for example, floppies
- **FAT16**   Used on volumes from 16MB through 2GB
- **FAT32**   Optionally used on volumes from 512MB through 2TB

Tip

FAT12 is not covered explicitly on the A+ exams. For more information on this structure, please reference Scott Mueller's eleventh edition of *Upgrading and Repairing PCs*, Chapter 27, "File Systems and Data Recovery."

FAT32

The primary advantage of the FAT32 file system is its capability to support larger hard drives. The original FAT system used 16-bit numbers to track the clusters or allocation units on a disk. Although this was fine when FAT was developed, it is not so now. A 16-bit long number is limited to managing 65,536 clusters. This might seem like a lot, but with the ever increasing capacity of hard disks, it has proven to be quite a severe limitation.

Before FAT32, all you could do was split the drive into multiple partitions or increase the size of the clusters in a given partition. Increasing cluster size created a lot of wasted space when storing smaller files. FAT32 addresses both these problems by supporting drives and individual partitions of up to 2TB (2 terabytes, or 2,000GB) in size and with much smaller clusters. A 2GB FAT16 partition uses 32KB clusters, whereas the clusters on the same size FAT32 partition are only 4KB. With FAT32, you have a 32-bit number for tracking clusters, meaning that you can have over 4.2 billion clusters total! Because you can split a drive into more separately manageable pieces, the pieces can be smaller, and there is less wasted space.

FAT32 volumes are implemented by the `FDISK` program included with the OSR2x Windows 95 and Windows 98 releases. When you attempt to create a partition larger than 512MB, the program asks if you want to enable large disk support. Choosing Yes causes all partitions larger than 512MB to use the FAT32 file system.

Formatting

The final step in the installation of a hard disk drive is the high-level format. Like the partitioning process, the high-level format is specific to the file system you've chosen to use on the drive. On Windows 9x and DOS systems, the primary function of the high-level format is to create a FAT and a directory system on the disk so that the operating system can manage files. You must run `FDISK` before formatting a drive. Each drive letter created by `FDISK` must be formatted before it can be used for data storage.

Usually, you perform the high-level format with the FORMAT.COM program or the formatting utility in Windows 9x Explorer. FORMAT.COM uses the following syntax:

```
FORMAT C: /S /V
```

This command high-level formats drive C:, writes the hidden operating system files in the first part of the partition, and prompts for the entry of a volume label to be stored on the disk at the completion of the process. The FAT high-level format program performs the following functions and procedures:

1. Scans the disk (read only) for tracks and sectors marked as bad during the LLF, and notes these tracks as being unreadable.

2. Returns the drive heads to the first cylinder of the partition, and at that cylinder (Head 1, Sector 1) writes a DOS volume boot sector.

3. Writes a FAT at Head 1, Sector 2. Immediately after this FAT, it writes a second copy of the FAT. These FATs essentially are blank except for bad-cluster marks noting areas of the disk that were found to be unreadable during the marked-defect scan.

4. Writes a blank root directory.

5. If the /S parameter is specified, copies the system files, IO.SYS, MSDOS.SYS (or IBMBIO.COM and IBMDOS.COM, depending on which DOS you run) and COMMAND.COM to the disk (in that order).

6. If the /V parameter is specified, prompts the user for a volume label, which is written as the fourth file entry in the root directory.

Now, the operating system can use the disk for storing and retrieving files, and the disk is a bootable disk.

Review

Cram Session

Operating systems' function and structure vary from one OS to another. There are three typical operating systems that can be installed for today's style of computing: DOS, Windows 3.x, and Windows 95.

- DOS (16-bit) and Windows 95 (32-bit) are true operating systems. Windows 3.x is just a shell interface that runs on top of DOS.

- The major components of DOS are the IO.SYS, MSDOS.SYS, and COMMAND.COM. IO.SYS and MSDOS.SYS provide interfaces to BIOS through the IO subsystem. COMMAND.COM provides the user interface by interpreting the command line.

- Windows 3.x provides a graphical user interface, or GUI, that resides on top of DOS. Windows for Workgroups includes built-in network clients and peer-to-peer networking capabilities.

- Time-slicing is the method used on a single processor that is simulating multitasking. True multitasking requires more than one processor. Windows 3.x uses cooperative multitasking, whereas Windows 9x uses the more reliable preemptive multitasking.

- The command interpreter provides access to internal commands such as `CLS`, `DIR`, and `COPY`, among others. These commands have no executable, unlike external DOS commands such as `FDISK.COM` and `FORMAT.COM`.

- Windows 95 uses a hierarchical database of all hardware and software settings that is called the Registry. This database is made up of the two files, `USER.DAT` and `SYSTEM.DAT`, and is modified through all manner of GUI interfaces such as the control panels, but it can also be directly manipulated through the use of `REGEDIT.EXE`.

- `AUTOEXEC.BAT` and `CONFIG.SYS` can exist in all three operating systems covered in this chapter but are not required in any of them except Windows 3.x, which requires a minimum files and buffers setting, if nothing else.

- Windows 3.x uses the `SYSTEM.INI` and `WIN.INI` to configure itself for hardware and software settings respectively.

- Navigating the file structures in any OS requires the understanding of the file cabinet drawer model. Files go into subfolders, into folders, into partitions, and into computers. This model is more commonly known as the directory tree.

- File attributes indicate what the properties of a given file or folder are. There are four types of attributes: Read-only, Archive, and System, and Hidden. In Windows 3x and 9x, these are accessed from the properties sheet.

- DOS and Windows 3.x use the 8.3 naming convention developed with the FAT partition scheme. Windows 9x uses the same scheme but manages to manipulate it into maintaining filenames up to 255 characters long by using multiple FAT entries for a single file.

- Low-level formatting should not be done on any IDE disk drive, except as a last resort to return it to serviceablity. Low-level formatting on SCSI drives must be done using software specific to the host adapter.

- Partitioning is the capability of the `FDISK` utility to create separate logical drives in a single partition. Making the partition bootable is also the responsibility of `FDISK`.

- FAT-16 is the original file allocation table system for DOS and Windows 3.x. Fat32 was able to replace it as part of Windows 9x for little, if any, cost due to its backward compatibility.

- FAT-32 uses 32-bit numbers to identify clusters, resulting in a potential maximum size for a single partition of 2,048GB, or 2TB, in size.

Review Questions

1. What is an operating system? What are some examples of an operating system?

2. What are the main components of DOS? What do they do?

3. What are the configuration files used in Windows 3.x?

4. Compare and contrast internal and external DOS commands.

5. What are the two configuration files used in DOS?

6. What is the Registry? How is it modified?

7. What is multitasking? Multithreading?

8. Compare preemptive and cooperative multitasking.

9. Explain the file cabinet theory of file and directory structures.

10. How does Windows 95 support long filenames on a FAT system that was never designed for any naming convention other than 8.3?

11. How do you prepare a hard disk for use? Give three steps.

12. How is FAT32 different from FAT16? What is it used for?

Review Answers

1. An operating system is an extension of BIOS that provides the interface between the user, the application, and the hardware. True operating systems covered on the A+ examination include DOS and Windows 9x. Windows 3.x is often called an operating system, but it lacks true OS features. It is simply a graphical user interface that sits on top of DOS.

2. DOS has two components: the hardware interface and the user interface. The hardware interface consists of the two system files IO.SYS and MSDOS.SYS. The user interface is COMMAND.COM—the command interpreter.

3. SYSTEM.INI and WIN.INI. These files provide system configuration and graphical user interface configuration settings, respectively.

4. Internal commands are built in to COMMAND.COM and are available whenever the DOS prompt is present. External commands are not resident in the computer's memory; the instructions to execute these commands must be located on a disk.

5. CONFIG.SYS and AUTOEXEC.BAT. These files are used to configure hardware and device drivers or user and system environment settings, respectively.

6. The Registry is a hierarchical database made up of two files: SYSTEM.DAT and USER.DAT. Any Control Panel applet or configuration setting modifies the Registry, but it can also be modified directly with REGEDIT.EXE.

7. True multitasking allows the processor to operate on two different instructions simultaneously. Multitasking on a single processor machine is achieved using time-slicing, or interleaving multiple programs into the processor so quickly that it looks as though it is servicing them all simultaneously. Multithreading, made possible through the use of the Win32 API, allows applications to spawn multiple threads of execution that can be processed independently of each other.

8. Cooperative multitasking (Windows 3.x) means that the applications maintain control and are supposed to cooperate concerning which one gets the processors time and for how long. One bad program can spoil the whole bunch. Preemptive multitasking, on the other hand, allows the OS to decide which program gets to use the CPU and when. This keeps the problematic program infighting from occurring because the programs generally don't even know that the other applications exist.

9. Navigating the file structures in any OS requires the understanding of the file cabinet drawer model. Files go into subfolders, folders, partitions, and computers. This model is more commonly known as the directory tree.

10. By creating multiple entries in the FAT. The number of entries is the number of characters in the name divided by 11 and plus 1 for the 8.3 name.

11. Low-level format, partition, high-level format.

12. FAT32 provides more efficient use of cluster sizes by increasing the number of sectors that can be addressed to a 32-bit value rather than a 16-bit value—an increase in sectors by a factor of 256 times as great as before.

Chapter 10

Memory Management

Types of Memory

The original PC had a total of 1MB of addressable memory, and the top 384KB of that was reserved for use by the system. Placing this reserved space at the top (between 640KB and 1,024KB) instead of at the bottom (between 0KB and 640KB) led to what is often called the *conventional memory barrier*. The constant pressures on system and peripheral manufacturers to maintain compatibility by never breaking from the original memory scheme of the first PC has resulted in a system memory structure that is (to put it kindly) a mess. Almost two decades after the first PC was introduced, even the newest Pentium II–based systems are limited in many important ways by the memory map of the first PCs.

The system memory areas discussed in this chapter, including the 384KB at the top of the first megabyte, which is used for video, adapter BIOS, and motherboard BIOS, as well as the remaining extended memory, are all part of the PC hardware design. They exist whether you are running 16-bit or 32-bit software; however, the limitations on their use in 16-bit (real) mode are much more severe. Because most people run 32-bit operating systems such as Windows 9x, NT, Linux, and so on, these operating systems automatically manage the use of RAM, meaning that you don't have to interact with and manage this memory yourself as you often did with the 16-bit operating systems.

The following sections are intended to give you an understanding of the PC hardware memory layout, which is consistent no matter which operating system you use. The only thing that changes is how your operating system uses these areas and how they are managed by the OS.

Someone who wants to become knowledgeable about personal computers must at one time or another come to terms with the types of memory installed on his system—the small and large pieces of different kinds of memory, some accessible by software application programs and some not. The following sections detail the different kinds of memory installed on a modern PC. The kinds of memory covered in the following sections include the following:

- Conventional (base) memory
- Upper memory area (UMA)
- High memory area (HMA)
- Extended memory (XMS)
- Expanded memory (obsolete)

If the processor is running in real mode, only the first megabyte is accessible. If the processor is in protected mode, the full 16MB, 4,096MB, or 65,536MB are accessible depending on the maximum memory addressable by your processor. These values were covered in Chapter 4, "Motherboards/Processors/Memory." Each symbol is equal to 1KB of memory, and each line or segment is 64KB. Figure 10.1 shows a map of the first two megabytes of system memory.

For more information on processor modes and addressable memory limits, please reference *Upgrading and Repairing PCs*, Chapter 3, "Microprocessor Types and Specifications."

Conventional Memory

The original PC/XT-type system was designed to use 1MB of RAM. This 1MB of RAM is divided into several sections, some of which have special uses. DOS can read and write to the entire megabyte, but it can manage the loading of programs only in the portion of RAM space called conventional memory, which was 512KB at the time the first PC was introduced. The other 512KB was reserved for use by the system, including the motherboard and adapter boards plugged into the system slots.

After introducing the system, IBM decided that only 384KB was needed for these reserved uses, and the company began marketing PCs with 640KB of user memory. Therefore, 640KB became the standard for memory that can be used by DOS for running programs, and is often termed the 640KB memory barrier. The remaining memory after 640KB was reserved for use by the graphics boards, other adapters, and the motherboard ROM BIOS.

This barrier largely affects 16-bit software, such as DOS and Windows 3.1, and is much less of a factor with 32-bit software and operating systems, such as Windows 95/98, NT, and so on.

Upper Memory Area

The term *Upper Memory Area* (UMA) describes the reserved 384KB at the top of the first megabyte of system memory. This memory has the addresses from A0000 through FFFFF. The way the 384KB of upper memory is used breaks down as follows:

- The first 128KB after conventional memory is called video RAM. It is reserved for use by video adapters. When text and graphics are displayed onscreen, the data bits that make up those images reside in this space. Video RAM is allotted the address range from A0000–BFFFF.

```
    . = Program-accessible memory (standard RAM)
    G = Graphics Mode Video RAM
    M = Monochrome Text Mode Video RAM
    C = Color Text Mode Video RAM
    V = Video ROM BIOS (would be "a" in PS/2)
    a = Adapter board ROM and special-purpose RAM (free UMA space)
    r = Additional PS/2 Motherboard ROM BIOS (free UMA in non-PS/2 systems)
    R = Motherboard ROM BIOS
    b = IBM Cassette BASIC ROM (would be "R" in IBM compatibles)
    h = High Memory Area (HMA), if HIMEM.SYS is loaded.

Conventional (Base) Memory:

        : 0---1---2---3---4---5---6---7---8---9---A---B---C---D---E---F---
000000: ................................................................
010000: ................................................................
020000: ................................................................
030000: ................................................................
040000: ................................................................
050000: ................................................................
060000: ................................................................
070000: ................................................................
080000: ................................................................
090000: ................................................................

Upper Memory Area (UMA):

        : 0---1---2---3---4---5---6---7---8---9---A---B---C---D---E---F---
0A0000: GGGGGGGGGGGGGGGGGGGGGGGGGGGGGGGGGGGGGGGGGGGGGGGGGGGGGGGGGGGGGGGG
0B0000: MMMMMMMMMMMMMMMMMMMMMMMMMMMMMMMMCCCCCCCCCCCCCCCCCCCCCCCCCCCCCCCCC
        : 0---1---2---3---4---5---6---7---8---9---A---B---C---D---E---F---
0C0000: VVVVVVVVVVVVVVVVVVVVVVVVVVVVVVVVaaaaaaaaaaaaaaaaaaaaaaaaaaaaaaaa
0D0000: aaaaaaaaaaaaaaaaaaaaaaaaaaaaaaaaaaaaaaaaaaaaaaaaaaaaaaaaaaaaaaaa
        : 0---1---2---3---4---5---6---7---8---9---A---B---C---D---E---F---
0E0000: rrrrrrrrrrrrrrrrrrrrrrrrrrrrrrrrrrrrrrrrrrrrrrrrrrrrrrrrrrrrrrrr
0F0000: RRRRRRRRRRRRRRRRRRRRRRRRRbbbbbbbbbbbbbbbbbbbbbbbbbbbbbbbRRRRRRRR

Extended Memory:

        : 0---1---2---3---4---5---6---7---8---9---A---B---C---D---E---F---
100000: hhhhhhhhhhhhhhhhhhhhhhhhhhhhhhhhhhhhhhhhhhhhhhhhhhhhhhhhhhhhhhhh

Extended Memory Specification (XMS) Memory:

110000: ................................................................
120000: ................................................................
130000: ................................................................
140000: ................................................................
150000: ................................................................
160000: ................................................................
170000: ................................................................
180000: ................................................................
190000: ................................................................
1A0000: ................................................................
1B0000: ................................................................
1C0000: ................................................................
1D0000: ................................................................
1E0000: ................................................................
1F0000: ................................................................
```

Figure 10.1 The logical memory map of the first 2MB.

- The next 128KB is reserved for the adapter BIOS that resides in read-only memory chips on some adapter boards plugged in to the bus slots. Most VGA-compatible video adapters use the first 32KB of this area for their onboard BIOS. Any other adapters installed can use the rest. Many network adapters also use this area for special-purpose RAM called *Shared Memory*. Adapter ROM and special-purpose RAM is allotted the address range from C0000–DFFFF.

In the Real World

These addresses for adapter ROMs were actually pointers to the physical ROM chips on the adapter itself. This way, the CPU was able to access the ROM chip for all the various adapters within its own memory address ranges. (Think of these addresses as shortcuts to the actual program in the ROM chip.) To speed up the ROM programs, the ROM could be *shadowed*, or copied into free upper memory blocks, and the pointer to the original ROM chip would be changed to point to the new RAM location. This enabled the ROM program to run much more efficiently from the shadow location on the system/memory bus rather than the expansion bus. For more information on system buses, refer back to Chapter 4 or to Scott Mueller's *Upgrading and Repairing PCs, Eleventh Edition*, Chapter 4, "Motherboards and Buses."

- The last 128KB of memory is reserved for motherboard BIOS (the basic input/output system, which is stored in read-only RAM chips or ROM). The POST (Power-On Self Test) and bootstrap loader, which handles your system at boot-up until the operating system takes over, also reside in this space. Most systems use only the last 64KB (or less) of this space, leaving the first 64KB or more free for remapping with memory managers. Some systems also include the CMOS Setup program in this area. The motherboard BIOS is allotted the address range from E0000–FFFFF.

Although the top 384KB of the first megabyte was originally termed *reserved memory*, it is possible to use previously unused regions of this memory to load 16-bit device drivers (such as the ANSI.SYS screen driver that comes with DOS) and memory-resident programs (such as MOUSE.COM, the DOS mouse driver), which frees up the conventional memory they would otherwise require. This requires the help of an EMM386.EXE driver as is described in the "Expanded Memory" section and is not the original intention of the UMA. Note that this does not affect 32-bit device drivers such as those used with Windows 95/98, NT, and so forth, because they load into extended memory with no restrictions. The amount of free UMA space varies from system to system, depending mostly on the adapter cards installed on the system. For example, most video adapters, SCSI adapters, and some network adapters require some of this area for built-in ROMs or special-purpose RAM use. For information on a specific adapter, consult the manufacturer's documentation.

Extended Memory

As mentioned previously in this chapter, the memory map on a system based on the 286 or higher processor can extend beyond the 1MB boundary that exists when the processor is in real mode. On a 286 or 386SX system, the extended memory limit is 16MB; on a 386DX, 486, Pentium, Pentium MMX, or Pentium Pro system, the extended memory limit is 4GB (4,096MB). Systems based on the Pentium II and III processors have a limit of 64GB (65,536MB).

For a system to address memory beyond the first megabyte, the processor must be in protected mode. Only programs designed to run in protected mode can take advantage of extended memory. Rather than allow all programs to interface directly with the extended memory, Lotus, Intel, and Microsoft created the XMS (eXtended Memory Specification) and the XMS memory manager.

Extended memory can be made to conform to the XMS specification by installing a device driver in the CONFIG.SYS file. The most common XMS driver is HIMEM.SYS, which is included with Windows 3.x and later versions of DOS, starting with 4.0 and up. Windows 95/98 and NT automatically provide for XMS functions in DOS prompt sessions, and you can configure full-blown DOS-mode sessions to allow XMS functions as well.

HIMEM.SYS becomes an arbitrator of sorts that first grabs all the extended memory for itself and then doles it out to programs that know the XMS protocols. In this manner, several programs that use XMS memory can operate together under DOS on the same system, switching the processor into and out of protected mode to access the memory. XMS rules prevent one program from accessing memory that another has in use. Because Windows 3.x is a program manager that switches the system to and from protected mode in running several programs at once, it has been set up to require XMS memory to function. Windows 95 operates mostly in protected mode, but it still calls on real mode for access to many system components.

High Memory Area

The High Memory Area (HMA) is an area of memory 16 bytes short of 64KB in size, starting at the beginning of the first megabyte of extended memory. It can be used to load device drivers and memory-resident programs to free up conventional memory for use by real-mode programs. You can load only one device driver or memory-resident program into HMA at one time, no matter what its size. Originally, it could be any program, but Microsoft decided that DOS could get there first and built that capability into DOS 5 and newer versions.

The HMA area is vital to those who use DOS 5 or higher because these DOS versions can move their own kernel (about 45KB of program instructions) into this area. This is done simply by first loading an XMS driver (such as HIMEM.SYS) and adding the line DOS=HIGH to your CONFIG.SYS file. Taking advantage of this DOS capability frees another 45KB or so of conventional memory for use by real-mode programs by essentially moving 45KB of program code into the first segment of extended memory. Although this memory was supposed to be accessible in protected mode only, it turns out that a defect in the design of the original 286 accidentally allows access to most of the first segment of extended memory while still in real mode. Fortunately, this defect has been propagated forward to the more recent processors as a "feature." The HIMEM.SYS or an equivalent driver controls the use of the HMA.

Expanded Memory

Some older programs can use a type of memory called *Expanded Memory Specification* or *EMS memory*. Unlike conventional (the first megabyte) or extended (the second through sixteenth megabytes) memory, expanded memory is not directly addressable by the processor. Instead, it can be accessed only through a 64KB window and small 16KB pages established in the UMA. Expanded memory is a segment or bank-switching scheme in which a custom memory adapter has many 64KB segments onboard, combined with special switching and mapping hardware. The system uses a free segment in the UMA as the home address for the EMS board. After this 64KB is filled with data, the board rotates the filled segment out and a new, empty segment appears to take its place. In this fashion, you have a board that can keep on rotating in new segments to be filled with data. Because only one segment can be seen or operated on at one time, EMS is very inefficient for program code and is normally used only for data.

Figure 10.2 shows how expanded memory fits with conventional and extended memory.

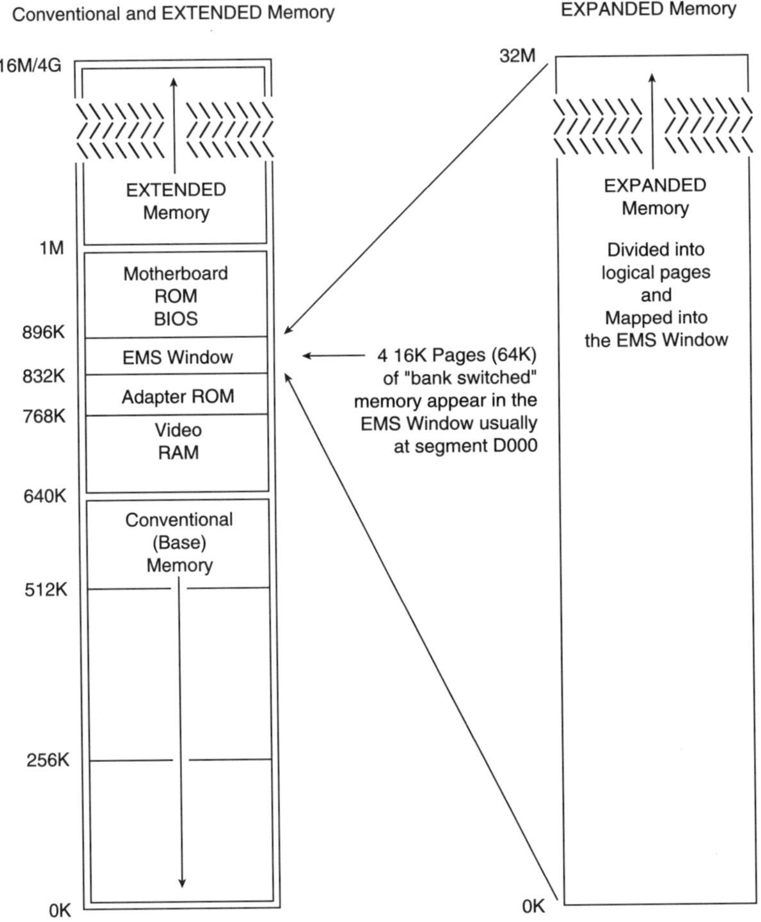

Figure 10.2 Conventional, extended, and expanded memory.

Intel originally created a custom memory board that had the necessary EMS bank-switching hardware. They called these boards Above Boards, and they were widely sold many years ago. EMS was designed with 8-bit systems in mind and was appropriate for them because they could not access extended memory. The 286 and newer systems, however, can have 15 or more megabytes of extended memory, which is much more efficient than the goofy (and slow) bank-switching EMS scheme. The Above Boards are no longer being manufactured, and EMS memory—as a concept and functionally—is obsolete.

If you have any antique software that still requires EMS memory, EMM386.EXE can convert extended memory to expanded memory by allocating some of the extended memory as the "above-board" memory pool. This memory can then be paged in and out of the UMA as with the old EMS boards. To get a clearer picture of this, imagine taking the entire column of expanded memory in Figure 10.2 and placing it in one large free block of extended memory above the HMA (above 1088KB).

EMM386.EXE also controls the upper memory area to allow some drivers to be loaded "high," as described in the previous section "Upper Memory Area." Today, EMM386.EXE is more likely to be used to map the free blocks in the UMA for the purpose of loading drivers, and not for EMS. The EMM386 driver is included with DOS versions 5 and higher as well as with Windows.

If you have several versions of EMM386.EXE on hand, as a rule always use the newest one. For more information on using EMM386.EXE, refer to Que's *Special Edition Using MS-DOS 6.2* or your DOS manual.

Virtual Memory

Much like the page swapping in the EMS specification, virtual memory is all about swapping pages into and out of memory. In this case, it is not existing extended memory that cannot be addressed, rather it is the opposite. The processor can now address far more memory than is commonly available in the system. To provide more memory for the processor to work with, portions of the physical extended memory are paged to the hard disk, where other pages are stored and swapped back as needed. Both Windows 3.x and 95 are very memory-intensive and allow multiple programs to "live" in RAM. Because the amount of RAM in the system cannot possible hold all the applications that run simultaneously, the active program is the page that is swapped into physical memory.

It is important to note that this process slows the efficiency of the system as compared to a system with the full amount of RAM being addressed. However, if the RAM is not available, paging it in and out of virtual memory is infinitely preferable to having no additional virtual RAM. In fact, in Windows 95 and 98, setting the computer to turn off virtual RAM can cause the system to slow down to a crawl and eventually crash. The only way to recover is to start up the computer in safe mode and change the setting back to Use Virtual Memory and to let Windows decide how much it needs and when.

Files, Buffers, and Stacks

These are operating system conventions for various aspects of memory that can be user-configured through the CONFIG.SYS file. These include files, buffers, and stacks.

Files indicate that the maximum number of files that the operating system can have open at any one time. Windows 3.x requires at least a setting of 30.

Buffers are allocations of memory blocks used for buffering disk access requests to and from the CPU. These act as a holding area for data that has just been or is about to be processed. You can think of these as the original L2 cache, albeit much slower because they are controlled by the operating system.

Stacks are special storage arrays used for placing data being processed on hold. When the CPU receives an interrupt request from a device, it is literally interrupted. The task being processed at that moment is placed on hold in one of the stacks. A typical stacks command is `Stacks=9, 256,` which creates nine individual arrays, each 256 bits long.

Memory Conflicts

As explained previously, C000 and D000 are reserved for use by adapter-board ROM and RAM. If two adapters have overlapping ROM or RAM addresses, usually neither board operates properly. Each board functions if you remove or disable the other one, but they do not work together.

With many adapter boards, you can change the actual memory locations to be used with jumpers, switches, or driver software, which might be necessary to allow two boards to coexist in one system. This type of conflict can cause problems for troubleshooters. You must read the documentation for each adapter to find out what memory addresses the adapter uses and how to change the addresses to allow coexistence with another adapter. Most of the time, you can work around these problems by reconfiguring the board or changing jumpers, switch settings, or software-driver parameters. This change enables the two boards to coexist and stay out of each other's way.

Additionally, you must ensure that adapter boards do not use the same IRQ (Interrupt Request Line), DMA (direct memory access) channel, or I/O port address. You can easily avoid adapter board memory, IRQ, DMA channel, and I/O port conflicts by creating a chart or template to mock up the system configuration by penciling on the template the resources already used by each installed adapter. You end up with a picture of the system resources and the relationship of each adapter to the others. This procedure helps you anticipate conflicts and ensures that you configure each adapter board correctly the first time. The template also becomes important documentation when you consider new adapter purchases. New adapters must be configurable to use the available resources in your system.

If your system has plug-and-play capabilities, and you use PnP adapters, it can resolve conflicts between the adapters by moving the memory usage on any conflict. Unfortunately, this routine is not intelligent and still requires human intervention—that is, manual specification of addresses to achieve the most optimum location for the adapter memory.

For more information on these system resources, see Chapter 1, "Installation, Configuration, and Upgrading" and *Upgrading and Repairing PCs, Eleventh Edition*, Chapter 4.

Upper Memory Usage

After you identify a conflict or potential conflict using one of the two methods discussed in the previous section, you might have to reconfigure one or more of your adapters to move the upper memory space used by a problem adapter or device driver that has been loaded into the UMA.

Most adapter boards make moving adapter memory a somewhat simple process, enabling you to change a few jumpers or switches to reconfigure the board. With plug-and-play cards, use the configuration program that comes with the board or the Windows Device Manager to make the changes. The following steps help you resolve most problems that arise from adapter boards conflicting with one another:

1. Determine the upper memory addresses currently used by your adapter boards and write them down.
2. Determine whether any of these addresses are overlapping, which results in a conflict.
3. Consult the documentation for your adapter boards to determine which boards can be reconfigured so that all adapters have access to unique memory addresses.
4. Configure the affected adapter boards so that no conflict in memory addresses occurs.

For example, if one adapter uses the upper memory range C8000–CBFFF and another adapter uses the range CA000–CCFFF, you have a potential address conflict. One of them must be changed. Note that plug-and-play cards enable these changes to be made directly from the Windows Device Manager.

Optimizing Upper Memory Use

On an ideal PC, adapter boards would always come configured so that the upper memory addresses they use would immediately follow the upper memory addresses used by the previous adapter, with no overlap that could cause conflicts. Such an upper memory arrangement would not only be "clean," but it would make it much easier to use available upper memory for loading device drivers and memory-resident programs. However, this is not the case. Adapter boards often leave gaps of unused memory between one another. This is, of course, preferable to an overlap, but still is not the best use of upper memory.

If you want to make the most of your upper memory, you might consider studying the documentation for each adapter board installed on your system to determine a way to compact the upper memory used by each of these devices. For example, the use of upper memory could be simpler if you configured your adapter boards so that the blocks of memory they use fit together like bricks in a wall, rather than like a slice of Swiss cheese, as is the case on most systems. The more you can reduce your free upper memory to as few contiguous chunks as possible, the more completely and efficiently you can take advantage of the UMA.

Memory optimization in this manner is not really necessary if you are running 32-bit drivers as you would in a normal Win95/98 or NT system. This is mostly useful for running older DOS applications, games, and so on.

MEMMAKER.EXE

On systems using an older 16-bit operating system, such as Windows 3.1 or DOS, memory-resident programs and device drivers can be moved into the UMA by using a memory manager such as the MEMMAKER utility or some other after-market utility. These memory management utilities examine the memory-resident programs and device drivers installed on your system, determine their memory needs, and then calculate the best way to move these drivers and programs into upper memory, thus freeing the conventional memory they used.

Using MEMMAKER is quite simple. Make a backup of your CONFIG.SYS and AUTOEXEC.BAT files so that you have usable copies if you need them to restore your system configuration; then run MEMMAKER from the DOS prompt. MEMMAKER installs required device drivers in your CONFIG.SYS file and then begins optimizing your memory configuration. It does a decent job of freeing up conventional memory; however, with careful fine-tuning, you can perform feats of memory management, using only the raw DOS HIMEM.SYS and EMM386.EXE drivers, that no automatic program can do.

Only driver programs that run in the processor's real mode must be loaded in the first megabyte of memory. Because real-mode drivers are made up of 16-bit real-mode program code, they cannot reside in extended memory because only the first megabyte (base memory) is accessible when in real mode. DOS and Windows 3.x are 16-bit programs and use drivers that run in real mode, hence the need for the base-memory optimization. With the number of drivers that people are using today, it can be difficult to fit them all in the available UMA space while leaving enough base memory free to run applications.

Things are different with the newer operating systems. Windows 95/98, for example, uses primarily 32-bit protected-mode drivers and program code, although there is still some 16-bit real-mode program code left. Windows NT and OS/2 are full 32-bit operating systems, and all their drivers and applications are made up of 32-bit protected-mode instruction code. If you are using all 32-bit programs, virtually no memory optimization is necessary in the first megabyte because 32-bit programs are free to run in extended memory.

SMARTDRV.EXE

Smartdrive is another memory-fooling application. This driver uses extended RAM to cache hard drive access in much the same way as the L1 and L2 cache work on data in RAM.

In fact, it is possible that one piece of data on a hard disk could be cached in RAM using SMARTDRV, loaded from SMARTDRV's RAM to main memory RAM when the data is loaded, which is in turn cached in L2 cache, which is in turn cached in L1 cache, which is in turn used in the processor!

All this caching is designed to keep hard drive access at a minimum and hard drive access while the CPU waits nonexistent.

Caching methods

There are several caching methods available to SMARTDRV as well as to other caching programs and utilities. These include two main categories: Write-back (or write-behind) and write-through caching.

Write-through caching is designed to provide the most secure caching available for the CPU when reading or writing data to the hard disk. Of course, SMARTDRV is intercepting calls to the hard disk and relaying them to the area in RAM designated by SMARTDRV as the hard disk cache. When the CPU calls for a read from the hard drive, the data is pulled from the cache and is delivered to the CPU at nanosecond speed. However, when data is written to the drive from the CPU, the CPU writes the data directly back onto the hard disk drive at millisecond speeds and copies it into the cache simultaneously at nanosecond speeds. As you would imagine, this makes the write process work even slightly slower than if SMARTDRV was not loaded at all.

Write-behind caching, on the other hand, provides the fastest caching available on both reads and writes. By allowing the CPU to read and write to the cache RAM area only, both read and writes are measured in nanoseconds. When the CPU has some idle time available, SMARTDRV will ask it to copy the new cached data back to the hard disk. The problem is that RAM loses all its data when the power is cut, whereas a hard disk does not. Unfortunately, because SMARTDRV has fooled the CPU into thinking that the data was written to a permanent location, all cached data is lost during a power failure. This usually does not, but can, result in a catastrophic loss—as I had when I forgot to save this document before the last power failure. Fortunately, Microsoft Word has a recovery option for this reason, whereas SMARTDRV does not.

Review

The following key points to remember and test questions will help you ready yourself for the A+ exams.

Cram Session

- Because of the original limitations of the first IBM PCs, and the industry's clamor for backward compatibility, today's memory usage is nothing short of a mess. In the newest Pentium III-based systems capable of addressing 64GB of RAM, the 640KB conventional barrier still exists.

- As system memory capacity grew, new memory conventions were created, always bending over backward to maintain compatibility. These memory types and their ranges included conventional, 0–640KB; Upper, 640KB–1,024KB; High, 1,024KB–1,088KB; Extended 1,024KB–64GB, and the now-obsolete page-swapping Expanded memory.

- Conventional memory is the memory location in which executable applications are loaded and run. This is also known as base memory.

- The UMA contains pointers to all ROM chips in the system, shadowed ROM code (if applicable), device drivers loaded high (if applicable), the page frame for expanded memory (if applicable), and the CMOS Setup program and ROM BIOS information.

- Extended memory is all memory above 1,024KB, including the HMA. Extended memory requires an extended memory manager such as HIMEM.SYS or Windows 95.

- The High Memory Area is the first 64KB above 1,024KB. Only one application can be loaded here at a time, most often DOS's kernel by the DOS=HIGH command in CONFIG.SYS.

- Expanded memory was the first method for expanding RAM outside the 1MB limitation on the PC. Special adapter cards were used to swap up to 32MB in 16KB pages to and from a 64KB-page frame in the UMA. Now obsolete, any application requiring expanded memory must use the Expanded memory emulator, EMM386.EXE. EMM386 uses 32MB of extended memory as the memory pool that used to be on a separate adapter card and swaps it in and out of the page frame in the same manner.

- EMM386 also enables drivers to be loaded into the free upper memory blocks in the UMA.

- Virtual memory uses hard disk drive space to simulate RAM much as EMM386 uses extended memory by swapping full portions of RAM into the page file on the hard disk for other data that thinks it is in RAM. Typically, only a few pieces of active programs are in RAM, whereas the remainder of open Windows applications are in the swap file.

- Memory conflicts can be resolved manually or by using a memory optimization application like MEMMAKER. MEMMAKER looks at all the drivers and adapter ROMs loaded in the UMA and HMA and shuffles them so that they all fit and leave the largest possible upper memory blocks available.

- SMARTDRV uses RAM to cache hard disk drive data for faster access by the processor. Write-behind cache is less secure but faster for writes than write-through cache, which takes the time to write the data to the hard drive instead of storing it in RAM.

Review Questions

1. What is the range of memory in kilobytes for conventional memory?

2. Why was expanded memory necessary? Why is it obsolete now?

3. What is the device driver required for XMS?

4. What is EMS and who created the specification for it?

5. What memory occupies the space between 640KB and 1,024KB?

6. What is required to load devices into the UMA?

7. What effect does turning off virtual RAM have on a Windows 95 computer?

8. What must you do to resolve a plug-and-play adapter's memory conflict if PnP fails to resolve it?

9. What does MEMMAKER do?

10. What is the benefit of write-behind caching? What is the detriment?

Review Answers

1. In the first PC, this was 0KB–512KB. Shortly thereafter, the industry standardized on the second revision, 0KB–640KB.

2. Expanded memory is RAM that is unaddressable by the CPU. It must be swapped into and out of a page frame window in the UMA. This enabled the CPU to work with far more memory than its 1MB limit. It became obsolete shortly after the introduction of the 286 with its addressable memory limit of 16MB.

3. XMS (eXtended Memory Specification) requires a memory manager called HIMEM.SYS in order for the system to use it.

4. EMS (Expanded Memory Specification) was developed by Lotus, Intel, and Microsoft. The LIM (for the founder's company names) specification defined how EMS worked.

5. The UMA (Upper Memory Area) resides in the 384KB of RAM below the 1MB mark.

6. EMM386.EXE must be loaded in the CONFIG.SYS, and the driver in question must be loaded into a free upper memory block with the CONFIG.SYS command DEVICEHIGH= DRIVERNAME.

7. Eliminating the page file slows the system down to a crawl. Often, this will cause a complete lockup of the system, and it will only start in safe mode until the setting has been changed back.

8. Manually change the memory configuration settings on the adapter, or if it has no jumpers, use the configuration software that came with the card.

9. MEMMAKER analyzes your current memory settings and load order for drivers and optimizes them to create the largest amount of free conventional and upper memory areas.

10. Write-behind caching has a performance increase during CPU data writes to the hard disk over write-through caching. The downfall is that the data in the cache is less secure in the face of a power failure.

Chapter 11

Operating Systems: Installation, Configuration, and Upgrading

Installing and Upgrading Operating Systems

This section discusses the steps necessary to prepare and load a computer with the operating system of your choice.

Preparing the System

As you learned in Chapter 9, "Function, Structure, Operation, and File Management," preparing the system is almost entirely composed of preparing the hard disk drive through low-level formatting (except on IDE drives), partitioning (using FAT or FAT32), and formatting the drive (using the correct operating system boot disk). In addition to the last format, an I/O subsystem must be installed. This is accomplished by using the SYS command from a command prompt or the /S option on the high-level format command.

Another large part of preparing the computer for the operating system involves system requirements. Each operating system, like each game or other program you buy at the store, has minimum operating requirements. The absolute minimum requirements for the three operating systems I will be discussing are compared in Table 11.1.

Table 11.1   Manufacturer's Minimum Requirements

Operating System	Processor	Memory	Hard Disk Available	Video
DOS	8088	384 Kilobytes	3–5 Megabytes	Any
Windows 3.x	80286 Real Mode/80386 Protected Mode	1 Megabyte	5–12 Megabytes	EGA
Windows 95	80386	4 Megabytes	40 Megabytes	VGA

In the Real World

It is very important to understand that minimum requirements are *not* real-world requirements. The requirements listed in the preceding table reflect the manufacturer's promise that these requirements will run the operating system, but it makes no promises that it will be able to run anything except the operating system. A better example of real-world requirements are listed for Windows 95 as follows:

- Processor: Pentium 133
- RAM: 32 Megabytes
- Hard Disk Space Available: 540 Megabytes
- Video: Super VGA

Running the Installation

After the system is prepared, the operating system can be installed. With the exception of DOS, which can boot itself entirely from one diskette, operating systems require a split process. Generally, a small pseudo-operating system is loaded first so that the main operating system choices can be chosen. Usually, this pseudo-operating system is a smaller version of the final system as is the case in Windows 95 and Windows NT.

DOS

The latest version of MS-DOS, which is the most popular variant, is version 6.22. Windows 95 and 98 have versions of DOS built in to them that are later revisions, but because these are truly encapsulated in the Windows operating system, they cannot rightly be called DOS versions.

Version 6.22 is installed by simply booting a freshly prepared machine with the first disk of the three 1.44MB floppy diskettes. After verifying that the system is properly prepped and creating a directory to put itself into, it expands all DOS files to the `C:\DOS` directory.

Windows 3.x

As mentioned before, Windows 3.x is a graphical shell that rides on top of DOS. Therefore, DOS must be installed first.

After following the preceding steps to install DOS, the Windows installation can begin. Windows 3.x can be installed from the original five (or six, seven, or eight, depending on which version you have) 3.5" floppy diskettes by running `SETUP.EXE`.

SETUP will guide you through selecting various options such as destination installation folder, desired Windows components, and hardware selection and verification for device drivers. After this is all complete, the SETUP program commences copying files and modifying DOS to suit its needs. After rebooting, AUTOEXEC.BAT calls Windows and its program manager for the first time.

Windows 95

As you learned in Chapter 9, much of Windows 95 is similar to DOS and Windows 3.x, with some very nice advancements. Not only are 32-bit OS code, kernel, and applications finally available, but so are plug-and-play configurations, as well as the elimination of the underlying DOS that was required in 3.x.

The hardware requirements were listed in the previous section, "Preparing the System." Aside from adhering to these specifications, the installation steps are as follows:

1. Boot from a Windows 95 Boot disk with the appropriate CD-ROM drivers loaded.
2. Switch to the CD-ROM drive. (The diskette and first release CD-ROM versions of Windows 95 required service packs and were known as version A and are no longer supported or recommended for use.)
3. Change directories to %Installation Path%\win95.
4. Run SETUP.EXE.
5. Provide all information requested in the installation menus. Windows will begin copying all necessary files to the hard disk.
6. After the system is rebooted, a few additional changes are made and all profile information is created.

Upgrading Windows 3.x to Windows 95 is fairly straightforward. If you choose this installation method, simply run the Windows 95 SETUP.EXE from the File menu, Run command in the Windows 3.x File Manager application. This method will migrate most applications and all user settings and configuration. There are a few things to keep in mind if you choose this:

- The amount of required free space is increased from 40MB to almost 80MB, preferably over 100MB to allow for virtual memory and other Windows options.
- Ensure that the system is functioning properly and that all applications other than the Program Manager are shut down.
- Make backup copies of all INI and GRP files. Pay close attention to the files that SYSEDIT.EXE loads (CONFIG.SYS, AUTOEXEC.BAT, SYSTEM.INI, WIN.INI, PROGMAN.INI, and PROTOCOL.INI).

In the Real World

Even though the upgrade process from Windows 3.x to Windows 95 is very well known and commonly used, this process leaves pieces of Windows 3.x code and configurations in the new operating system. I recommend that *any* operating system be installed to a clean, freshly formatted partition, or at the very least, a new subdirectory.

Loading Drivers

The device drivers required in each of the operating systems differ greatly. Typically, DOS uses real-mode, 16-bit device drivers loaded in `CONFIG.SYS`.

Windows 3.x uses protected-mode, 16-bit virtual device drivers and some real mode DOS-style drivers as well.

Windows 95 is the most complex operating system of these three and typically uses protected-mode, 32-bit, plug-and-play, virtual device drivers, but it can support some of the 16-bit version device drivers and real mode drivers as well.

Booting the OS

The term *boot* comes from the word bootstrap and describes the method by which the PC becomes operational. Just as you pull on a large boot by the small strap attached to the back, a PC loads a large operating system by first loading a small program that can then pull the operating system into memory. The chain of events begins with the application of power and finally results in a fully functional computer system with software loaded and running. Each event is triggered by the event before it and initiates the event after it.

Boot Sequences

Tracing the system boot process might help you find the location of a problem if you examine the error messages that the system displays when the problem occurs. If you see an error message that is displayed only by a particular program, you can be sure the program in question was at least loaded and partially running. Combine this information with the knowledge of the boot sequence, and you can at least tell how far along the system's startup procedure has progressed before the problem occurred. You usually want to look at whatever files or disk areas were being accessed during the failure in the boot process. Error messages displayed during the boot process and those displayed during normal system operation can be hard to decipher. However, the first step in decoding an error message is to know where the message came from—what program actually generated or displayed it. The following programs are capable of displaying error messages during the boot process:

- Motherboard ROM BIOS
- Adapter card ROM BIOS extensions
- Master partition boot sector
- DOS volume boot sector
- System files (`IO.SYS.`/`IBMBIO.COM` and `MSDOS.SYS`/`IBMDOS.COM`)
- 16-bit device drivers (loaded through `CONFIG.SYS`)
- Shell program (`COMMAND.COM` in DOS)
- Programs run by `AUTOEXEC.BAT`

If Windows 3.x or 9x are installed, the following pieces are also part of the boot process following the previous steps:

- Windows (`WIN.COM`)
- Windows 9x Registry, 32-bit devices and drivers
- Windows 9x Startup group

The following sections examines the system startup sequence and provides a detailed account this process.

DOS

The following steps occur in a typical DOS startup after turning on system power:

1. The microprocessor begins executing the ROM BIOS code, starting at memory address FFFF:0000.

2. The ROM BIOS performs a Power-On Self-Test of the central hardware to verify basic system functionality. Any errors that occur are indicated by POST audio beep codes or video error codes as discussed in Chapter 2, "Diagnosing and Troubleshooting," and Scott Mueller's *Upgrading and Repairing PCs*, Chapter 5, "Motherboard BIOS."

3. The ROM BIOS searches for a partition or volume boot record at cylinder 0, head 0, sector 1 (the very first sector) on the default boot drive.

4. The MBR searches its partition table for a boot indicator byte marking an active partition and then loads and tests it.

5. The partition boot record is executed as a program. This program checks the root directory to ensure that the first two files are `IO.SYS` (or `IBMBIO.COM`) and `MSDOS.SYS` (or `IBMDOS.COM`). If these files are present, they are loaded.

6. `IO.SYS` runs first and loads `CONFIG.SYS` and all its device drivers.

7. `MSDOS.SYS` loads `COMMAND.COM` and `AUTOEXEC.BAT`, if present. If `AUTOEXEC.BAT` is not present, `COMMAND.COM` executes the internal `DATE` and `TIME` commands, displays a copyright message, and displays the DOS prompt.

Windows 3.x

Because Windows 3.x loads on top of DOS as a graphical shell, the following steps occur in a typical startup *after* all the steps for DOS occur and the `AUTOEXEC.BAT` loads:

1. By typing `WIN` at the DOS prompt or including it as the last line of the `AUTOEXEC.BAT`, the system executes the `WIN.COM` program that examines the capabilities of the hardware in the system and loads Windows in the appropriate mode to support that hardware.

2. `WIN.COM` executes a file called `WIN386.EXE` that in turn loads the drivers specified in the `[386enh]` section of the `SYSTEM.INI` file.

3. `WIN.COM` continues by loading `KRNL386.EXE`, `USER.EXE`, and `GDI.EXE`.

4. `USER.EXE` and `GDI.EXE` in turn load `WIN.INI` for user settings and `PROGMAN.EXE` and `PROGMAN.INI` to start the Windows interface.

Windows 95

During the system startup process, the initial procedures are very similar to those of a DOS system, as outlined earlier in this chapter through step 5. In Windows 9x, however, IO.SYS automatically loads the equivalents of HIMEM.SYS, IFSHLP.SYS, and SETVER.EXE into memory. You can still use CONFIG.SYS and AUTOEXEC.BAT files to load real-mode device drivers and memory-resident programs, but the 32-bit device drivers designed specifically for use with Windows 9x, as well as most of its configuration settings, are loaded from entries in the Windows 9x Registry. This process is outlined as follows:

1. IO.SYS loads the boot initialization text from the hidden ASCII text file calls MSDOS.SYS. Please note that this MSDOS.SYS is quite different from the DOS version of the same.

2. A Loading Windows 95... message is displayed to provide a pause for the user to hit a boot option key. These keys are discussed in the next section.

3. After loading the title screen, the Registry is loaded. Specifically, the SYSTEM.DAT portion of the Registry is loaded. After loading SYSTEM.DAT, a backup copy is made called SYSTEM.DA0.

4. CONFIG.SYS and AUTOEXEC.BAT are loaded for backward compatibility with 16-bit device drivers.

5. WIN.COM is loaded and calls all 32-bit virtual device drivers necessary like the virtual memory manager and the kernel.

6. The commands in the RUN portions of the Registry are launched.

7. USER.DAT is loaded and backed up in the same way that SYSTEM.DAT was.

8. All shortcuts and applications in the Startup group are executed.

Further information on Boot sequences can be found in *Upgrading and Repairing PCs, Eleventh Edition*, Chapter 26, "Operating Systems."

Boot Options

There are several tricks to use when starting an operating system. All of these steps must be performed during the Starting MS DOS... or Starting Windows 95... messages.

In DOS and Windows 95, Microsoft has provided the capability to bypass loading the operating system and startup files, dropping straight to a plain DOS prompt. On DOS systems, this function key is F5.

Another option for both operating systems is to step through the CONFIG.SYS and AUTOEXEC.BAT startup files. In this manner, you can selectively load lines from these files to eliminate potential conflicts without editing and saving the files differently each time. This option is invoked by pressing the F8 key during the Starting MS-DOS... message.

On Windows 9x, pressing F8 gives you some other options specific to Windows 95 and 98. These are displayed in Figure 11.1.

```
        Microsoft Windows 95 Startup Menu
        ================================
        1.   Normal
        2.   Logged (\BOOTLOG.TXT)
        3.   Safe  mode with Network Support
        4.   Safe Mode with Network Support
        5.   Step by Step Confirmation
        6.   Command Prompt Only
        7.   Safe Mode Command Prompt
        8.   previous Version of MS-DOS

        Enter a Choice: ___

F5=Safe mode Shift+F5=Command prompt
Shift+F8=Step-by-step confirmatoin [N]
```

Figure 11.1   Windows 95 Startup menu options.

Windows 95's safe mode enables you to start the computer with a the most basic configuration available. In many cases, this mode is the only option when a user mistakenly creates a conflict or causes some other OS failure. The stored configurations are not used to boot the system in safe mode, but they *are* available to modify for the next normal startup.

The Logged option also provides an insight into the troubled operating system. By using this option, a file called `BOOTLOG.TXT` is created that contains a map of each subcomponent that was successfully loaded during startup. If the startup fails, the last component to successfully load is listed in the `BOOTLOG.TXT`.

Other options include Command Prompt Only and Step-by-Step Configuration. These menu options are as described under the F5 and F8 keys previously mentioned.

Emergency Boot Disks

Boot disks are very useful in the undesirable event of a hard disk failure or operating system failure. Because you must be prepared for these failures before they happen, most people are caught unawares and might lose a great deal of time or even data. *Always make an emergency boot disk!*

To create an emergency boot diskette for DOS, simply format a blank floppy using the `FORMAT A: /S` command to include the system files, and copy these additional files to it for future use:

- `CONFIG.SYS`
- `AUTOEXEC.BAT`
- `FDISK.EXE`
- `FORMAT.COM`
- `SYS.COM`
- `EDIT.COM`
- `CHKDSK.EXE` or `SCANDISK.EXE`
- `DEBUG.EXE`
- `MSD.EXE`
- `MEM.EXE`

For Windows 3.x, add all INI and GRP files, but especially these:

- `WIN.INI`
- `SYSTEM.INI`
- `PROGMAN.INI`
- `PROTOCOL.INI`

For Windows 95, the process is made somewhat easier. Microsoft included an applet that creates the diskette for you and includes most of the preceding programs as well as the `REGEDIT.EXE` command. It is recommended that you also create a backup copy of `AUTOEXEC.BAT`, `CONFIG.SYS`, `WIN.INI`, `SYSTEM.INI`, `SYSTEM.DAT`, and `USER.DAT` and place these on your emergency startup diskette or another backup disk as well.

To create this emergency startup disk, simply go to the Control Panels, Add/Remove Programs applet, and select the third tab titled Startup Disk as pictured in Figure 11.2. Have a blank diskette ready and click the Create Disk button.

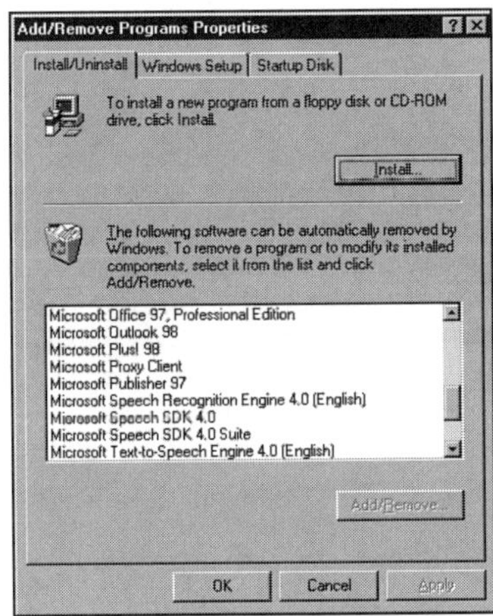

Figure 11.2   Creating an emergency startup diskette.

Configuring Device Drivers in Windows

Configuring device drivers in Windows 95 is an essential skill for passing the A+ Operating Systems Exam. This section will discuss both the manual and plug-and-play methods.

The Old-Fashioned Way

To manually configure a device in Windows 95, use the Add New Hardware applet in the Windows 95 Control Panel. For comparison, Windows 3.x also used the Control Panel extensively, but it did not automate nearly as much as Windows 95. DOS however, uses real-mode device drivers loaded through the `CONFIG.SYS` file.

Tip

Avoid real-mode device drivers loaded in **CONFIG.SYS** for Windows 95. Although this feature is provided for backward compatibility, these real-mode drivers degrade Windows' performance heavily.

When the applet, or wizard, has been started, you will be given several screens that inform you about the system and some questions regarding your hardware. The wizard will attempt to locate your hardware by searching all available ports for new devices. If a device is found, Windows will load the driver from its own sources, or if the driver was not available at your Windows version's release date, it will prompt you for the device driver. After this is specified, if the wizard can determine what resource settings the new device requires, these will be configured. (Although not considered plug-and-play, this method is extremely automated and much closer to plug-and-play than manual configuration.) If at any point along the process Windows cannot determine the proper configuration, the user will be prompted to provide the correct information.

This process can be modified at a later date using the Windows 95 Device Manager. Windows 9x's Device Manager is a far more useful configuration tool than any operating system has had before. When you select the Device Manager page from the System Control Panel, you see an expandable list of the types of devices found in the system (see Figure 11.3). Expanding each type displays the actual hardware installed in the computer. Each entry has a Properties dialog box that enables you to configure the device, view the hardware resources that it is using, and update its driver.

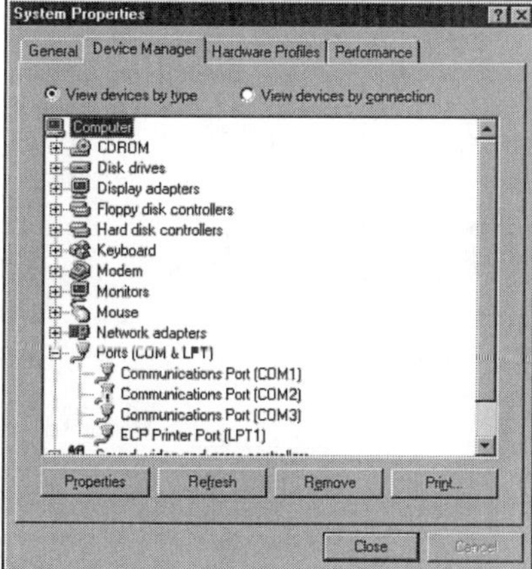

Figure 11.3   The Windows 9x Device Manager.

By clicking the View Devices by Connection option button, the display is sorted by the computer's various ports and interfaces.

Plug and Play

Perhaps the largest improvement in Windows 9x from a hardware standpoint is the introduction of support for Plug and Play (PnP). Plug and Play is a standard that enables the operating system to automatically negotiate for the system resources needed by a particular device and configure the hardware to use them, thereby eliminating many, if not all, of the manual steps described previously. Most of the PC peripherals manufactured today support PnP, making the installation of new hardware as simple as inserting an expansion card into a slot or plugging it into a port.

When this inventory of the system hardware is completed, the Configuration Manager loads a driver for each device in the hardware tree. The Windows 9x drivers are all 32-bit, protected-mode modules, permitting them to be loaded into system memory much more easily than their real-mode counterparts from Windows 3.1, which require conventional memory (memory below 640K) to load.

With the drivers loaded, the Configuration Manager then uses resource arbitrators to negotiate the hardware resources that are to be allocated to each device. These arbitrators reconcile any resource conflicts that might exist between devices and determine the best combination of operational settings for the hardware.

Installing and Configuring Printers

As with many peripherals, printers are highly reliant on a driver installed on the PC. The printer driver provides the software interface between the printer and your application or operating system. The primary function of the driver is to inform the PC about the capabilities of the printer, such as the PDLs it uses, the types of paper it handles, and the fonts installed. When you print a document in an application, the print options you select are supplied by the printer driver, although they appear to be part of the application.

Printer Drivers

In DOS, printer drivers are integrated into individual applications. A few major software packages provide drivers for a full range of printers, but most include only a few generic drivers. At times like these, the best thing to do is to select a driver that supports the same PDL revision as your printer. For example, a LaserJet III driver uses PCL 5, which will support all the LaserJet III and 4 models, even if it does not use all the printer's features. It is quite possible that a DOS application that doesn't have a driver for your exact printer model might not be able to take advantage of all your printer's capabilities.

In all versions of Windows, you install the printer driver as part of the operating system, not in the individual applications. The Windows product includes drivers for a wide range of printers, and individual drivers are almost always available from the printer manufacturer's online services. Note that the drivers included with Windows are usually developed by the manufacturer of the printer, not by Microsoft, and are included in the Windows package for the sake of convenience.

Although the printer manufacturer develops the drivers for any printer model used with Windows 9x, there might be significant differences between the printer drivers included with Windows 9x and those shipped with the printer or available online. Drivers included with Windows normally provide access to a printer's basic features, whereas the enhanced drivers provided by the manufacturer on CD-ROMs included with the printer or via download might include deluxe color-matching, enhanced spooling, improved dialogs, or other benefits. Be sure to try both types of drivers to see which one works best for you.

Installing Printers in Windows

All the Windows operating systems have a Printers Control Panel that is the central location for all printer driver configuration activities. You can install drivers for as many printers as you need, including multiple drivers for the same printer, drivers for network printers, and even drivers for printers that do not exist.

Windows 9x and Windows NT include a wizard for installing printer drivers that walks you through the entire process. The procedure in Windows 3.1 is fundamentally the same, although the screens are somewhat different in appearance. When you click the Add Printer icon in the Printers Control Panel, the wizard first asks whether you are installing a driver for a printer connected to the local machine or to the network. Then, you are presented with a dialog box as in Figure 11.4 in which you can select the manufacturer of your printer and the specific model.

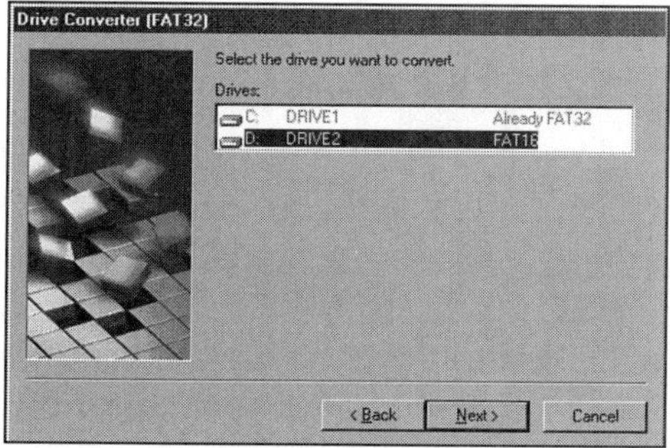

Figure 11.4   The Printer Selector screen from the Windows 95 Add Printer Wizard.

The operating systems include a comprehensive selection of printer drivers and a Have Disk button that enables you to install drivers that you have obtained from the manufacturer of your printer or from other sources.

After selecting the printer type, you specify the port to which the printer is attached. The Available Ports option (see Figure 11.5) lists all the COM and LPT ports installed on your system and the FILE entry for saving print jobs to disk files.

The wizard also asks whether you intend to use the printer with DOS applications. If you answer yes, the wizard configures your system to intercept all output sent to the default LPT1 printer port and redirect it to the Windows printer driver (see Figure 11.6). This is needed when you are configuring a network printer because certain 16-bit DOS or Windows applications might not have support for long filenames or network printing.

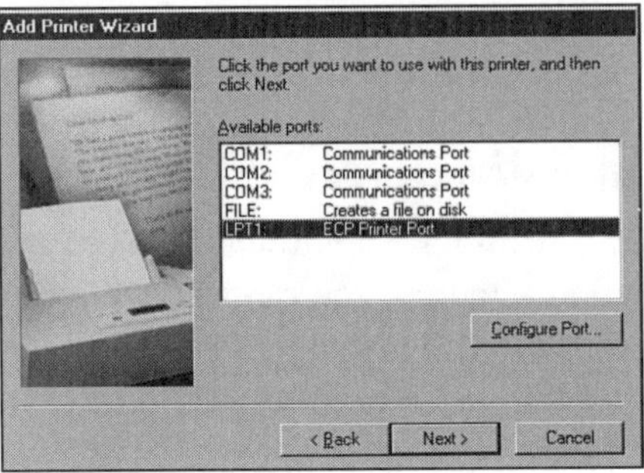

Figure 11.5 The Add Printer Wizard's Available Ports dialog box.

After you specify whether you want to make the new printer your default Windows printer, the wizard creates a new icon in the Printers control panel. This makes the printer available to all your Windows applications and provides access to the printer's Properties dialog box, which you can use to configure the driver and manipulate your print jobs.

Configuring Printers in Windows

Additional configuration of various printers and printer drivers vary greatly among different manufacturers and even different models of the same manufacturer.

The Properties dialog box for a particular printer typically contains numerous settings apart from those for selecting the port that the printer is to use. The features and the appearance of this dialog box are dependent on the printer driver you have installed; however, in most cases, it enables you to select items such as the size and orientation of the paper that the printer will use, the tray that the paper is loaded in, and the number of copies of each page to print.

Many printer drivers provide settings that enable you to adjust the way that the driver handles print elements such as fonts and graphics. A typical Graphics page such as that for the HP LaserJet 5P driver might contain the following parameters:

- **Resolution**   Enables you to select from the print resolutions supported by the printer. A lower resolution provides faster printing and uses less printer memory. This setting doesn't affect text quality on most recent laser printers; the text will still print at the printer's maximum resolution (600 dpi on this model).

- **Dithering**   Enables you to select various types of dithering for the shades of gray or colors produced by your printer. The various dithering types provide different results depending on the nature of the image and the resolution at which you are running the printer.

- **Intensity**   Enables you to control how dark the graphic images in your documents should be printed.

- **Graphics mode**   Enables you to select whether the driver should send graphic images to the printer as vectors to be rasterized by the printer or the driver should rasterize the images in the computer and send the resulting bitmaps to the printer. If you're printing complex slides from a program such as Lotus Freelance Graphics to an HP LaserJet printer, you might find that the layers become "transparent" if you use the default vector graphics setting but print as intended with the bitmap setting.

Caution

If you're planning to use the printer to produce multiple copies of pages with vector graphics from presentation or draw-type software such as Freelance Graphics, Microsoft PowerPoint, CorelDRAW, or Adobe Illustrator, do a single-copy test print first to see if you have problems before running your high-volume print job.

Many printer drivers include a Fonts page that enables you to control how the driver treats the TrueType fonts in the documents you print. The usual options are as follows:

- **Download TrueType fonts as outline soft fonts**   Causes the driver to send the fonts to the printer as vector outlines so that the printer can rasterize them into bitmaps of the proper size. This option generally provides the fastest performance.

- **Download TrueType fonts as bitmap soft fonts**   Causes the driver to rasterize the fonts in the computer and send the resulting bitmaps to the printer. This option is slightly slower than sending the font outlines but uses less printer memory.

- **Print TrueType as graphics**   Causes the driver to rasterize the fonts into bitmaps and send them to the printer as graphic images. This is the slowest of the three options, but it enables you to overlap text and graphics without blending them.

The Device Options provided by many printer drivers enables you to specify values for the following options:

- **Print quality**   Enables you to select the level of text quality for your documents. Lower qualities print faster but have a coarser appearance.

- **Printer memory**   Enables you to specify how much memory is installed in the printer. The setting displays the amount of memory that ships with the printer, but if you install additional memory, be sure to modify this setting. This setting is used by the Printer Memory Tracking feature (see the following option) to calculate compression and the likelihood of the print job's being completed successfully.

- **Printer memory tracking**   Enables you to control how aggressively the printer driver will use the amount of memory configured in the printer memory parameter. When it processes a print job, the driver computes the amount of printer memory needed and compares it to the amount installed in the printer. If the job requires a great deal more memory than the printer has, it will abort the job and generate an error message. When the amount of memory required is close to the amount installed, this setting determines whether the driver will attempt to send the job to the printer, at the risk of incurring an out-of-memory error, or behave conservatively by aborting the job.

Review

Cram Session

- Preparing the computer for the installation of the operating system centers on preparing the hard disk: Low-level format, partitioning, and formatting.

- Minimum system requirements for the operating systems are progressively more advanced. For details on specific requirements, see Table 11.1.

- Installing the operating system requires a system startup disk (boot disk) and the installation media for the operating system in question. As with DOS, these might be one and the same, or as in the case of Windows 3.x and 9x, they might not be.

- In all three operating systems, starting the system from the boot diskette and launching `SETUP.EXE` from the initialization media is the basic procedure for installation.

- Knowledge of the boot order for your operating system can assist greatly in troubleshooting. DOS boot sequences start with `IO.SYS`, `CONFIG.SYS`, `MSDOS.SYS`, `COMMAND.COM`, and `AUTOEXEC.BAT`. Windows 3.x appends the following to that list: `WIN.COM`, `KRNL386.EXE`, `USER.EXE`, `GDI.EXE`, `SYSTEM.INI`, and `WIN.INI`. Windows 95 differs from these others by loading the `IO.SYS`, text from `MSDOS.SYS`, `SYSTEM.DAT`, `COMFIG.SYS`, `AUTOEXEC.BAT`, `WIN.COM`, and `USER.DAT`.

- Boot options for DOS and Windows 3.x include bypassing the startup files using F5 or stepping through these same configuration files line by line using F8.

- Boot options for Windows 95 are more complex. The options include safe mode, logged mode, command prompt, line-by-line configuration, and previous DOS version. Of these, safe mode and logged mode are most important for the exam.

- Emergency boot diskettes are great to have in the event of a drive or operating system failure. Windows 95 has an application button in the Add/Remove Programs applet that creates this diskette for you.

- Configuring device drivers in Windows 95 is normally handled using Plug and Play. Plug and Play requires three things: a PnP device, a PnP Operating System, and a PnP BIOS.

- If Plug and Play fails, manual configuration using the Add New Hardware wizard is the next step. This will automate the steps required to install device drivers, prompting the user for information as necessary.

- Printer installation in DOS requires nothing more than attaching to the parallel port and sending it output. Each DOS application will use a unique and built-in printer driver.

- In Windows 3.x and 9x, printers are installed using the Control Panel. This process is more automated in Windows 95 with the Add Printer Wizard.

- LPT port redirection is the process of assigning a Windows printer and driver to a parallel port for legacy DOS applications. This causes all output sent to the LPT1 port to be intercepted and redirected to the Windows printer driver chosen.

Review Questions

1. Compare and contrast the minimum system requirements for DOS, Windows 3.x, and Windows 9x.

2. Why are minimum requirements not a good mark by which to judge a system?

3. Explain the installation process for Windows 3.x.

4. After Windows 95 loads IO.SYS and MSDOS.SYS, what file is loaded next?

5. How does Windows 95 make a backup copy of the Registry?

6. What is Windows 95 safe mode used for?

7. What is the procedure to create a Windows 95 boot disk?

8. If a manual configuration needs modification at a later date, what system utility is used in Windows 95?

9. What printer setting should be configured for DOS-based applications? How?

Review Answers

1. Minimum system requirements for the operating systems are progressively more advanced. For details on specific requirements, see Table 11.1.

2. Minimum requirements for operating systems are often the manufacturer's bare minimums to load the OS and not the requirements for additional applications running on top of the OS.

3. After following the preceding steps to install DOS, the Windows installation may begin. Windows 3.x can be installed from the original five (or six, seven, or eight, depending on which version you have) 3.5" floppy diskettes by running SETUP.EXE.

4. SYSTEM.DAT is loaded and initializes all 32-bit protected-mode virtual device drivers.

5. After loading SYSTEM.DAT and USER.DAT, backup copies are made and saved in the user's default profile directory as SYSTEM.DA0 and USER.DA0.

6. Some devices or errant user settings might cause a system conflict. Safe mode is the boot option that loads default drivers but enables the errant configurations to be modified.

7. Emergency boot diskettes are great to have in the event of a drive or operating system failure. Windows 95 has a button in the Add/Remove Programs applet on the Startup Disk Tab that creates this diskette for you.

8. When you select the Device Manager page from the System Control Panel, you see an expandable list of the types of devices found in the system. Expanding each type displays the actual hardware installed in the computer. Each entry has a Properties dialog box that enables you to configure the device, view the hardware resources that it is using, and update its driver.

9. LPT port redirection is the process of assigning a Windows printer and driver to a parallel port for legacy DOS applications. This causes all output sent to the LPT1 port to be intercepted and redirected to the Windows printer driver chosen.

Chapter 12

Operating Systems: Diagnosing and Troubleshooting

Interpreting Error Messages

Interpreting error messages correctly is a large part of your troubleshooting process. Following are some of the most common error messages for various operating systems and their most common causes. This list is not intended to be all-inclusive:

- `Incorrect Dos version`   This message is commonly caused by attempting to run an external DOS command that was distributed with a different version of DOS than was loaded during boot.

- `Bad or Missing Command Interpreter`   This indicates that `COMMAND.COM` is missing, corrupt, or sometimes the wrong version as compared to `IO.SYS` and `MSDOS.SYS`.

- `Unrecognized Command in CONFIG.SYS`   Typically, a command has been mistyped, although any DOS command line in the `CONFIG.SYS` will yield this error as well.

- `HIMEM.SYS not loaded`   This is generally a precursor to a larger error. Without `HIMEM.SYS`, Windows 3.x and 9x will not load. Either the file is corrupt or you have a hardware memory error.

- `Username not found`   When logging into Windows 95, a profile is created for each user. If the login is required and is miskeyed, the system will not allow access.

Note

Many of the steps for diagnosing and troubleshooting were discussed in Chapter 2, "Diagnosing and Troubleshooting." Most of this chapter will use the fundamentals discussed there as applied to operating systems and other software.

Software-Based Printing Errors

These errors are typically associated only with Windows because basic DOS printing is cut and dried. Printer managers/spoolers/queues and printer drivers are the typical culprits of these software problems.

To get an understanding of these two software components, you need to be able to see where they function between pressing the print button and the printer receiving output.

Typically, the application sends the raw data to the printer driver. This driver formats the data as necessary for the printer to understand it. The newly formatted data is passed on to the print spooler, also known as a queue, or the print manager in Windows 3.x. The queue receives the data exactly as the printer would and relays a message back to the application that the printer is done printing the requested document, even though it has not yet been completed. When the printer is ready, the print spooler feeds the data to the printer in more manageable chunks until the print job is complete.

Print Spooler

The most common print spooler error is when the print spooler stalls and the printer ceases to print. Generally, this is caused by a "stuck" job at the head of the line in the queue. Remove the first job in the queue and the printer should start printing again.

Another common problem with the printer spooler is low disk space. When this occurs, the spooler has no place to store the print jobs being sent to it and will not even store them in line. To resolve this, simply free up some space, or change the printer properties, details tab, and spool settings to print directly to the printer. This will cause the application to stall while waiting for the printer to complete the job, but it is better than nothing.

Printer Drivers

Using the wrong printer driver can have effects as benign as not all the options being available to something as malignant as the printer printing garbage on every page—and won't stop printing pages. Make sure that you are using the latest release version printer driver from the manufacturer. (Before upgrading, it is important to create a backup copy of the previous driver in case the new driver has problems.)

Printer drivers and troubleshooting were covered in Chapter 5, "Printers." Most of the software-based material also applies to the Operating Systems Exam.

Common Problems and Their Resolution

Although I cannot possibly include specific problems or even all the general ones, some of the more common categories of problems are discussed in this section.

GPF

A general protection fault occurs when a Windows application attempts to use an unallocated or previously occupied memory location. When this happens in 16-bit applications, a blue screen is displayed with text indicating what application caused the problem and at what memory location. For 32-bit applications, the Windows dialog box with a red × circle appears as a system fault.

Recovering from GPFs in Windows 3.x was chancy at best. Windows 95 resolved some of the problems with 16-bit application faults, but system lockups still occasionally occur. Regardless of whether the system locks up, it is recommended that you close all applications and exit the system to maintain your system integrity and reliability.

Illegal Operation

An illegal operation is an error in the code of the application that you are running. This can be caused by an invalid mathematical or algorithmical error. Dividing by zero is a good example of this error.

Usually, the manufacturer of the application will have a fix for the illegal operation because chances are good that you are not the first person to find the problem.

System Lockup

System lockups can be caused by any number of things. Typically, a soft memory error or GPF causes a system lockup.

Soft memory errors were discussed in Chapter 10, "Memory Management."

If lockups continue to occur, the problem might be hardware-related or heat-related, although again, most system lockups are software configuration issues.

DOS and Windows Utilities

In many cases, it might not be necessary to purchase third-party diagnostic software because your operating system has all the diagnostic tools you need. Windows 95, and to a lesser degree, DOS and Windows 3.x, include a large selection of programs that enable you to view, monitor, and troubleshoot the hardware in your system. The following sections examine some of these tools and their functions.

The *CHKDSK* Command

The useful and powerful DOS CHKDSK command is frequently misunderstood. To casual users, the primary function of CHKDSK seems to be providing a disk space allocation report for a given volume as well as a memory allocation report. CHKDSK does those things, but its primary value is in discovering, defining, and repairing problems with the DOS directory and FAT system on a disk volume. In handling data recovery problems, CHKDSK is a valuable tool, although it is crude and simplistic compared to some of the after-market utilities that perform similar functions.

The output of the CHKDSK command when it runs on a typical hard disk is as follows:

```
Volume 4GB_SCSI     created 01-31-1998 5:05p
Volume Serial Number is 1882-18CF

2,146,631,680 bytes total disk space
      163,840 bytes in 3 hidden files
   16,220,160 bytes in 495 directories
  861,634,560 bytes in 10,355 user files
1,268,613,120 bytes available on disk

       32,768 bytes in each allocation unit
       65,510 total allocation units on disk
       38,715 available allocation units on disk

      655,360 total bytes memory
      632,736 bytes free
```

The real function of CHKDSK is to inspect the directories and FATs to see whether they correspond with each other or contain discrepancies. CHKDSK does not detect (and does not report on) damage in a file; it checks only the FAT and directory areas of a disk. Checking the files and the actual media is the responsibility of the next command: SCANDISK.

SCANDISK

It's a good idea to check your FAT partitions regularly for the problems discussed in this chapter and any other difficulties that might arise. By far, an easier and more effective solution for disk diagnosis and repair than CHKDSK and RECOVER is the SCANDISK utility included with DOS 6 and higher versions as well as with Windows 9x. This program is more thorough and comprehensive than CHKDSK or RECOVER and can perform the functions of both of them—and a great deal more. Windows 95 OSR2 and Windows 98 include SCANDISK versions that support FAT32 partitions.

SCANDISK is like a scaled-down version of third-party disk repair programs such as Norton Disk Doctor, and it can verify both file structure and disk sector integrity. If SCANDISK finds problems, it can repair directories and FATs. If the program finds bad sectors in the middle of a file, it marks the clusters (allocation units) containing the bad sectors as bad in the FAT, and it attempts to read the file data by rerouting around the defect.

SCANDISK provides two basic testing options: Standard and Thorough. The difference between the two is that the Thorough option causes the program to scan the entire surface of the disk for errors in addition to the items just mentioned. You can also select whether to run the program interactively or let it automatically repair any errors that it finds.

SCANDISK also has an Advanced Options dialog box that enables you to set the following parameters:

- Whether the program should display a summary of its findings
- Whether the program should log its findings
- How the program should repair cross-linked files (two directory entries pointing to the same cluster)

- How the program should repair lost file fragments
- Whether to check files for invalid names, dates, and times

Defrag

The entire premise of the FAT file systems is based on the storage of data in clusters that can be located anywhere on the disk. This enables the computer to store a file of nearly any size at any time. The process of following a FAT chain to locate all the clusters holding the data for a particular file can force the hard disk drive to access many different locations on the disk. Because of the physical work involved in moving the disk drive heads, reading a file that is heavily fragmented in this way is slower than reading one that is stored on consecutive clusters.

As you regularly add, move, and delete files on a disk over a period of time, the files become increasingly fragmented, which can slow down disk performance. You can relieve this problem by periodically running a disk defragmentation utility on your drives, such as the one included with Windows 9x. When you run Disk Defragmenter, the program reads each of the files in the disk, using the FAT table to access its clusters, wherever they might be located.

The program then writes the file to a series of contiguous clusters and deletes the original. By progressively reading, erasing, and writing files, the program eventually leaves the disk in a state where all its files exist on contiguous clusters. As a result, the drive is capable of reading any file on the disk with a minimum of head movement, thus providing what is often a noticeable performance increase.

The Windows 95 Disk Defragmentation utility provides this basic defragmenting function. It also enables you to select if you want to arrange the files on the disk to consolidate the empty clusters into one contiguous free space (which takes longer). The Windows 98 version adds a feature that examines the files on the disk and arranges them with the most often used program files grouped together at the front of the disk, which can make programs load faster.

Before you defragment your disks, it is a good idea to run a disk repair program such as Windows 9x's SCANDISK or Norton Disk Doctor, even if you are not experiencing any problems. This ensures that your drives are in good working order before you begin the defragmentation process.

In the Real World

Windows 98 includes a Task Scheduler program that enables you to schedule programs for automatic execution at specified times. (A similar feature is included in Windows 95's Plus Pack called the System Agent.) The Windows 98 Maintenance Wizard walks you through the steps of scheduling regular disk defragmentations, disk error scans, and deletions of unnecessary files. You can schedule these processes to execute during nonworking hours, so regular system activities are not disturbed.

MSD.EXE

MS-DOS 6.x, Windows 3.1, and Windows for Workgroups all include a basic tool called Microsoft Diagnostics (MSD). MSD is a simple, DOS-based program that displays information about your system hardware. Designed in 1993 for use with these older operating systems, MSD does not recognize much of the new hardware in use today, such as Pentium processors.

Although MSD has garnered a reputation for incorrectly identifying certain hardware, such as the UART chips in PC serial ports and the interrupt usage listing, it is one of the best tools for identifying memory usage in the Upper Memory Area, which is a common source of conflicts between add-on adapter cards. It is also quite useful for documenting the version numbers of the system BIOS, Video BIOS, and other drivers.

MSD also ships on the Windows 9x CD-ROM, although it is somewhat hidden and is not automatically installed during the Windows setup procedure. You can copy MSD from the CD-ROM directly to your hard drive and run it from any DOS prompt. It provides better information if you first shut down Windows and choose Restart the Computer in MS-DOS Mode.

Using Safe Mode

The Windows 9x boot menu provides a safe mode option. This option bypasses the loading of the drivers for the specific hardware in the system and instead loads a set of generic drivers designed to get the system up and running with only minimal functionality. This enables the computer to boot the Windows GUI in situations where a malfunctioning driver or device would otherwise prevent access to the system.

When booted from the standard and generic drivers, the Device Manger (discussed later in this section) and other configuration applications allow changes to be made to the failed configuration, rather than the pristine one that was used to boot the system. This allows the erroneous drivers or configuration settings to be changed even if they affect the video driver or halt the system on a normal startup.

Windows 9x Device Manager

Windows 9x's Device Manager is a far more useful hardware inventory tool than MSD. When you select the Device Manager page from the System Control Panel, you see an expandable list of the types of devices found in the system (see Figure 12.1). Expanding each type displays the actual hardware installed in the computer. Each entry has a Properties dialog box that enables you to configure the device, view the hardware resources that it is using, and update its driver.

By clicking the View Devices By Connection option button, the display is sorted by the computer's various ports and interfaces.

Another lesser-known feature of the Device Manager is that when you double-click the Computer entry at the top of the list, you see the Computer Properties dialog box, shown in Figure 12.2. From this dialog box, you can examine all the IRQs, I/O ports, DMA channels, and memory addresses in your system and the devices that are using them.

In cases where Windows 9x's plug-and-play feature cannot assign system resources for you, the Device Manager is an excellent tool for resolving device conflicts. The Properties dialog box for each device displays the resources supported by that particular device and indicates if other devices are already using those resources and which resources the device hardware is configured to use.

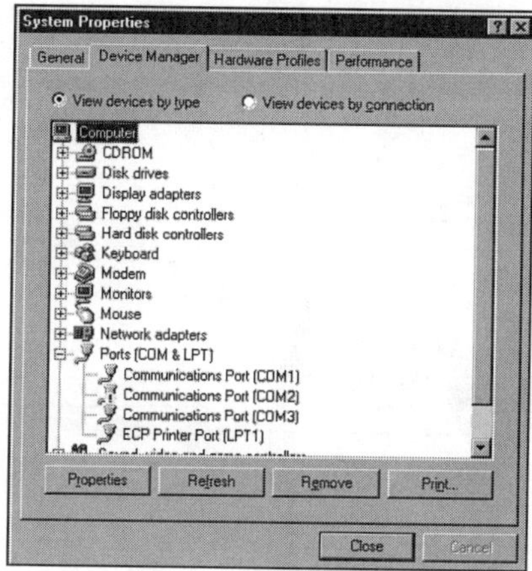

Figure 12.1 The Windows 9x Device Manager.

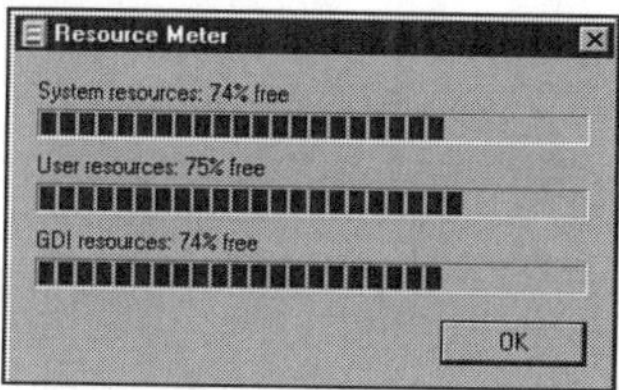

Figure 12.2 The Computer Properties dialog box.

Windows 9x Resource Meter

The Windows 9x Resource Meter launches as an icon in the tray area of the toolbar. This application continually monitors the Windows 9x system, user, and GDI (graphics device interface) resources. As you load more programs and open more windows, the icon in the tray indicates the diminishing available resources in the system by growing smaller. When you double-click the tray icon, you see a more detailed presentation, as shown in Figure 12.3.

System Monitor/Performance Monitor

The Windows 9x System Monitor and the Windows NT Performance Monitor perform roughly the same function. Both programs track specific elements of a system's performance and display them in a graphical format, as shown in Figure 12.4. By default, you can choose to display various statistics pertaining to the computer's kernel, memory manager, file system, and other core functions.

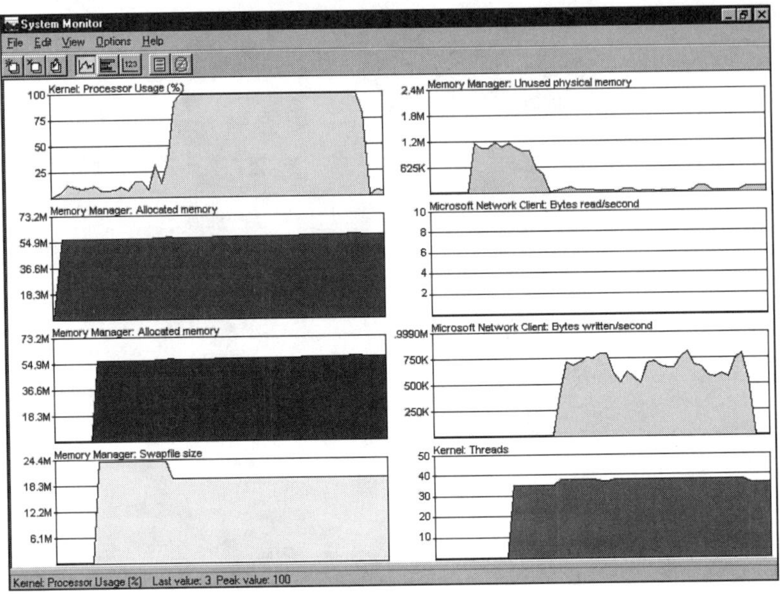

Figure 12.3 The Windows 9x Resource Meter.

Both of these programs, however, are extensible. Installing additional applications and services on the computer can add new categories of statistics. For example, installing a NetWare client on the system adds a collection of statistics regarding incoming and outgoing traffic generated by that client.

SYSEDIT.EXE

Windows 3.x and 9x (although somewhat unnecessary in 9x) have a utility that opens all the major initialization and configuration files for editing. SYSEDIT.EXE opens AUTOEXEC.BAT, CONFIG.SYS, WIN.INI, SYSTEM.INI, and PROTOCOL.INI in cascading Notepad-style windows.

Viruses

Viruses are little programmed "gremlins" in your machine. In some cases malignant, in some cases simply amusing, viruses are man-made computer pranks. Programmers have created a whole new industry based on these pranks. It seems to be a game of one-upmanship: The bad guys create a virus, the good guys create a cure, and it starts all over again. In fact, many individuals have accused the virus detection companies of writing viruses just to increase their business.

What exactly is a virus? A virus is a type of resident program designed to replicate itself. Usually at some later time when the virus is running, it causes an undesirable action to take place.

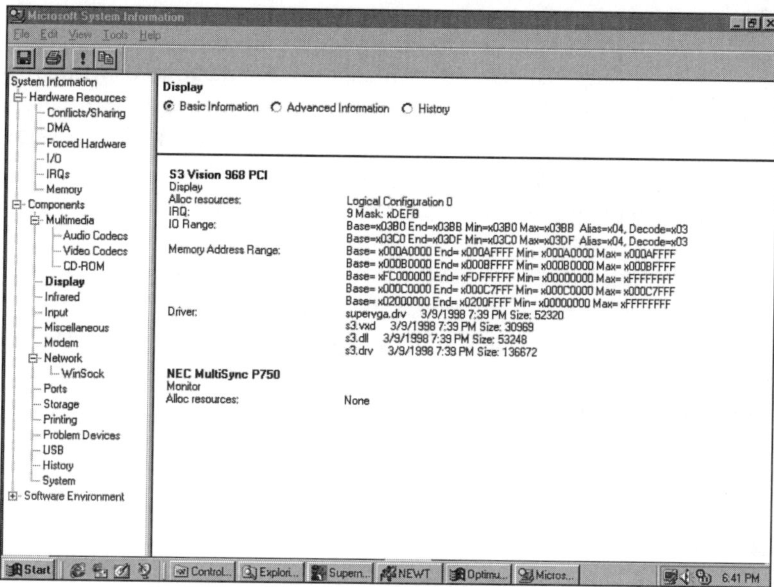

Figure 12.4 The Windows 9x System Monitor.

Types of Viruses

There are several types of viruses, but they all boil down to three categories: replication method, activation method, and payload.

Replication methods can be anything from a user copying an infected file unknowingly to a self-propagating email chain.

In the Real World

One virus that is not considered to be one by most antivirus companies is the "virus scare" that seems to perpetually be passed around in email. The Good Times virus is a good example. An email from a fake "reliable" source warns about a terrible computer virus that should be avoided at all costs. The interesting thing is that the virus cited doesn't exist. It is a hoax. However, by passing this email to all your friends and they to all theirs, the user community has become the replication method for this email. No antivirus program can stop this pseudovirus. Granted, the payload is relatively harmless: It takes up space on the server and causes panic among the users temporarily. By my definition, this is a virus nonetheless. Only by verifying a virus report before relaying the message can this replication of panic be stopped.

Activation methods range from as simple as the user loading it (as in a Trojan Horse) to it being invoked by loading an infected file (common memory-resident virus), to starting based on some time algorithm or other criteria.

Payloads might be as simple and harmless as playing "Yankee Doodle Dandy" from the PC speaker on July 4th to as complex as randomly replacing one word on each page of Word documents with a virus keyword to as dangerous as permanently erasing your hard disk or FlashBIOS.

Detecting and Removing

Viruses are a danger to any system, and it's a good idea to make scans with an antivirus program a regular part of your preventative maintenance program. Although both Microsoft and IBM provide antivirus software in MS- and PC-DOS, respectively, if you run Windows 9x or Windows NT, you must obtain a third-party program to scan your system. There are many after-market utility packages available that scan for and remove viruses. No matter which of these programs you use, you should perform a scan for virus programs periodically, especially before making hard-disk backups. This helps ensure that you catch any potential virus problem before it spreads and becomes a major catastrophe. In addition, it is important to select an antivirus product from a vendor that provides regular updates to the program's virus signatures. The signatures determine which viruses the software can detect and cure, and because there are new viruses constantly being introduced, these updates are essential.

Review

Cram Session

- For diagnosis and troubleshooting fundamentals, please review Chapter 2.

- Interpreting errors correctly is key to resolving your problems. Most of the common errors are associated with the boot process.

- Printing errors (software-based) are typically problems with the printer driver or the printer queue. Resolving queue problems usually requires the administrator to remove the "stuck" job from the queue.

- Printer drivers can be incorrect even if they are only a revision or two off the norm.

- General protection faults occur when a Windows application attempts to use an unallocated or previously occupied memory location. When this happens in 16-bit applications, a blue screen is displayed with text indicating what application caused the problem and at what memory location. For 32-bit applications, the Windows dialog box with a red × circle appears as a system fault.

- Illegal operations are generally the province of software bugs. These tend to cause divide-by-zero and other similar errors.

- Many things can cause a system lockup, although hard and soft memory errors tend to cause this the most.

- Your operating system has all the diagnostic tools you need for most jobs.

- SCANDISK, defrag, CHKDSK, MSD, Safe mode, and Device manager are all examples of operating system prevention and resolution utilities.

- A virus is a type of resident program designed to replicate itself. Usually at some later time when the virus is running, it causes an undesirable action to take place.

Review Questions

1. What are the three steps for troubleshooting?

2. What are some of the common error messages found during startup?

3. What happens when you use a LaserJet II driver to send data to the LaserJet IV? Vice versa?

4. Compare and contrast GPFs in Windows 3.x and Windows 95.

5. What is the most likely cause for system lockups?

6. Which utility provides the capability to scan the surface area of the hard disk?

7. How does Windows 9x device manager assist users in configuring new hardware?

8. What are the various type of viruses?

9. What is a virus hoax?

Review Answers

1. As indicated in Chapter 2, define, isolate, and resolve with documentation occurring during all phases.

2. Although these vary from system to system, they include DOS version errors, unrecognized commands in configuration files, and `HIMEM.SYS` or other drivers not loading. What are some common errors that you have run across?

3. Using a Laserjet II driver to print to a Laserjet IV will yield a good printout, although some specialized features might not be available. Using a Laserjet IV driver to print to a Laserjet II might cause erratic print commands and other communication issues.

4. In 16-bit applications, a blue screen is displayed with text indicating what application caused the problem and at what memory location. For 32-bit applications, the Windows dialog box with a red × circle appears as a system fault.

5. Memory errors, hard or soft. For more on memory and possible errors, see Chapter 10, "Memory Management."

6. `SCANDISK.EXE`. If the program finds bad sectors in the middle of a file, it marks the clusters (allocation units) containing the bad sectors as bad in the FAT, and it attempts to read the file data by rerouting around the defect.

7. When you select the Device Manager page from the System Control Panel, you see an expandable list of the types of devices found in the system. Each entry has a Properties dialog box that enables you to configure the device, view the hardware resources that it is using, and update its driver.

8. There are several types of viruses, but they all boil down to three categories: replication method, activation method, and payload. Replication methods can be anything from a user copying an infected file unknowingly to a self-propagating email chain. Activation methods range from as simple as the user loading it (as in a Trojan Horse) to it being invoked by loading an infected file (common memory-resident virus), to starting based on some time algorithm or other criteria. Payloads can be as simple and harmless as playing "Yankee Doodle Dandy" from the PC speaker on July 4th to as complex as randomly replacing one word on each page of Word documents with a virus keyword to as dangerous as permanently erasing your hard disk or FlashBIOS.

9. A virus hoax is generally an email advertising a new "deadly" strain of computer virus that does not exist. This is generally propagated due to the collective users' fear.

Chapter 13

Networks

Introduction to Configuring Windows for Networking

A local area network (LAN) enables you to share files, applications, print-ers, disk space, modems, faxes, tape backup drives, and CD-ROM drives among different systems; use client/server software products; send elec-tronic mail; and otherwise make a collection of computers work as a team.

In most cases, however, computers are connected to a network using a net-work interface adapter that either takes the form of an expansion card or is integrated into the computer's motherboard. The adapter in each computer then connects to a cable installation in such a way as to permit any com-puter on the network to communicate with any other.

Much of these networking basics were covered in Chapter 7, "Basic Networking." This chapter will deal specifically with the operating system and software side of networking.

Tip

For more in-depth networking certification information, please read the *Network+ Exam Guide*, ISBN# 0-7897-2157-0, also available from Que. More information on CompTIA's A+ and Network+ certifications can be found in Chapter 14, "Preparing for the Exam."

Perhaps because Windows 95 has inherent support for networking or because it is the predominant client operating system today, CompTIA's A+ certification typically asks questions only about Windows 95 or generic questions that might apply to either Windows version. This is especially true on the A+ Operating Systems Exam, Networking objectives. For this reason, the majority of this chapter will cover Windows 95 material exclu-sively.

Setting Up for a Local Area Network

Client Configuration

You might have few problems installing your NICs. They might pass their diagnostics flawlessly. However, until each station on your network can speak the same language, has correct client or server software setups, and uses the same protocols, your network will not function properly.

Table 13.1 shows the minimum network software configuration you must install for Windows 9x peer-to-peer networking depending on whether your machine will have network resources (a server) or not (a workstation):

Table 13.1   Minimum Network Software for Peer-to-Peer Networking

Item	Workstation	Server
Windows Network client	Yes	Yes
Networking protocol (NetBEUI, IPX, TCP/IP)	Yes	Yes
File and Print Sharing for Microsoft Networks	No	Yes
NIC installed and bound to protocols and services above	Yes	Yes
Workgroup identification (same for all PCs in workgroup)	Yes	Yes
Computer Name (each PC needs a unique name)	Yes	Yes

Use the Network Control Panel to choose your network settings as shown in Figure 13.1. You need the following software to set up the network: operating system CDs, diskettes or hard-disk image files, and NIC drivers. You'll be prompted to insert a CD or diskette or browse to the appropriate files during the installation procedure if they're not available on the Windows 9x CD-ROM.

After you complete the installation of the items listed previously, click OK in the Networks protocol. You need to reboot your PC to complete the process. After this is completed, you're ready to share resources.

Note

Networking is covered only briefly on the CompTIA A+ Certification exams. CompTIA has created a new certification called Network+ for an industry standard network certification. For those professionals needing a higher level of networking certification knowledge, consult Que's *Network+ Exam Certification Guide*.

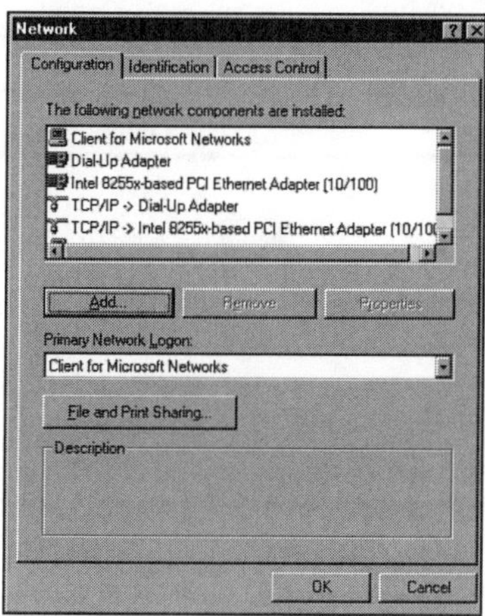

Figure 13.1 Network Control Panel.

Accessing Shared Resources

Network access requires some form of a unique identifier so that the resources you are attempting to access can verify that you deserve access. This is called a login identification. In share-level access, this is not used except on the user's local machine to save a list of passwords to which resource the user has already attached. In user-level access, the user ID is passed to the server with the user's unique password for verification by the server's security database. These methods for sharing (and accessing) resources are discussed next.

Share-Level Access

Peer-to-peer Windows 9x-style networking (and also Windows for Workgroups) provides access control on a resource-by-resource basis called share-level access.

Client/server-based networks, such as Windows NT, Windows 2000 Server, and Novell NetWare, control resources on a user-permission or group-permission basis. The following example demonstrates the differences in these approaches:

- Users 1, 2, 3, and 4 need to access a CD-ROM drive, two network hard drives, a laser printer, and an inkjet printer.

- Users 1 and 4 need read/write/create access to the \Msoffice folder on hard disk 1 and access to the laser printer. User 4 also needs read-only access to the \Photoshop folder on hard disk 2 and access to the inkjet printer.

- User 3 needs read-only access to the \Msoffice folder on hard disk 1, read/write/create access to the \Photoshop folder on hard disk 2, and access to the inkjet printer.

- User 2 needs access to the laser printer only.

The security settings that would be required to secure the resources with a peer-to-peer network are shown in Table 13.2.

Table 13.2   Number of Passwords Necessary for Peer-to-Peer Resources

Resource	Passwords	Reason for Second Password (If Used)
CD-ROM	One	
\Msoffice	Two	1 password for full access
		1 password for read-only access
\Photoshop	Two	1 password for full access
		1 password for read-only access
Laser printer	One	
Inkjet printer	One	

This means that there are a total of seven passwords on the system. The number of passwords needed by each user would be as follows:

User 1—two passwords needed
User 2—one password needed
User 3—three passwords needed
User 4—four passwords needed

This simple example demonstrates the not-so-simple problem of trying to control network resources. The Windows 9x–type peer-to-peer network has no way to create user lists or group permissions, and it therefore must assign a password to every resource. Even if all the users can remember their passwords (or store them in a password list), the challenge isn't over. Suppose that the passwords are revealed to others who shouldn't have access. The authorized users will need to memorize up to four additional (new) passwords after the passwords are changed, assuming that the unauthorized users don't take over the system first.

In addition to the limitations of what Microsoft calls share-level access control, another flaw in the peer-to-peer network scheme is that nobody is really in charge of the network. There is no administrator or superuser who can set up and change passwords for all resources. Instead, the user of the computer with the shared resource can add, change, or delete shared resource settings unless user profiles are set up on each machine that eliminate access to the Windows Explorer and Printers folder for the normal users of that computer.

User-Level Access

With a client/server network, a single password is assigned to each user's network login ID by a network administrator, and users can be divided into groups based on similar access needs. Using the previous example, this scenario would create security settings as demonstrated in Table 13.3.

Table 13.3   Client/server User Rights Example

User	Groups Belonged To	
User 1	OfficeCreate, Laserprinter	
User 2	Laserprinter	
User 3	OfficeRead, PhotoCreate, Inkjet	
User 4	OfficeCreate, Laserprinter, PhotoRead, Inkjet	

Group	Rights	Members
Laserprinter	Use	User 2, User 1, User 4
Inkjet	Use	User 4, User 3
OfficeCreate	Read, write, create	User 1, User 4
Office	Read, Read	User 3
PhotoCreate	Read, write, create	User 3
PhotoRead	Read	User 4
Administrator	Full control of network	

Although the client/server network's user-level access looks more complex at first glance, it's actually an easier and more secure network. It's easier because each user has a single password, regardless of the number of resources she will access. It's easier to administer because rights can be changed for an entire group or for any member(s) of a group. It's more secure because a full-time Network Administrator is able to set up and control all user and group rights to access of all network devices. It's more secure because access rights can be controlled more precisely than with a peer-to-peer network's full access, read-only access, or no access options. Because users can have read/write/create but not delete access to a specified resource, a program can be used without the possibility of it being deleted by the user.

This discussion is not designed to minimize the benefits of peer-to-peer networking. Fast, easy to set up, and flexible, peer-to-peer networking should be used in situations in which low cost is an important factor, and security is a relatively unimportant concern. If security and performance are important, use a client/server network instead.

Note

To learn more about client-server networking, see *Upgrading and Repairing Networks, Second Edition*, published by Que.

Setting Up for an Internet Connection

You can also network with Windows 9x PCs using modems and the operating system's Dial-up Networking feature. Dial-up Networking, or DUN, uses the same network client software as standard Windows 9x networking, but it substitutes a modem connection for the network interface adapter. You can use this technology to connect to the Internet from your home computer through an ISP, or Internet service provider. The following steps will walk you through creating a dial-up connection:

1. On the desktop, open My Computer.
2. Open the special folder Dial-up Networking.
3. To start the Connection Wizard, select Make New Connection.
4. On the first dialog box, name the connection. Generally, the name of your ISP is a good choice. Also, the modem that you will use is probably already set as the default, but verify this to be sure. This is shown in Figure 13.2.

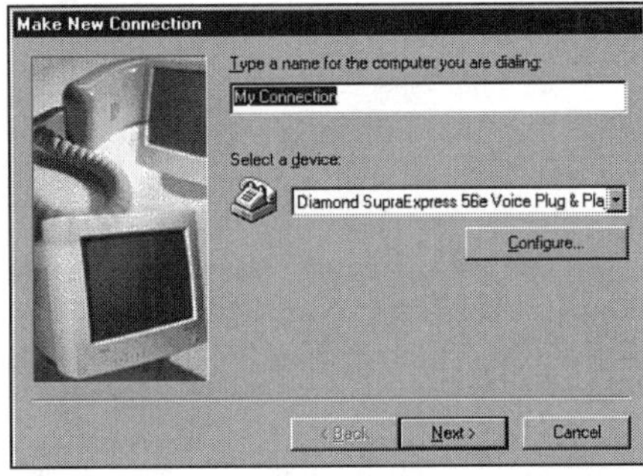

Figure 13.2   Creating a dial-up connection.

5. Choose Next and enter the phone number with area code on the next screen.
6. Select Finish.

Next, you will need to configure the protocols and addressing properties for the connection you just created. Go back to the DUN folder in My Computer and right-click the connection you just created. Select properties from the drop-down menu list. You will see a screen similar to Figure 13.3.

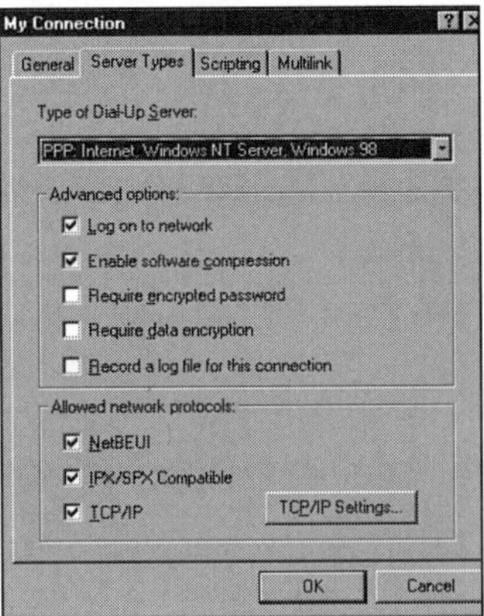

Figure 13.3 Configuring a dial-up connection.

Most of these configuration settings will be defined by your ISP, which should give you some installation instructions. If no instructions were given, the default settings will generally work with most ISPs.

In the Real World

If you are experiencing a slow link to the Internet through your ISP but your connection speed seems normal, try disabling unneeded protocols. Even though TCP/IP, IPX, and NetBEUI are the default protocols, most ISPs only support TCP/IP. Enabling TCP/IP only should increase your access times.

The TCP/IP settings button on the Server Types tab is probably the most important. It is shown in Figure 13.4.

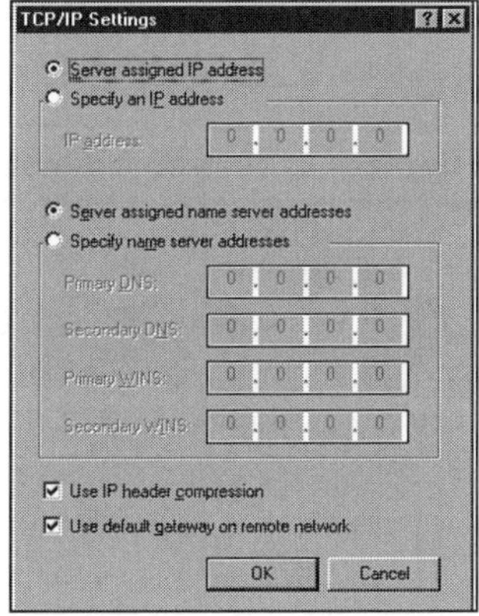

Figure 13.4 Configuring TCP/IP settings for a dial-up connection.

Most ISPs will assign these values to you automatically, but if not, you will need to enter them onto this page in each of your DUN connections.

Caution

Although it can be done, Microsoft does not recommend entering the TCP/IP configuration values for Dial-up Connections in the Network Control Panel. The Network Control Panel is designed for LAN and permanent connection management. Entering settings into this location for the Dial-up Adapter will hinder you in creating multiple functioning Dial-up connections—for instance, one DUN connection to your ISP for home use and one DUN connection to your office to retrieve email.

Internet Protocols and Applications

The most widely used protocol for the Internet is TCP/IP. This protocol rides on top of the PPP, or point-to-point protocol, connection that is used for the physical connections between you and your ISP as established in the preceding section.

An older protocol that is becoming obsolete is SLIP, or serial line interface protocol. SLIP and PPP were discussed in Chapter 7.

TCP/IP

TCP/IP is a protocol often used by people who have never seen a network interface card. People who access the Internet via modems with Dial-up Networking use TCP/IP just as those who get their Web access through their existing LAN. Although the same protocol is used in both cases, the settings vary a great deal.

Table 13.4 summarizes the differences you're likely to encounter. If you access the Internet with both modems and a LAN, you will need to make sure that the TCP/IP properties for modems and LANs are set correctly. You might also need to adjust your browser settings to indicate which connection type you are using. Table 13.4 only provides general and typical guidelines; your ISP or network administrator will give you the specific details.

Table 13.4   TCP/IP Properties by Connection Type—Typical

TCP/IP Property	Setting	Modem Access ("Dial-up Adapter") Modified in Dial-Up Connection	LAN Access ("XYZ Network Card") Modified in Network Control Panel
IP Address	IP Address	Probably automatically assigned by ISP but can be entered statically	Probably specified by network administrator, can be assigned using DHCP
WINS Configuration	Enable/ Disable WINS Resolution	None, but can be entered if necessary	Indicate server or enable DHCP to provide address
Gateway	Add Gateway/ List of Gateways	None (PPP is used to connect modem to Internet) Internet)	IP Address of Gateway used to connect LAN to Internet
DNS Configuration	Enable/ Disable		
Host Domain	Usually automatically assigned by ISP, but can be entered statically	Usually disabled or if enabled, with host and domain specified (get value from network administrator)	

As you can see from the preceding chart, correct settings for LAN access to the Internet and dial-up networking (modem) settings are almost always completely different. In general, the best way to get your dial-up networking connection working correctly is to use your ISP's automatic setup software. This is usually supplied as part of your ISP's signup software kit. After the setup is working, view the properties.

HTML

Hypertext Markup Language is a language used to describe and format plain-text files on the Web. HTML is based on pairs of tags that enable you to mix graphics with text, change the appearance of text, and create hypertext documents with links to other documents.

HTTP

Hypertext Transfer Protocol (HTTP) operates at the application layer and is the fundamental protocol of the World Wide Web. When you type a URL in your Web browser, the program transmits an HTTP request to the server you've specified. The server then responds with an HTTP reply containing the file you requested.

FTP

File Transfer Protocol (FTP). FTP is an application-layer protocol used to transfer files between TCP/IP systems. Unlike most protocols, FTP actually defines the user interface for an application. Virtually every TCP/IP implementation includes a text-based FTP program, and many of the commands are the same no matter what operating system you are using.

Email

Email is a method of transferring messages from one user to another using a client/server application. An example of an email client is Microsoft Outlook, which resides on the client computer, whereas the database that contains all messages and the transports that deliver them are on a server loaded with an email service such as Microsoft Exchange Server.

Internet email is similar in that your ISP provides the email service, and its message delivery connects to and uses the Internet for transport. Unlike business email, Internet email does not remain on the ISP's server. After being downloaded to your email client, the message on the server is discarded. Most business retain email in varying amounts, but it's usually 10–20MB per employee. This is generally for data recovery and legal purposes.

Web Browsers and Web Sites

What good is the Internet? How do you use it? The Internet has many, many possibilities and uses. The single most common use today is email (which I have already discussed) and Web access.

The World Wide Web (WWW) is a graphical information system based on hypertext that enables a user to easily access documents located on the Internet. In laymen's terms, this is a vast and dynamic information bank with no single administration point. It contains the combined knowledge (or lack thereof) of millions of people. Because no single index can contain everything available on it today, this amount of data requires thousands of administrators each working on their own piece of the "world."

All logical organizations of this knowledge organized by a single administrator constitute a Web *site*. The information is made up of pages of data called Web *pages* that are linked to other pages of data within the site.

To access a Web site, you need a Web *browser*. There are several available, but the two most popular browsers are Internet Explorer and Netscape Navigator. In addition to the browser, you need to know the address of the page that you are trying to reach.

This Web address is in the format *protocol://service.domain name.classification/Web page name*. In the case of Web browsing, the protocol is HTTP, as explained in the previous section on protocols. For Web browsing, the service name is usually www, which stands for World Wide Web, but other services exist as well. The domain name is unique to the organization hosting the Web site. This name is registered by the organization with the InterNic to ensure that no duplicates exist. The classification is also assigned by the InterNic as one of the following:

- `.com`—Commercial business
- `.org`—Non-profit organization
- `.edu`—Educational institution
- `.gov`—Government
- `.net`—Network providers and ISPs

The Web page name is also a unique identifier. These pages are written in HTML and usually have the extension `.htm` or `.html`, although some Web applications and search engines use their own codes to represent data. Either way, this is the name of the page that you want to view.

Review

Cram Session

- DOS and Windows 3.1 have no inherent networking capabilities. Windows for Workgroups and Windows 9x do have these capabilities.
- A basic client installation for Windows 9x requires a few software components installed and configured, at minimum. These are Windows Networking client, Network Adapter Driver, Networking protocol, and File/Print sharing.
- To configure the network, you must use the network control panel applet to install and configure the required software components. You will need the installation media for the operating system and any additional manufacturer's network card drivers or network operating system clients.
- Network access requires some form of secure identifier in the form of a user ID and password.
- Share-level access enables users access to resources based on a common shared password.
- User-level access authenticates users to resources based on a central security database that compares access permission lists to the user ID and unique password for each user.
- Internet connections are most commonly described as dial-up connections. Dial-up connections in Windows 95 are created using Windows 95 Dial-up Networking Connection Wizard.

- To create and configure a connection, you need the phone number for your ISP, its TCP/IP configuration, and a modem.

- To connect to your ISP, you need to launch the created connection and supply your assigned user ID and password from the ISP.

- Configuration of an individual dial-up connection's TCP/IP information should occur in the dial-up connection itself and not in the network control panel.

- TCP/IP is generally configured to have the ISP assign everything for dial-up connections, but it must be fully configured in standard LAN configurations. This requires an IP address, subnet mask, default gateway, DNS server, and WINS server.

- HTML is the language in which Web pages are written. HTTP provides the transport protocol for these pages to be communicated to your Web browser.

- FTP is a file transfer protocol and an application that enables logging in and putting or getting files from the server over the Internet.

- Email and Web browsing are the two most common uses for the Internet by the average person today.

- Web sites are logical groupings of Web pages (HTML pages) that are interlinked and administered by the same person or group.

- Web addresses are in the format *protocol://service.domain name.classification/Web page name*.

Review Questions

1. What is a network?

2. What are the minimum software-based network requirements?

3. What is a login ID used for? When is it used?

4. Compare and contrast the differences between share-level access and user-level access.

5. If share-level access is being used and a user quits, what is necessary to change administratively? Explain.

6. What does the dial-up adapter do?

7. How do you set up an Internet connection?

8. Why do most ISP's automatically assign IP addresses?

9. What language is a Web page commonly written in? What protocol is associated with the transport of this data?

10. What is email? How do Internet email and business email differ?

11. Explain how a Web browser retrieves a particular Web page.

Review Answers

1. A local area network (LAN) enables you to share files, applications, printers, disk space, modems, faxes, tape backup drives, and CD-ROM drives among different systems; use client/server software products; send electronic mail; and otherwise make a collection of computers work as a team.

2. Network client software, NIC driver, Networking Protocol, and Resource sharing protocol. See Table 13.1.

3. Network access requires some form of a unique identifier so that the resources you are attempting to access can verify that you deserve access. This is called a login identification. In share-level access, this is not used except on the user's local machine to save a list of passwords to which resource the user has already attached. In user-level access, the user ID is passed to the server with the user's unique password for verification by the server's security database.

4. Share-level access provides users access to resources based on a common shared password. User-level access authenticates users to resources based on a central security database that compares access permission lists to the user ID and unique password for each user.

5. Because all users use the same passwords to access the resource, the authorized users will need to be given new passwords to memorize for each resource that was affected.

6. The dial-up adapter redirects commands intended for a network card to the modem. It essentially uses the modem to emulate an NDIS-compliant network card.

7. First, create a dial-up connection. This is done through the Connection Wizard. Provide the name and phone number for your ISP. Then, the connection will need to be configured with the proper IP information. This is done by choosing the properties of the connection in question. Lastly, the connection must be launched, and the ISP-assigned login ID and password will be required.

8. Because users do not remain online constantly and there is a shortage of true IP addresses for the Internet, most ISPs will create a pool of addresses that will be delivered on an as-needed basis and recovered after the user hangs up. Essentially, this means that an ISP need only provide a single IP address for each phone line that they have.

9. Web pages are written in Hypertext Markup Language, or HTML. These pages are copied across the Internet to your computer using the HTTP protocol, or hypertext transport protocol.

10. Email is a method of transferring messages from one user to another using a client/server application. Most businesses retain email in varying amounts, usually 10—20MB per employee for legal and data security reasons. Unlike business email, Internet email does not remain on the ISP's server. When downloaded to your email client, the message on the server is discarded.

11. The individual address for a Web page is made up of `protocol://service.domain name.classification/Web page name`. To access this page, the browser queries the classification DNS server to determine what the IP address for the domain name server is. From there, the browser queries the service on that domain server to get the HTML document. Then, your computer retrieves a copy of the HTML document using HTTP.

So You're Ready to Take the Exam?

Chapter 14

Preparing for the Exam

Exam Overview

The Computing and Technology Industry Association (CompTIA) is the organization that sets the objectives for the A+ and Network+ certifications.

What is the A+ certification? Before the CompTIA standard, many individual manufacturers had their own testing courses. Each company had to provide their own 100-level introduction required course before they could advance into the specific courses on their own equipment. You can imagine the confusion and repetitive work that would arise when students had to take two different manufacturers' basic computing courses. CompTIA stepped into the gap in 1993 to standardize these introductory-level courses into one industry standard certification. The exams were revised in 1998 to include newer and more advanced technology. It is these 1998 revisions that this book covers.

In many computing fields, earning either of these certifications can increase your job security or increase your value to prospective employers. For more information on CompTIA, A+, or Network+ certifications, please check the Web site FAQ reprinted later in this chapter or go to their Web site at www.comptia.org. Que also publishes a Network+ exam guide that will be very helpful if you intend to pursue the Network+ certification after the A+ examination.

The A+ exam consists of two parts: Hardware and Operating Systems. To acquire your certification, both tests must be passed. The Core, or Hardware, exam is test number 220-101, and the DOS/Windows exam is test number 220-102. Table 14.1 describes the format of each exam.

Table 14.1   Exam Specifics

Category	Hardware Exam	DOS/Windows Exam
Exam number	220-101	220-102
Total questions	69	70
Allotted time	60 minutes	75 minutes
Single-answer questions	Yes	Yes
Multiple-answer questions	Yes—with correct number of answers listed	Yes—with correct number of answers listed
Matching	No	No
Multi-question scenarios	No	No
Exhibit-based questions	Yes	Yes
Adaptive examination	No	No
Performance-based simulation questions	No	No
Objective categories	8	5
Scored objective categories	7	5
Passing score	65%	66%

Exam Objectives—Core Technologies

(reprinted with CompTIA's permission)

Table 14.2 lists the domains measured by this examination and the approximate extent to which they are represented.

Table 14.2   Core Exam Breakdown

Objective Category	Percent of Examination
Installation, Configuration, and Upgrading	30%
Diagnosing and Troubleshooting	20%
Safety and Preventative Maintenance	10%
Motherboard/Processors/Memory	10%
Printers	10%
Portable Systems	5%
Basic Networking	5%
Customer Satisfaction	10%[1]
Total	100.00%

1 *The Customer Satisfaction domain will be scored but will not impact final pass/fail score on the A+ Core examination.*

The CompTIA organization has established the following objectives for the Core portion of the A+ Certification exam.

1.0 Installation, Configuration, and Upgrading

This section challenges the test taker to identify, install, configure, and upgrade microcomputer modules and peripherals. Established procedures for system assembly and disassembly must be followed. Test elements include the ability to identify and configure IRQs, DMAs, and I/O addresses and to properly set configuration switches and jumpers. This section is broken down as follows:

- **1.1** Identify basic terms, concepts, and functions of system modules, including how each module should work during normal operation. Examples of concepts and modules include the following:

System board	Modem
Power supply	Firmware
Processor/CPU	Boot process
Memory	BIOS
Storage devices	CMOS
Monitor	

- **1.2** Identify basic procedures for adding and removing field-replaceable modules. Examples of modules include the following:

  System board

  Power supply

  Processor/CPU

  Memory

  Storage devices

  Input devices

- **1.3** Identify available IRQs, DMAs, and I/O addresses with procedures for configuring them for device installation. Examples include the following:

  Standard IRQ settings

  Modems

  Floppy disk drives

  Hard drives

- **1.4** Identify common peripheral ports, associated cables, and their connectors. Examples include the following:

  Cable types

  Cable orientation

  Serial versus parallel

  Pin connections

Examples of connector types include the following:

DB-9

DB-25

RJ-11

RJ-45

BNC

PS2/Mini-DIN

■ **1.5** Identify proper procedures for installing and configuring IDE/EIDE devices. Examples include the following:

Master/slave

Devices per channel

■ **1.6** Identify proper procedures for installing and configuring SCSI devices. Topics include the following:

Address/termination conflicts

Cabling Types

Internal versus external

Switch and jumper settings

■ **1.7** Identify proper procedures for installing and configuring peripheral devices. Topics include the following:

Monitor/video card

Modem

Storage devices

■ **1.8** Identify procedures for upgrading BIOS. Topics include the following:

Methods for upgrading

When to upgrade

■ **1.9** Identify hardware methods of system optimization and when to use them. Examples include the following:

Memory

Hard drives

CPU

Cache memory

2.0 Diagnosing and Troubleshooting

This item requires the test taker to apply knowledge relating to diagnosing and troubleshooting common module problems and system malfunctions. This includes knowledge of the symptoms relating to common problems.

- **2.1**   Identify common symptoms and problems associated with each module and how to troubleshoot and isolate the problems. Contents might include the following:

Processor/memory symptoms

Mouse

Floppy drive failures

Parallel ports

Hard drives

Sounds card/audio

Monitor/video

Motherboards

Modems

BIOS

CMOS

Power supply

Slot covers

POST audible/visual error codes

Troubleshooting tools; for example, multimeter

- **2.2**   Identify basic troubleshooting procedures and good practices for eliciting problem symptoms from customers. Topics include the following:

Troubleshooting/isolation/problem determination procedures

Determine whether hardware or software problem

Gather information from the user regarding the following:

Customer environment

Symptoms/error codes

Situation when the problem occurred

3.0 Safety and Preventative Maintenance

This section requires the test taker to show knowledge of safety and preventative maintenance. With regard to safety, it includes the potential hazards to personnel and equipment when working with lasers, high-voltage equipment, ESD (Electrostatic Discharge), and items that require special disposal procedures that comply with environmental guidelines. With regard to preventative maintenance, this includes knowledge of preventative maintenance products, procedures, environmental hazards, and precautions when working on microcomputer systems.

- **3.1**   Identify the purpose of various types of preventative maintenance products and procedures and when to use or perform them. Examples include the following:

Liquid cleaning compounds

Types of materials to clean contacts and connections

Vacuum out systems, power supplies, fans

■ **3.2**   Identify procedures and devices for protecting against environmental hazards. Examples include the following:

UPS (uninterruptible power supply)/suppressors

Determining the signs of power issues

Proper methods of storage of components for future use

■ **3.3**   Identify the potential hazards and proper safety procedures relating to lasers and high-voltage equipment. Examples include the following:

Lasers

High-voltage equipment can cause electrocution; for example, power supply/CRT

■ **3.4**   Identify items that require special disposal procedures that comply with environmental guidelines. Examples include the following:

Batteries

Toner kits/cartridges

Chemical solvents and cans

CRTs

MSDS (Material Safety Data Sheet)

■ **3.5**   Identify ESD (Electrostatic Discharge) precautions and procedures, including the use of ESD protection devices. Examples include the following:

What ESD can do and how it can be apparent or hidden

Common ESD protection devices

Situations that could present a danger or hazard

4.0 Motherboard/Processors/Memory

This section requires the test taker to demonstrate knowledge of specific terminology and facts, ways, and means of dealing with classifications, categories, and principles of motherboards, processors, and memory in microcomputer systems.

■ **4.1**   Distinguish between the popular CPU chips in terms of their basic characteristics. Characteristics include the following:

Physical size

Voltage

Speeds

Onboard cache or not

Sockets

Number of pins

■ **4.2**   Identify the categories of RAM (Random Access Memory) terminology, their locations, and physical characteristics.

Terminology includes the following:

EDO RAM (Extended Data Output RAM)

DRAM (Dynamic Random Access Memory)

SRAM (Static RAM)

VRAM (Video RAM)

WRAM (Windows Accelerator Card RAM)

Locations and physical characteristics include the following:

Memory bank

Memory chips (8-bit, 16-bit, and 32-bit)

SIMMS (Single Inline Memory Module)

DIMMS (Dual Inline Memory Module)

Parity chips versus nonparity chips

■ **4.3**   Identify the most popular type of motherboards, their components, and their architecture (for example, bus structures and power supplies).

Types of motherboards include the following:

AT (Full and Baby)

ATX

Motherboard components include the following:

Communication ports

SIMM and DIMM

Processor sockets

External cache memory (Level 2)

Bus architecture includes the following:

ISA

EISA

PCI

USB (Universal Serial Bus)

VESA local bus (VL-BUS)

PC Card (PCMCIA)

Basic compatibility guidelines

■ **4.4**   Identify the purpose of CMOS (Complementary Metal-Oxide Semiconductor), what it contains, and how to change its basic parameters. Examples include the following:

Printer parallel port: Unidirectional/bidirectional, disable/enable, ECP/EPP

COM/serial port: memory address, interrupt request, disable

Hard drive: size and drive type

Floppy drive: enable/disable drive or boot, speed, density

Boot sequence

Memory: parity, nonparity

Date/time

Passwords

5.0 Printers

This domain requires knowledge of basic types of printers, basic concepts, printer components, how they work, how they print onto a page, paper path, care and service techniques, and common problems.

■ **5.1** Identify basic concepts, printer operations, printer components, and field-replaceable units in primary printer types. Types of printers include the following:

Laser

Inkjet

Dot matrix

Paper feeder mechanisms

■ **5.2** Identify care and service techniques and common problems with primary printer types. Examples include the following:

Feed and output

Errors

Paper jam

Print quality

Safety precautions

Preventative maintenance

■ **5.3** Identify the types of printer connections and configurations. Topics include the following:

Parallel

Serial

Network

6.0 Portable Systems

This section requires the test taker to demonstrate knowledge of portable computers and their unique components and problems.

■ **6.1** Identify the unique components of portable systems and their unique problems. Examples include the following:

Battery

LCD

AC adapter

Docking stations

Hard drive

Types I, II, III cards

Network cards

Memory

7.0 Basic Networking

This section requires the test taker to demonstrate knowledge of basic network concepts and terminology, ability to determine whether a computer is networked, knowledge of procedures for swapping and configuring network interface cards, and knowledge of the ramifications of repairs when a computer is networked.

- **7.1** Identify basic networking concepts, including how a network works. Examples include the following:

  Network access

  Protocol

  Network Interface Cards

  Full duplexing

  Cabling/Twisted-Pair, Coaxial, Fiber-Optic

  Ways to network a PC

- **7.2** Identify procedures for swapping and configuring network interface cards.
- **7.3** Identify ramifications of repairs on the network. Examples include the following:

  Reduced bandwidth

  Loss of data

  Network slowdown

8.0 Customer Satisfaction

No one can underestimate the value and importance of customer satisfaction, especially personal computer repair technicians who must deal with customers who are often under stress because their computer has crashed. The CompTIA A+ Core exam has several objectives dealing with customer service. As important as this topic is, it is not covered in this book, which is really about the nuts and bolts of PC repair.

Exam Objectives—DOS/Windows

Note

The A+ exam objectives are reprinted by permission of CompTIA's.

Table 14.3 lists the categories measured by this examination and the approximate extent to which they are represented.

Table 14.3 Test Categories and How Each Is Weighted

Objective Category	Percent of Examination
Function, Structure, Operation, and File Management	30%
Memory Management	10%

(continues)

Table 14.3   Test Categories and How Each Is Weighted

Objective Category	Percent of Examination
Installation, Configuration, and Upgrading	30%
Diagnosing and Troubleshooting	20%
Networks	10%
Total	100%

Tip

Approximately 75% of the test items will relate to Windows 95 and the remaining 25 percent will relate to DOS and Windows 3.x.

1.0 Function, Structure Operation and File Management

This domain requires knowledge of DOS, Windows 3.x, and Windows 95 operating systems in terms of their functions and structure, for managing files and directories, and for running programs. It also includes navigating through the operating system from DOS command-line prompts and Windows procedures for accessing and retrieving information.

Content Limits

1.1   Identify the operating system's functions, structure, and major system files. Content might include the following:

- Functions of DOS, Windows 3.x, and Windows 95
- Major components of DOS, Windows 3.x, and Windows 95
- Contrasts between Windows 3.x, and Windows 95
- Major system files: What they are, where they are located, how they are used, and what they contain
- System, Configuration, and User Interface files
- DOS

  `AUTOEXEC.BAT`

  `CONFIG.SYS`

  `IO.SYS`

  `ANSI.SYS`

  `MSDOS.SYS`

  `EMM386.EXE`

  `HIMEM.SYS`

  `COMMAND.COM` (internal DOS commands)

- Windows 3.x

  `WIN.INI`

  `SYSTEM.INI`

  `USER.EXE`

  `GDI.EXE`

  `WIN.INI`

  `WIN.COM`

  `PROGMAN.INI`

  `PROGMAN.EXE`

  `KRNLXXX.EXE`

- Windows 95

  `IO.SYS`

  `MSDOS.SYS`

  `COMMAND.COM`

  `REGEDIT.EXE`

  `SYSTEM.DAT`

  `USER.DAT`

1.2 Identify ways to navigate the operating system and how to get to needed technical information. Content might include the following:

- Procedures (for example, menu- or icon-driven) for navigating through DOS to perform such things as locating, accessing, and retrieving information
- Procedures for navigating through the Windows 3.x/Windows 95 operating system, accessing, and retrieving information

1.3 Identify basic concepts and procedures for creating, viewing and managing files and directories, including procedures for changing file attributes and the ramifications of those changes (for example, security issues). Content might include the following:

- File attributes
- File naming conventions
- Command syntax
- Read Only, Hidden, System, and Archive attributes

1.4 Identify the procedures for basic disk management. Content might include the following:

- Using disk management utilities
- Backing up
- Formatting
- Partitioning
- Defragmenting

- ScanDisk
- FAT32
- File allocation tables (FAT)
- Virtual file allocation tables (VFAT)

2.0 Memory Management

This domain requires knowledge of the types of memory used by DOS and Windows and the potential for memory address conflicts.

Content Limits

2.1 Differentiate between types of memory. Content might include the following:

- Conventional
- Extended/upper memory
- High memory
- Expanded memory
- Virtual memory

2.2 Identify typical memory conflict problems and how to optimize memory use. Content might include the following:

- What a memory conflict is
- How it happens
- When to employ utilities
- System Monitor
- General Protection Fault
- Illegal operations occurrences
- MemMaker or other optimization utilities
- `HIMEM.SYS`
- `SMARTDRV`
- Use of expanded memory blocks (using `EMM386.EXE`)

3.0 Installation, Configuration, and Upgrading

This domain requires knowledge of installing, configuring and upgrading DOS, Windows 3.x, and Windows 95. This includes knowledge of system boot sequences.

Content Limits

3.1 Identify the procedures for installing DOS, Windows 3.x, and Windows 95 and for bringing the software to a basic operational level. Content might include the following:

- Partitioning
- Formatting drive

- Running appropriate set-up utility
- Loading drivers

3.2 Identify steps to perform an operating system upgrade. Content might include the following:

- Upgrading from DOS to Windows 95
- Upgrading from Windows 3.x to Windows 95

3.3 Identify the basic system boot sequences and alternative ways to boot the system software, including the steps to create an emergency boot disk with utilities installed. Content might include the following:

- Files required to boot
- Creating emergency boot disk
- Startup disk
- Safe mode
- DOS mode

3.4 Identify procedures for loading/adding device drivers and the necessary software for certain devices. Content might include the following:

- Windows 3.x procedures
- Windows 95 Plug and Play

4.0 Diagnosing and Troubleshooting

This domain requires the ability to apply knowledge to diagnose and troubleshoot common problems relating to DOS, Windows 3.x, and Windows 95. This includes understanding normal operation and symptoms relating to common problems.

Content Limits

4.1 Recognize and interpret the meaning of common error codes and startup messages from the boot sequence, and identify steps to correct the problems. Content might include the following:

- `Safe Mode`
- `Incorrect DOS version`
- `No operating system found`
- `Error in CONFIG.SYS line XX`
- `Bad or missing COMMAND.COM`
- `HIMEM.SYS not loaded`
- `Missing or corrupt HIMEM.SYS`
- `Swap file`
- `A device referenced in SYSTEM.INI could not be found`

4.2 Recognize Windows-specific printing problems and identify the procedures for correcting them. Content might include the following:

- Print spool is stalled
- Incorrect/incompatible driver for print

4.3 Recognize common problems and determine how to resolve them. Content might include the following:

- Common problems
- General protection faults
- Illegal operation
- Invalid working directory
- System lock up
- Option will not function
- Application will not start or load
- Cannot log on to network
- DOS and Windows-based utilities
- ScanDisk
- Device manager
- `ATTRIB.EXE`
- `EXTRACT.EXE`
- `DEFRAG.EXE`
- `EDIT.COM`
- `FDISK.EXE`
- `MSD.EXE`
- `MEM.EXE`
- `SYSEDIT.EXE`

4.4 Identify concepts relating to viruses and virus types—their danger, their symptoms, sources of viruses, how they infect, how to protect against them, and how to identify and remove them. Content might include the following:

- What they are
- Sources
- How to determine presence

5.0 Networks

This domain requires knowledge of network capabilities of DOS and Windows, and how to connect to networks, including what the Internet is about, its capabilities, basic concepts relating to Internet access and generic procedures for system setup.

Content Limits

5.1 Identify the networking capabilities of DOS and Windows, including procedures for connecting to the network. Content might include the following:

- Sharing disk drives
- Sharing print and file services
- Network type and network card

5.2 Identify concepts and capabilities relating to the Internet and basic procedures for setting up a system for Internet access. Content might include the following:

- TCP/IP
- Email
- HTML
- `HTTP://`
- FTP
- Domain names (Web sites)
- ISP
- Dial-up access

Scheduling the Exam

These exams are administered by Sylvan Prometric and can be scheduled and taken at any SP testing center.

To schedule your examination, call Sylvan Prometric at 1-800-77-MICRO (1-800-776-4276). You will need to provide your Sylvan testing identification number (usually your social security number), your name, address, employer, phone number, and credit card number. They will give you a list of testing centers in your area and a choice of dates at the center closest to you.

Caution

It is important to remember that when you pass one of the exams, the second exam must be passed within 90 days or the first exam will need to be retaken as well.

Don't forget that you will need two forms of identification, one with a picture ID, in order to sit for the exam. **You will be turned away if you forget to bring this identification.** This is to ensure that no one can pay someone else to take the exam for him, maintaining the integrity of the certification process and the certification itself.

Exams can be cancelled up to 24 hours before the previously scheduled time. Within 24 hours of the scheduled time, no refunds will be given.

More information about Sylvan Testing Centers and Sylvan Prometric can be found at `www.educate.com`.

Testing Strategies

As with any test, the strategies that you learned in high school and college still apply:

- Get a good night's sleep and a healthy breakfast.

- Arrive at the testing center early and in full preparation. If you feel that you really need it, re-read the Cram Session sections at the end of each chapter. Relax. When you sit down at the testing computer, take off your shoes and get comfortable. You will gain nothing by being tense, except maybe an ulcer.

- Read each question and all the answers thoroughly. Some answers might be "more correct" than others. Answer only after reading all the possibilities.

- Do not second-guess yourself. There are no trick questions. Try not to read too deeply into the questions to see where CompTIA is trying to fool you.

- When in doubt, eliminate the wrong answers. CTIA tends to have three distractors. Two will obviously be incorrect, whereas the third might be more subtle. When all the wrong answers are eliminated, the one that is left is the right one.

- Even if you are not sure of the correct answer, fill in all the questions. You can choose to mark the question by clicking in the small "Mark" box on the screen and come back to it if you have time. If you do run out of time, you still have a 25% chance of getting the right answer on those questions.

CompTIA Web Site FAQ

Note

The CompTIA FAQ is reprinted by permission of CompTIA.

Do you suggest any study materials for the A+ certification?

CompTIA has not developed any materials to prepare for the examination. However, study materials are sold by third party vendors and a list of these training sources can be found on CompTIA's Web site under Training Resources. These sources have paid to appear on the CompTIA Web page. CompTIA has not reviewed or approved, and does not endorse any of the publications listed. CompTIA makes no representation or warranty with respect to the accuracy or completeness of the contents of any such publications, and specifically disclaims any warranties of merchantability or fitness for a particular purpose. CompTIA makes no guarantee concerning the success of persons using any of such publications in order to prepare for an A+ Certification examination.

What technologies are covered on the new exam?

Your best source of information for this would be to look at the test objectives that are posted on our Web site. These are located by going to CompTIA's home page at www.comptia.org.

Please remember that the Core and the DOS/Windows exams completely changed on July 31, 1998. If you took any portion of the exam prior to this date and did not earn your A+ Certification, you will have to re-take both modules to become A+ certified.

What qualifications are needed to take the exams?

A+ Certification is open to anyone who wants to take the tests. The A+ exam is targeted for entry-level computer service technicians with at least 6 months on-the-job experience. No specific requirements are necessary, except payment of the fee.

Who do I call to register for the test?

Please call Sylvan Prometric at 1-800-776-4276 if you reside in the United States, Canada or Puerto Rico. If your company is a member of CompTIA you can register for the A+ test via Internet Registration at `http://www.2test.com`.

For international registrations call your regional Sylvan Prometric office.

The Netherlands: 31-320-239-890 or 0800-022-7584
Sydney: 61-2-9414-3663
Dusseldorf: 31-320-239-800
Paris: 33-1-4289-3122
Japan: 813-3269-9620
Latin America / Caribbean: 410-843-4300

How many questions are on the new A+ tests?

There are 69 questions on the Core portion. There are 70 questions on the DOS/Windows portion. To pass the Core, a score of at least 65% is required. To pass the DOS/Windows, a score of at least 66% is required. Candidates are given 1 hour to complete the Core. Candidates are given 1 hour and 15 minutes to complete the DOS/Windows.

What is the passing percentage that I need for the Core and the DOS/Windows?

To pass the Core, a score of at least 65% is required. To pass the DOS/Windows, a score of at least 66% is required. Candidates are given 1 hour to complete the Core. Candidates are given 1 hour and 15 minutes to complete the DOS/Windows. There are 69 questions on the Core portion. There are 70 questions on the DOS/Windows portion.

How much time will I get to take the tests?

Candidates are given 1 hour to complete the Core. Candidates are given 1 hour and 15 minutes to complete the DOS/Windows. There are 69 questions on the Core portion. There are 70 questions on the DOS/Windows portion. To pass the Core, a score of at least 65% is required. To pass the DOS/Windows, a score of at least 66% is required.

What is the 90 calendar days rule?

The 90-calendar day's rule states that a candidate must take the Core and DOS/Windows portion within 90 calendar days of each other. If the two parts are taken outside of the 90-calendar day window, the candidate will re-take both sections in order to receive the A+ designation. It is the responsibility of the candidate to count the days, and to take the portion of the exam that is needed by the 90th calendar day. The first day to count would begin with the day the test was taken. CompTIA and Sylvan Prometric will not count you days for you. Be careful that you give yourself enough time. It is for this reason that we strongly encourage candidates to take the Core and DOS/Windows portion at the same time. The only exception to the 90-day rule is if there has been a death in the family or if a family member has been hospitalized. CompTIA will require proof as in a death certificate or a doctor's note on proper stationery.

I am currently A+ Certified with the Mac OS Specialty, and would like to become A+ Certified with the DOS/Windows Specialty. Can I take only the DOS/Windows portion of the exam? Will I receive another certificate?

Yes. CompTIA is allowing A+ Certified Mac technicians to earn the A+ DOS/Windows certification by taking only the DOS/Windows portion of the A+ Service Technician exams. When you call to register for your exam, however, you must notify the customer service representative that you are currently A+ Certified with the Mac OS Specialty. Please be prepared to furnish your A+ verification number at this time. If you cannot provide a valid A+ verification number, you will have to take both exams to earn the A+ DOS/Windows certification. After passing the exam, you will receive the standard fulfillment package.

Are customer service questions included?

There are customer service questions on the Core exam. These questions are not included in the final score. The scores from this section are reported at the bottom of the score report so that employers and clients know how the candidate performed on this section.

Are networking questions on the exam?

Yes, there are some basic networking questions. Please see the test objectives found on the CompTIA Web site for further details.

If I failed, may I see my answers?

As an internationally recognized entry-level professional certification for service technicians, the test must remain secure at all times. Thus, no test questions or answers are ever released. In order to maintain the high quality of the exam, no exceptions are made.

If I failed a portion of the test, will I have to pay to retake that portion?

Yes, each time you take the test, there will be a fee. Call Sylvan Prometric at 1-800-776-4276 to re-register if you live in the United States, Canada or Puerto Rico.

For international retests call your regional Sylvan Prometric office.

The Netherlands: 31-320-239-890 or 0800-022-7584
Sydney: 61-2-9414-3663
Dusseldorf: 31-320-239-800
Paris: 33-1-4289-3122 Japan: 813-3269-9620
Latin America / Caribbean: 410-843-4300

What if I am unhappy with a test question?

If you are unhappy with the wording of a test question, or are unhappy with a test question, you may comment these at the time you take the exam. Furthermore, we invite your comments in writing. Please fax them to: (630) 268-1384, to the attention of the Certifications Department.

How long is my test voucher good for?

The vouchers are valid for one calendar year and expire after that period.

Can I take the Core and the DOS/Windows at separate times?

Although it is possible, we strongly recommend that you take both parts of the exam at the same time. * Both parts of the A+ test must be completed within 90 calendar days. The only exception to the 90-day rule is if there has been a death in the family or if you or a family member has been hospitalized. CompTIA will require proof, as in a death certificate or a doctor's note on proper stationery.

What do I do if my certificate is late, misspelled or I have lost my certificate or ID card?

If you reside in the United States, Canada or Puerto Rico, please call Sylvan Prometric at 1-800-776-4276 and request a replacement.

If you reside outside of these areas please call your regional office for assistance.

The Netherlands: 31-320-239-890 or 0800-022-7584
Sydney: 61-2-9414-3663
Dusseldorf: 31-320-239-800
Paris: 33-1-4289-3122
Japan: 813-3269-9620
Latin America / Caribbean: 410-843-4300

If you need a new certificate within 3 months of the original printing, the first copy is free. Each subsequent printing carries a $15 charge. This charge is also instituted for any reprint requested after 6 months of certifying.

How long is the A+ certification good for?

Once you are A+ certified, you are certified for life.

There is a new A+ logo in use on your Web site. Is my current A+ logo still good?

Yes, the current A+ logo is valid indefinitely.

What are the new exam codes for the new A+ tests?

The exam code for the Core is 220-101. The exam code for the DOS/Windows is 220-102.

I took the Macintosh OS Module to earn my A+ certification and I know that you are no longer offering this module. However, I lost my certificate. Can I get a reprint?

Yes, A+ certificates with the Macintosh OS Specialty will continue to be printed indefinitely. However, you will receive a certificate and logo sheets (with the new A+ logo) only. Pins and ID cards will not be provided. Please call Sylvan Prometric at 1-800-776-4276 to request a reprint.

If you reside outside of these areas please call your regional office for assistance.

The Netherlands: 31-320-239-890 or 0800-022-7584
Sydney: 61-2-9414-3663
Dusseldorf: 31-320-239-800
Paris: 33-1-4289-3122
Japan: 813-3269-9620
Latin America / Caribbean: 410-843-4300

I earned my certification under the previous version of the exam. All the other techs have certified under the test version as of July 31 and our certificates do not look the same. Can I get my certificate reprinted on the new certificate paper?

Yes, this option is available to you. There will be a $15 charge for this printing, however, as this is considered a request for a duplicate. Please call Sylvan Prometric at 1-800-776-4276 to request a copy if you live in the United States, Canada or Puerto Rico. If you live outside these areas see the question above for your Sylvan Prometric regional office phone number.

Can I take the A+ test outside the United States, Canada or Puerto Rico?

Yes, the A+ test is live throughout the world in English. We have translated the A+ test into the following languages: Spanish, French, German, Portuguese, Japanese, simplified Chinese and Traditional Chinese.

Does CompTIA make any accommodations for people with disabilities who want to take the test?

It is CompTIA's policy to make reasonable accommodations for individuals with disabilities. If you need special accommodations, please contact us 30 days before scheduling your exam.

Are there A+ lapel pins available?

At this point in time, the pins are not available, but will be considered for future merchandise.

We are a training provider and a member of CompTIA. How can we give our students the member discount price for the A+ exam?

In order for your students to receive the discount on the A+ test, the training provider will need to purchase vouchers from Sylvan Prometric. Their phone number is 1-800-776-4276. The training provider can then sell the vouchers to their students.

If your company is outside of these areas please call your regional Sylvan Prometric office for assistance.

> The Netherlands: 31-320-239-890 or 0800-022-7584
> Sydney: 61-2-9414-3663
> Dusseldorf: 31-320-239-800
> Paris: 33-1-4289-3122
> Japan: 813-3269-9620
> Latin America / Caribbean: 410-843-4300

What languages has the A+ test been translated into?

The A+ test has been translated into: German, French, Portuguese, traditional Chinese, simplified Chinese and Japanese. You may request the A+ test in any of these languages worldwide.

Who do I call to get my verification or sp number after I take and pass the test?

If you reside in the United States, Canada or Puerto Rico, please call Sylvan Prometric at 1-800-776-4276.

If you reside outside of these areas please call your regional office for assistance.

> The Netherlands: 31-320-239-890 or 0800-022-7584
> Sydney: 61-2-9414-3663
> Dusseldorf: 31-320-239-800
> Paris: 33-1-4289-3122
> Japan: 813-3269-9620
> Latin America / Caribbean: 410-843-4300

Once I have passed the test, how long will it be before I receive my certificate and ID card?

Sylvan Prometric generates the certificates and it takes 3 - 4 weeks. If you do not receive your certificate and ID card after 5 weeks please call your regional Sylvan Prometric office.

Chapter 15

Sample Test Questions

Before You Begin

This chapter should be used when your studying is complete. There are two practice exams here, one for the Hardware exam and the other for the Operating Systems exam. Try taking the two following exams in about 30 minutes each. This will give you an approximation of the actual exam questions as well as time frames.

One last note: Beware of taking them more than once because this might not provide an accurate evaluation of your testing ability.

Good luck!

Core Technologies Examination

1. **A SCSI bus supports how many device IDs?**

   a. 6

   b. 7

   c. 8

   d. 9

2. **What is a cylinder?**

   a. Pie-shaped portion of a platter

   b. Concentric circles on a single platter

   c. 512 bytes

   d. A vertical stack of tracks

3. **Which of the following is a description of a Full Duplex option?**

   a. One unit always transmits, and the other unit always receives

   b. One unit transmits only after the other unit stops transmitting

   c. Both units can transmit at the same time, but only one can receive at a time

   d. Both units can transmit at the same time and receive at the same time

4. **What type of chip is also known as FlashROM?**

   a. DRAM

   b. PROM

   c. SIMM

   d. EEPROM

5. **IBM's MCA bus architecture provided which of the following?**

   a. Bus mastering

   b. Software configuration

   c. Backward compatibility

   d. Inexpensive equipment manufacturing

6. **What is the single best ESD protection in the field?**

   a. Ionization machines

   b. Antistatic sprays

   c. Touching the power supply while it is plugged in

   d. Using an ESD wrist strap and common ground

7. **Today's computers have two DMA Controllers, DMA1 and DMA2. DMA1 has CH0–CH3. DMA2 has CH4–CH7. DMA2 is cascaded from DMA1 through CH4. There are only two channels of the eight channels used, while all others are available. Which channel is used for the Floppy Disk Drive Controller?**

   a. 0

   b. 1

   c. 2

   d. 3

8. **What order are the three steps of the troubleshooting process in?**

   a. Diagnosing, Troubleshooting, Repair

   b. Isolation, Resolution, Duplication

   c. Diagnosing, Troubleshooting, Documentation

   d. Definition, Isolation, Resolution

9. **What does a 3xx POST code indicate has a problem?**

   a. Monitor

   b. Keyboard

   c. Floppy

   d. CPU

10. With IDE devices, what must the boot drive be configured as?

   a. master

   b. slave

   c. cable select

   d. boot

11. What is the name of the process that laser printers use to create the image?

   a. Electrophotographic

   b. Photomorphic

   c. The Guttenberg process

   d. Electrophotostatic

12. Which type of cable uses eight wires to transfer data from one device to another and is limited to approximately 10 feet to ensure data integrity?

   a. Serial

   b. Parallel

   c. Video

   d. SCSI

13. What is the data path of a DIMM?

   a. 16-bit

   b. 32-bit

   c. 64-bit

   d. 168-bit

14. When connecting a digital multimeter to a circuit to measure amperage, what must the connection be?

   a. Parallel

   b. Open

   c. Series

   d. A multimeter does not measure amperage

15. What is the first step in replacing the power capacitor in a sealed power supply?

   a. Break the seal on the supply

   b. Use a voltmeter to check the electrical potential of the capacitor

   c. Order a new capacitor

   d. Take it to an authorized service technician

16. How many hard drives can be installed in an Enhanced IDE system?

   a. 2

   b. 3

   c. 4

   d. As many open drive bays as you have available

17. What is the single most common cause for printer preventative maintenance in dot matrix printers?

a. Paper

b. Ink

c. Heat

d. Power

18. Mice commonly use which of the following ports? Choose all that apply.

a. Centronics 50

b. DB25

c. PS/2

d. Proprietary bus connector

19. One classification for memory uses capacitors that require refreshing, whereas the other type uses transistors that do not require refreshing. These are which of the following?

a. RAM, ROM

b. SDRAM, EDORAM

c. DRAM, SRAM

d. WRAM, St. Louis RAM

20. You find a 486D×4100 processor. At what speed in MHz does its external (system) bus run?

a. 25

b. 33

c. 50

d. 100

21. Which of the following batteries has the notorious "memory effect?"

a. NiCd

b. NiMH

c. AA

d. Li-ion

22. What could cause video distortion?

a. Monitor is configured incorrectly

b. Video card has a bad character generator on it

c. Display is next to a fluorescent light

d. Monitor is unplugged

23. Which of the following protocols is routable?

a. MAC

b. IP

c. IPX

d. NetBEUI

24. **While configuring your modem, one thing you need to consider is what the COM port you are using's IRQ setting is. If you are using COM port 3, what is the IRQ that is used?**

    a. 2

    b. 3

    c. 4

    d. 5

25. **Token Ring uses a token-passing access method on a ring topology. What access method and logical topology does Ethernet use?**

    a. Busmastering, bus

    b. FIFO, star

    c. CSMACD, bus

    d. LIFO, dual independent rings

26. **Which step should you perform first before discharging a CRT?**

    a. Remove the CRT from its housing

    b. Disconnect the CRT from the computer

    c. Remove the video assembly

    d. Turn off power before removing power source

27. **Which of the following is the correct IRQ, port address, and DMA channel for the FDD Controller?**

    a. IRQ3, 3E8h, Ch2

    b. IRQ4, 2E8h, Ch4

    c. IRQ5, 378h, Ch3

    d. IRQ6, 3F7h, Ch2

28. **In the Binary numbering system, a (1) represents a jumper being shorted and a (0) represents a jumper being open. On a three-bit jumper block on a SCSI drive, how would an ID of logical 3 be set?**

    a. 100

    b. 010

    c. 011

    d. 101

Operating Systems Examination

1. **What are the two hidden system files for MS-DOS?**

    a. `IO.SYS`

    b. `BIOS.SYS`

    c. `OS.SYS`

    d. `MSDOS.SYS`

2. **What two files make up the Windows 95 Registry?**

   a. `REGISTRY.DAT`

   b. `SYSTEM.DAT`

   c. `WIN.DAT`

   d. `USER.DAT`

3. **Which of the following is a valid DOS filename?**

   a. `THIS IS A.TST`

   b. `HOOSIER.DDY`

   c. `SCOTT's.FILE`

   d. `12/99.XLS`

4. **What utility must be used before defragmentation can occur?**

   a. `FDISK.EXE`

   b. `SCANDISK.EXE`

   c. `CHKDSK.EXE`

   d. `SMARTDRRV.EXE`

5. **The concept of using hard disk storage as swappable RAM storage is called which of the following?**

   a. Hard RAM

   b. Caching RAM

   c. Virtual RAM

   d. Illegal

6. **What is the key combination required during the boot process to bypass all startup files immediately in DOS 6.22?**

   a. F1

   b. DEL

   c. F8

   d. F5

7. **What Windows 95 utility is used to set up additional Windows components?**

   a. Device Manager

   b. Network Installation Applet

   c. System Information

   d. Add/Remove Programs

8. **After the network adapter has been installed, what three main components must be configured in the Network applet?**

   a. Network client

   b. Network protocols

   c. Computer name

   d. Username

9. **Which security model is more secure?**

   a. Share-level

   b. Password-level

   c. Workgroup

   d. User-level

10. **What is the built-in MS-DOS virus-detection utility?**

    a. `NAV`

    b. `MWAVE`

    c. `AUNTIE VIRUS`

    d. `MSAV`

11. **What must be configured in order to connect to the Internet if you have no LAN?**

    a. DUN

    b. WAN

    c. CAN

    d. LUN

12. **Plug and Play requires a plug-and-play–compatible device. What other two plug-and-play–compatible components are required?**

    a. PnP BIOS

    b. PnP RAM

    c. PnP OS

    d. PnP Manual Configuration Utility

13. **In Windows 95 networking, how do workgroup computers share resources?**

    a. By default

    b. By advertising the NetBIOS and share name

    c. By distributing the data to a central file server

    d. Very carefully

14. **What is the utility used to optimize your system's usage of memory?**

    a. RAM doubler

    b. Memmaker

    c. `MEM /C`

    d. Scandisk

15. **Adding a printer in Windows 95 creates what?**

    a. Printer configurator

    b. Printer driver

    c. Printer queue

    d. Financial burden

16. **What area of RAM does conventional memory occupy?**

    a. 0—384KB

    b. 0—640KB

    c. 640—1024KB

    d. 1,024—1,088KB

17. **What Windows utility can be used to modify all the common configuration files simultaneously?**

    a. Regedit

    b. Sysdiff

    c. Sysedit

    d. Device Manager

18. **What is the proper order for initializing a hard disk?**

    a. Low-level format, high-level format, partition

    b. Low-level format, partition, Windows System Format

    c. High-level format, detail-level format, partition

    d. Low-level format, partition, high-level format

19. **If you are in the directory `c:\windows\options\cabs`, what files are most likely to be there?**

    a. Windows option diskettes for use with MCA reference diskettes

    b. The cab company rates for Redmond Washington

    c. Windows installation disks

    d. Windows optional configuration settings

20. **What is used to modify the Registry?**

    a. `REGEDIT.EXE`

    b. Control Panels

    c. Add Printer Wizard

    d. All of the above

21. **If you are in the directory `c:\windows\options\cabs`, how would you switch to the root of the `A:` drive?**

    a. `Switchdir a:`

    b. `Move a:\root`

    c. `CHDIR a:\`

    d. `cd\ a:`

22. **What two files in Windows 3.x provide for the configuration of the user and computer environment?**

    a. `WIN.COM`

    b. `WIN.INI`

    c. `USER.INI`

    d. `SYSTEM.INI`

Answers

Core Technologies Examination

1. **C.** There are 8 total IDs supported by a single SCSI–2 channel. (Although later revisions of SCSI support 16 IDs, the exam will only cover SCSI basics that include the 8 ID versions.) One ID is always taken for the host adapter, so there are 7 IDs available for SCSI devices.

2. **D.** A vertical stack of tracks on both sides of the platters constitutes a cylinder. Imagine an invisible tube intersecting the entire drive vertically. Every track it touches makes a cylinder.

3. **D.** Full duplex provides simultaneous two-way communication, much like a standard telephone conversation.

4. **D.** A FlashROM or FlashBIOS chip is an electrically erasable programmable ROM, or EEP-ROM.

5. **A and B.** MCA provided the first software-configurable bus-mastering 32-bit expansion bus, but it was not backward compatible with ISA and was fairly expensive because of IBM's licensing arrangements.

6. **D.** Although ionization is the best method, it is usually restricted to controlled factory areas due to the expense of equipment and setup. Antistatic sprays help, but they do not protect the equipment from you—only from the surface that you have sprayed. Touching the power supply is better than nothing, but only marginally so. The only adequate ESD protection for field use is an ESD wrist-strap and mat properly grounded to the system.

7. **C.** The floppy disk drive uses DMA channel 2.

8. **D.** Although answer B is in the correct order, duplication is actually part of the resolution stage.

9. **B.** The keyboard error range is 300–399. Most commonly seen is the 301 error, which indicates a generic keyboard failure.

10. **A.** In a two-drive IDE pair, one drive is the master, and one is the slave. The master drive is always the boot device.

11. **D.** The electrophotostatic process is used by laser printers and copiers alike. The Guttenberg printing press, incidentally, was the first printing press ever created in the mid-16th century.

12. **B.** Parallel cabling transfers an entire byte with each cycle. Because of the wider data path, the distance traveled cannot be more than 10–15 feet.

13. **C.** The 168-pin DIMM has a 64-bit data path to equal the path of today's Pentium-class processors.

14. **C.** Amperage is current. Current is the total amount of electrons flowing past a given point in a specified amount of time. To get all the electrons to flow through the meter, it must be an integral part of the circuit itself. The circuit must be cut and the meter inserted in series to complete the circuit.

15. **D.** Power supplies are to be serviced by experienced personnel only.

16. **C.** Assuming that the question implies only one EIDE controller in the system, there are positions available for two drives per each of two channels.

17. **A.** The tractor-fed, perforated paper leaves much paper dust. This dust accumulates in the bottom of the printer, on the print head, in the gears, and on the platen, gathering oil and other residue and creating a hazard to printing.

18. **B, C, and D.** Centronics 50-pin connections are SCSI. There are no "scuzzy" mice except those that need a bath.

19. **C.** DRAM requires refreshing circuitry and is commonly used for main memory. SRAM does not require the refreshing circuitry, is much faster, and is consequently used mostly for memory cache.

20. **B.** Despite the multiplication symbol and the number four, these processors ran at a clock tripled rate, rather than quadrupled. The DX4-100 was actually a 33 MHz external bus with a 99MHz CPU.

21. **A.** Nickel-Cadmium batteries require you to fully drain them before recharging or they might not fully recharge the next time. NiMH and Li-ion do not exhibit this behavior, and of course, AA batteries are a battery size rather than technology.

22. **C.** Fluorescent lights and electrical motors generate an oscillating magnetic field that causes the display to distort.

23. **B and C.** MAC is a data link–layer protocol and is broadcast-based. NetBEUI is a network-layer protocol that relies on NetBIOS name broadcasts for address resolution.

24. **C.** Remember that that COM ports use IRQs 3 and 4. All even-numbered COM ports (2, 4, 6, and so on) should use the odd-numbered IRQ (3), whereas all odd numbered COM ports (1, 3, 5, and so on) should use the even numbered IRQ (4).

25. **C.** Ethernet uses a carrier-sense, multiple-access, collision-detection method on a single shared bus with a 10 or 100Mbps bandwidth.

26. **D.** Turning off the monitor power before unplugging it is an important step in allowing the CRT to dissipate most of the stored charge in the tube. You can then unplug the device and proceed with the high-voltage probe discharge process.

27. **D.** Knowing any of these settings eliminates virtually all other possibilities. Look to use this method of elimination on the exam.

28. **C.** The least significant binary position represents a 1, followed by a 2, followed by a 4, and so on, each position doubling the value represented by the position to its immediate right.

Operating Systems

1. **A and D.** `IO.SYS` (`IBMBIO.COM`) and `MSDOS.SYS` (`IBMDOS.COM`) are the hidden system files for MS-DOS (or IBM's PC-DOS).

2. **B and D.** `SYSTEM.DAT` and `USER.DAT` together form the Windows 95 Registry.

3. **B.** Answers A, C, and D all have invalid characters for the DOS 8.3 filename format.

4. **B.** In Windows 95, `SCANDISK.EXE` will actually be called by `DEFRAG.EXE` prior to any starting defragmentation work. `CHKDSK` will also check most of the same things that `SCANDISK` will. However, `CHKDSK` even recommends that `SCANDISK` be run instead.

5. **C.** Virtual RAM is what Windows calls a swap file. This allows Windows to "page" RAM to and from the hard disk as necessary to simulate more RAM than the machine actually has.

6. **D.** F1 or Delete generally will access CMOS for you, whereas F8 will step you through your startup files one line at a time. F5 is used to immediately bypass all startup files and go straight to a DOS prompt.

7. **D.** The Add/Remove Programs applet has a tab for Windows Setup. At this tab, you can choose all options that were not chosen during the initial setup of Windows 95.

8. **A, B, and C.** The username is not a required configuration. This is only required during the login process.

9. **D.** User-level security uses a network security provider (Novell or NT) that has a security database in which all users have a unique user identification and password. Both are needed to access any network resource.

10. **D.** Microsoft Anti-virus (`MSAV.EXE`) is a licensed version of the Central-Point Anti-virus software.

11. **A.** Dial-up networking must be configured to access the Internet over a phone connection. WAN and CAN are classifications of networks, whereas LUN is the abbreviation for a mainframe-based logical unit number.

12. **A and C.** There is no such thing as PnP RAM and manual configuration is the opposite of PnP. For Plug and Play to function, a PnP device, operating system, and BIOS are all required.

13. **B.** NetBIOS is required for Microsoft peer-to-peer workgroup computing. Share-level permissions are used in which all users use the same password to access the resource.

14. **B.** Memmaker will reboot your machine and reorganize your memory-resident applications and memory-management software to the best possible arrangement. Windows 95 memory management has made this process somewhat obsolete, although it is very helpful in DOS and Windows 3.x environments.

15. **C.** Windows 95 creates a logical printer device that uses a provided printer driver and creates a printer queue for the printer object. This works in much the same way as the Windows 3.x Print Manager.

16. **B.** 0–640K is Conventional memory, 640–1024K is Upper memory, and 1024K–1088K is the High memory area as discussed in Chapter 10.

17. **C.** `SYSEDIT.EXE` simultaneously opens `WIN.INI`, `SYSTEM.INI`, `PROTOCOL.INI`, `AUTOEXEC.BAT`, and `CONFIG.SYS` for modification.

18. **D.** As discussed in Chapter 9, a low-level format must occur first, followed by a partition, and then finally prepared with the high-level format.

19. **C.** The `WINDOWS\OPTIONS\CABS` directory is the default location for copying the Windows installation disks (or cabinet files—thus the name "cabs").

20. **D.** Almost all system configuration utilities and applets modify specific Registry settings. Although `REGEDIT.EXE` is used to directly modify the Registry, all the utilities listed record their information in the Registry.

21. **C.** Although answer D might work if the two commands were entered on different command lines, this would rely on the hope that the default directory on the `A:` drive is the root. The only correct answer is C (although `CHDIR` could be replaced with `CD`, the more common form of the command).

22. **B and D.** `WIN.INI` provides user environment information, whereas `SYSTEM.INI` provides system environment information.

Index

Special Characters and Numbers

S

X-Y-Z